ROSE MARIE JONES

The
FATHER'S
VOICE

The Father's Voice

Copyright © 1999 Rose Marie Jones

ISBN 0-9669396-1-1
Library of Congress Catalog Card Number: 98-61673

Printed in the United States of America

Published by Voice Publishing
54 Albion Street
Jacksonville, Illinois 62650
All rights reserved.

D. M. Headen, editor
S. E. Edwards, copyeditor
M. R. Jones, graphic designer and cover artist
O. G. Crowder, pastoral consultant
J. K. Kafer, Branstiter Printing Co.

Publisher's Cataloging-in-Publication
(Provided by Quality Books, Inc.)

Jones, Rose Marie.
    The Father's Voice / Rose Marie Jones. -- 1st
ed.
        p. cm.
        Includes index.
        LCCN: 98-61673
        ISBN: 0-9669396-1-1

    1. Devotional calendars. 2. Meditations.
I. Title.

BV4811.J66 1999   242.2
                                QBI99-1898

Introduction

When I was a little girl, I would climb onto my daddy's lap, and he would read Bible stories to me. I listened to his tender, gentle voice, and I would be comforted in his love. Now that I am older, I find myself doing the same thing with my Heavenly Father.

The Father's Voice is dedicated to my own earthly "daddy" whose example of gentle goodness has helped me to understand and hear my heavenly Abba's voice.

It has been a privilege to receive Father's love letters, and I have marveled at his ability to express himself through my language—but his words. These love songs were received by my listening spirit's ear, like gifts, after much careful prayer and time spent before the presence of our Lord. Only minimal editing has been allowed.

To the best of my ability, with the faith God has given me, I have recorded these words on different occasions, sometimes for certain individuals in trying circumstances—but always because God loves us and wants to communicate his love to his children.

Many of the entries in this book are dedicated to precious friends or loved ones, and they are placed on their birthday or anniversary dates. It is to you that I say "thank you" for being a part of the vine that God has wrapped around my life, for being an inspiration to me, and touching my life with your love.

"But everyone who prophesies speaks to men for their strengthening, encouragement, and comfort." I Corinthians 14:3, NIV.

My prayer is that you will be strengthened, encouraged, and comforted through this daily devotional, and that as a child of God, you may more deeply come to know and understand your Heavenly Father's love for you.

Like ivy, may *the Father's voice* wrap his love songs around you and entwine his heart with yours. *"I am the true vine, and my Father is the vinedresser." John 15:1, AMP.*

Rose Marie Jones

Prelude to
The Father's Voice

The words recorded within this book are the soothing salve of *the Father's voice*, songs that heal and comfort. These words from the Father must be read with the heart (or else they will bounce off a wall and roll away).

The anointed word is incorruptible. The voice of the Father rings throughout the chronicles of heaven, resounding and echoing against the walls and halls of eternity. His words have always existed and will forever reverberate from amidst the throne of God.

Gather up these words into your soul, and allow the sheer presence of God to fill your tank with his fuel from heaven that is laced with his power and dynamite energy! These words are his love songs to us, his children.

"He will rejoice over you with singing." Zephaniah 3:17, NKJV.

The Father sings over us always, weeping joy-drops into our souls as we hear his voice and delight in his love songs to us.

The Bride of Christ is cherished! The love letters flow from the throne room seeking the open heart of his beloved.

We must respond with receptivity to our Father's passion for his children and with the Son's love cry for his Bride. We are his creation, and we are loved tenderly and passionately by our Holy Creator who sings and makes melody over us through his love songs—*The Father's Voice.*

Just by Being You!

"Every branch in Me that does not bear fruit He takes away; and every branch that bears fruit He prunes, that it may bear more fruit."　　　　　　　　　　**John 15:2 NKJV**

Beloved, I love you beyond human words of explanation. All of the volumes of love songs and poetry accumulated through the centuries of man's existence could not sufficiently express my devotion to you.

I am pleased with you because you love Me and serve Me with all of your heart. Man looks on the outward appearance, but I look into your heart. My vision is not through the world's eyes, for I see you through the blood of my Son Jesus Christ.

You are a light in darkness. Your candle shines, and I need your light in the dark world. Your light shines *just by being you!* You bring Me glory. You bring Me honor, just by being you.

You are significant to Me and my Kingdom's plans. It is not by chance that you reside in your present corner. I have placed you there to be a light of mine, to shine the light of Jesus in the dark world around you . . . just by being you! Repent when you "flub up," then glory in my shining and reigning presence that touches lives through you.

Can you manufacture the Holy Spirit's anointing? No. Can you break the yoke that the anointing destroys? No. Are you the power? No. You are merely the conduit. We have been working on purifying the heart, "roto-rootering" your heart canals so that my anointing might flow unhindered through you. This comes in just by being you!

True holiness spawns from the root system of your heart, grounded in my Word. The soil of your heart will produce the fruit of your branches. You can only yield to the deep roots that swallow up the rain of my Spirit and the meat of my Word. It is the authentic Lordship of Jesus Christ that precisely prunes for maximum perfection on the vine. You may only allow the Vinedresser to garden his vines according to my perfect will.

In time, my hand of perfection produces a sweet crop. This has been the Vinedresser's purpose: to serve the sweet platter of grapes and hear announced, "Well done!"

The vine can only yield and respond, hunger and thirst. Even when pruned, the branches will humbly bow in repentance. The vine understands to welcome the "snip" of the pruning tools. Humility is her response. The Bride of Christ welcomes the pruning and brings forth fruit worthy of her Father's pleasure and Groom's delight! Amen.

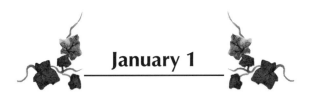

January 1

Father's Favor

"By this I know that thou favourest me, because mine enemy doth not triumph over me."   *Psalm 41:11 KJV*

What is favor? It is a daddy's listening ear that cannot say no! It is a father's heart that pounds when his child expresses love and adoration for him. It is a host of angels that waits to hear a command to protect you, and they do that at the sound of Father's voice.

My favor first begins with the blood of the Lamb. The washing away of sin opens the door of my favor!

Your response to Me is what pulls the heart strings of your Father. I am not so difficult to rope in! I cannot resist love songs, heartfelt praise, and your honor of Me.

A father likes to know that he is loved by his children. His long hours of labor have paid for his child's provision. He rejoices to hear appreciation. "Thank you" are tender words to his heart. Like salt sprinkled on a steak, praise flavors a daddy's attitude towards his child.

When a child likes to do what his dad does, that also wins the father's heart. Two who hunt together (father-son), hunt amiably and build comradeship. The wise son will pace himself with his dad and seek his father's voice on matters of concern in their conversation. The son will honor the dad with respect, not ridicule. In this atmosphere of honor, the father's heart is won, and favor is granted.

What the son needs, he receives. What the son asks for, he gets. The father bends over backwards to assist the son in reaching his goals. After all, favor means unceasing giving and support . . . so it is with Me, your Heavenly Father. The enemy absolutely will not triumph over you if you have won your *Father's favor* by loving, honoring, and cherishing Me! Amen.

January 2

Hasten My Word

"I will hasten my word to perform it."   *Jeremiah 1:12 KJV*

I love to perform my Word, for in doing so, my divine destiny for my beloved creation unfolds.

Performing my will is like sending warm sunshine upon a rose garden of budded bushes. It is the blossoming of the buds that cries "glory!" The petals unfold and emit my sweet fragrance of heaven. The beauty is most exquisite in the blossoming roses whose petals have given their unfolded plant-loveliness for all to behold, enjoy, and cherish!

My Word is my will for your life. As your Heavenly Father, my purpose is to guide your steps upon my path of destiny that reflects your Father's heart. When I first created you, I had in mind a specific plan and purpose and calling for you to fulfill. Each man is given to, so that he might give again. My gifts are placed in you so that you might be my hand extension on earth.

As my Word is performed through you, my "Father's heart" is overjoyed! I become excited when my will is acted out on the stage of life. Your audience in the heavenlies gives applause for your fulfillment of my Word performed!

I send my angels to assist you in your everyday tasks. I hasten to perform my Word through you and in behalf of your prosperity and health.

When my Word is spoken through your lips in faith, a supernatural chemical explosion transpires that releases divine energy in your behalf!

Speak my Word. Profess my promises. Pray my love songs! I, in turn, will *hasten my Word* to be performed, both in your behalf and in behalf of your loved ones for whom you have interceded with my Word. I love you! Amen.

January 3

Your Children Are Blessed

"The just man walketh in his integrity; his children are blessed after him."
Proverbs 20:7 KJV

The meaning of this promise is simple. If you walk in my integrity as an upstanding citizen in my Kingdom, then my blessing will fall upon your children.

Indeed, I honor my promise to the man and woman of integrity in Me. My blessings follow obedience. You are able to purchase a flow from heaven of goodness and splendid gifts by walking uprightly before Me and living according to my Word.

Blessings flow, like a river, meandering about each family member, for it is certain that you cannot outgive Me. My blessing on your seed is just one way I can give back to you your own gift of loving and serving Me with all of your heart.

I do love you, and I desire only good to come to your offspring and descendants. *Your children are blessed* because I love you!

January 4

Glorify My Name

"I will praise you, O Lord my God, with all my heart; I will glorify your name forever."
Psalm 86:12 NIV

This is the heartbeat cry of my beloved one, my saint who loves and honors Me with a complete attitude of surrender.

I say in return, "And I love you, too! It is my great pleasure to know you and love you. You are a child that brings Me gladness, unlike some other children who lie against my truths."

The soul who will *glorify my name* forever understands his eternal value; that whether on earth or in heaven, his destiny is to give Me glory!

To be only earthly minded is to be shortsighted. I give you eyes of eternity that see beyond the crust of the earth.

Your spirit eyes understand life's longevity, and the works done in your flesh fade in light of my eternal glory calling to you, "Come, come home, my love, come home!"

January 5

Keep Silent

"The Lord is in his holy temple: let all the earth keep silent before him."
Habakkuk 2:20 KJV

Reverence is a lost art in your contemporary world. The speed of which daily life travels blinds the moments of worship I daily offer in the artistry of my angels' early sunrise or the silhouette of silver designed on a full moon's night. Yes, even in nature, I send you glimpses of my glory and moments of worship, that which your eyes may behold and your heart may embrace.

Reverence stems from the inner man. It is an attitude of awe and respect for who I am with an understanding of what it is I do for you daily. It defies the presumptuousness of man and places deity back on my throne. I long to be recognized and worshipped because I dwell within my holy temple.

Earth does not understand holiness. The counterfeiter has tempted the world to design a lifestyle completely lacking of holiness and purity, but he cannot touch the sunrise or sunset. He cannot affect the moon or the stars—nor even the eternal spirits of my saved ones washed in the blood of my Son.

Oh, that the earth would *keep silent* before Me! It is the realization of my holiness that creates the silence of reverence. Behold your God! Even in your corporate worship, I desire to be honored by your reverenced silence before Me.

I am holy! I am holy! I am holy! Let all the earth keep silent before Me! Amen.

January 6

New Home Heaven's Side

"For our light and momentary troubles are achieving for us an eternal glory that far outweighs them all."   *2 Corinthians 4:17 NIV*

The difference between a rotten boiled egg and a solid golden egg is the difference between your earthly suffering and your heavenly reward.

Beloved, pure suffering turns into gold in heaven. It comes with you and transforms into living jewels and stones about your neck and upon your crown, and it far outweighs your momentary troubles.

There is not one tear on earth that is not saved and recorded in heaven.

Beloved, I want to comfort you with my promise of heaven. It is like preparing for a vacation. You study maps, make reservations, plan out a schedule, save your money, and in your heart, anticipation grows and excitement builds in your expectation of the fun holiday event.

It is the same way with heaven—only you never return home!

No sacrifice you make in saving and preparing for your trip to heaven is too great. Your wildest imaginations cannot humanly fathom the ultimate sheer glory of your *new home heaven's side.* You will love it! Amen.

January 7

The Stripes

"Who his own self bare our sins in his own body on the tree, that we, being dead to sins, should live unto righteousness: by whose stripes ye were healed."
                    I Peter 2:24 KJV

Understand the cross. Realize the purpose of my Son's suffering for you! It is more than salvation, more than a ticket to heaven. Because He bore your sin, you and I can begin our father-son eternal relationship. "Live unto righteousness" means that you can fellowship with Me. We can converse and enjoy our love for one another. Cleansed in the blood of the Lamb, you become aware of my "Fatherhood" and my intense love for you. Our mutual friendship grows.

My Son bore *the stripes* in your behalf. We loved you, and the purchase of your good divine health was made at the cross. The price has been paid. The enemy's right to afflict your body is no more. You need only FAITH to exercise the privilege of walking in good health.

You only have to believe to receive. I have already made the purchase. Let not the stripes be for naught!

January 8

In the Desert

"I am like an owl of the desert."   *Psalm 102:6 KJV*

What man has not walked through a desert?

I am with you, even in the driest of times when your throat is parched and there is no quenching of your thirst.

Beloved, I am with you. When or where you veered onto the desert plain, you may not clearly recall. Only, one day you noticed the sweat on your brow and the dry, crusty earth beneath your feet.

It is *in the desert* that I am able to allow segments of your humanity to dry up. Like unnecessary baggage, in the desert, you rid yourself of weight and burden that you carried voluntarily without my direction.

In the desert, we have long walks, even though it seems that you are talking to an empty sky. I am with you! It is in these desert days that I prepare areas of repentance that would not have surfaced any other time.

All you know to do is look forward and perpetually step in the same direction utilizing all the skills you have learned prior to this moment. The thrill of new revelation is silenced. The intimacy and fellowship with Me is quieted. You are alone, it seems, even though I am with you!

No man enjoys the desert when he is in the middle of it and has no choice but to proceed forward to its edge. Remembrances of past streams flowing with cool, clear water come to the forefront of your mind.

My encouragement is that what you learn in the desert is important to Me, necessary for your growth. The fruit of repentance will be sweet-tasting to Me— and to you. Hold true to what you have already attained. I will guide you out of the dry place and set again your feet in my wells of salvation.

January 9

Practice for Eternity

"Speak to one another with psalms, hymns, and spiritual songs. Sing and make music in your heart to the Lord."　　　　　　　　　*Ephesians 5:19 NIV*

I admonish you to speak with psalms, hymns, and spiritual songs because this will be your eternal conduct in Me when the full glory of my presence is realized.

Being about your Father's business in heaven will entail extensive song between you and other beloved saints. Your language will be praise and song of Me.

Praise and worship are the business of heaven. When you sing psalms and hymns to Me, you are joining yourself with a host of unseen angels and saints that have gone before you.

I like always for you to be practicing on earth those attitudes and arts of heaven . . . on earth as it is in heaven.

It is with great difficulty that I can sway my people to practice such hospitality on earth. You are carnally inclined to "chat and discuss" the issues of life's pressures and the weather nonsense, when you should, on the contrary, be addressing one another in song and making melody in your hearts unto Me. That is what you will do in heaven. Oh, that you would *practice for eternity* in your spare time!

January 10

Never Give Up

"He who overcomes shall be clothed in white garments, and I will not blot out his name from the Book of Life; but I will confess his name before My Father and before His angels."   *Revelation 3:5 NKJV*

To overcome is to not give up. *Never give up* on Me and my ability to cleanse, heal, and deliver you.

Beloved, to overcome is to keep striking out time and time again, believing always in your potential for a home run. Then, suddenly, the moment comes, the ball soars out of the stadium, and you are the hero!

Beloved, to overcome is to resist evil every day of your life.

To overcome is to face temptation but to turn away from its appealing pleasures.

To overcome is to say "no!" repeatedly to the enemy's offers.

To overcome is to stand in faith, believing my promises and knowing that I always honor and respond to faith.

To overcome is to trust my time scale and not anxiously rush ahead of my foreordained plan for your life.

To overcome is to patiently wait as I line up all circumstances and priorities to work together.

To overcome is to fall one hundred times, get back up 100 times, and try again 100 times . . . until finally, the 101'st time, you ride for miles.

To overcome is to absolutely never give up!

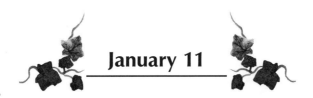

January 11

Precept upon Precept

"For precept must be upon precept, precept upon precept; line upon line, line upon line; here a little, and there a little."   *Isaiah 28:10 KJV*

Beloved, I have been and I am perfecting you, line upon line, *precept upon precept.* I am the Master Carver who has had a design in mind for your spirit man since the beginning of time.

I am creating in you the Kingdom of Heaven, one precept upon another—one gentle carve after another, one revelation after another. I am preparing you for the Eternal City where no frostbite exists, where no venom poisons, where no man dies but lives eternally.

Beloved, I love you, and I will perfect both your natural life and your spiritual walk.

I will never forsake the works of your hands—never! This means that my Spirit will work alongside you, in you, through you, and around you to produce fruit.

Only ask, and I will breathe upon the works of your hands and cause the "ordinary" to become "extraordinary"—because that is the kind of God I am! Amen.

January 12

A Good Thing to Fast

"But the time will come when the bridegroom will be taken from them; in those days they will fast."   *Luke 5:35 NIV*

It is *a good thing to fast*, to wait upon the Lord, to seek Me with your whole heart and your whole body. I love you, beloved. When you fast, you set yourself apart in a special way unto Me. You know you cannot displease Me in your fast, for I have mercy on the weak. When you fast, your vessel is weakened that your spirit might be strengthened. Rejoice! There is a way by which you are able to "speed up" your pace of growth in Me—by fasting, says your Lord.

Wait, be still, listen, allow Me to speak. Fasting in itself is not dynamic, but what I do in your spirit man will shake the earth. The more dimension I am able to inhabit within you, the more your prayers will shake the face of the earth.

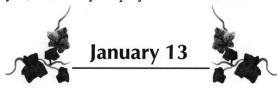

January 13

I Love to Stretch You!

"I can do everything through him who gives me strength."

Philippians 4:13 NIV

There is nothing you cannot accomplish in my strength, for that which I call you to do, I will always equip you. Nothing shall be impossible when you have my will backing your exploits.

It is my anointing that causes all that you do to sparkle with that Holy Ghost excellence. That which you do in my strength and will has my glory shining through it crying, "Holy!"

Philippians 4:13 should be the motto engraved across the forefront of your heart. If you know nothing is impossible with Me, then you can do the impossible through Me. *I love to stretch you!* I am in the stretching business. If you are mine, I will stretch you with circumstances and a calling that demands your absolute dependency upon my promise of Philippians 4:13.

You bring me great JOY when you entrust your uneasiness to faith's challenge and believe this verse. I am glorified when you entrust the giant, Goliath, into my sling shot, simple but mighty.

I love to empower you to do the impossible! Your flesh cries out, but your spirit soars as an eagle. I love you, beloved. Believe and reach with Me to higher heights. Nothing is impossible in my strength!

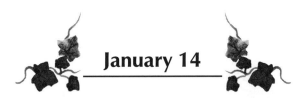

January 14

Power, Love, and a Sound Mind

"For God has not given us a spirit of fear, but of power and of love and of a sound mind."   *2 Timothy 1:7 NKJV*

Whenever you are afraid, you need to remember that you have laid down your sword of faith, and the enemy's foot is upon your back.

It is not my will for you to ever fear—never! I have not given you this spirit of fear. No! I give you a spirit of POWER—a spirit of LOVE—and a SOUND MIND.

The truth of the matter is, despite your feelings, I equip you with love and power. I do not give you depression and confusion. No. I give you a sound mind.

You have two simple choices. Walk in fear, or walk in faith. Walk with Me, or walk with the enemy. Walk in victory, or walk in defeat.

There is no excuse for misery because my promise is for your *power, love, and a sound mind*.

The choice is yours!

January 15

I Will Send Comfort

"For the Lord comforts his people and will have compassion on his afflicted ones."   *Isaiah 49:13 NIV*

When my people are afflicted, my heart is pierced. Then is when my angels send the needy ones increased grace to endure and strengthened heart to withstand the hardships.

When outer circumstances deny the manifestation of victory, I supply the supernatural presence of inner victory.

You cannot outgive Me in your devotion and dedication. The more you commit your hardship to Me, the more I will assist in your deliverance.

No matter what the affliction, if you turn to Me, *I will send comfort*—and that is the manifest presence of God in you!   Amen.

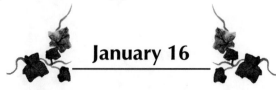

January 16

I Am My Word

"I cannot go beyond the word of the Lord my God, to do less or more."
Numbers 22:18 KJV

This oath is to be worn as your badge of honor. Do you solemnly swear not to go beyond my Word to do even more or less? Delight to do my will, and I will write my laws within your heart!

Beloved, I love you, and I see your earnest, sincere love for my Word. I am my Word! In the beginning was the Word, and the Word was with God, and the Word was God. You love my Word because you love Me. You love my Son because you love Me. My Son is the Bread of Life. Your spirit consumes this bread and brings forth spiritual fruit.

All the secrets of my universe are hidden within my Word. They are locked and sealed up and given to those who earnestly seek Me with all of their hearts.

Beloved, I love you! My Word is the light unto your path so you never have cause to stumble. My Word of promise will never fail or disappoint you. Have faith in my Word, and the performance of my promises will follow.

Beloved, my Word is my love letter to you, a record of your inheritance in the spirit and your eternal genealogy.

My Word is eternal. In heaven, my Word breathes spiritual life continually, sings constantly, speaks always. Heaven is an atmosphere of my Word, like the oxygen you breathe on earth. All things in heaven consist of my Word.

That is why you should highly prize it now on earth. Grow accustomed to living Word-centered, for this is a reflection of your eternal life in heaven with Me. If you want more of heaven on earth for yourself, incorporate more of my Word into your life. *I am my Word.* We eternally breathe together. I love you. Amen.

January 17

Your Father's Eyes

"Your eye is the lamp of your body. When your eyes are good, your whole body also is full of light. But when they are bad, your body is full of darkness."
Luke 11:34 NIV

Let Me give you my eyes, beloved,
  for then you will look upon life
    the way I do.

My eyes discern.
  They view with wisdom,
    ready with answers and decisions.

My eyes, beloved,
  see past the waves
    to the destination of the boat.
My eyes never rest upon the waves,
  thus depression never comes.
    Darkness is the perfect word for depression,
      but there is only light in my eyes.

If you are wanting
  to be filled with my love,
    and if you are desiring to be a light
      that shines to all men—
  like a city set on a hill,
    then you shall be!

Only yield to my sight,
  and seek Me to place upon you
    your Father's eyes.

With my eyes,
  you will see and pursue
    peace and love toward your neighbor.

In my strength,
  shall this vision
    be accomplished.

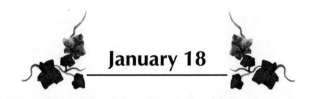

January 18

Taproot of Jesus

"And He shall be like a tree Planted by the rivers of water, That brings forth its fruit in its season, Whose leaf also shall not wither, And whatsoever he does shall prosper."   *Psalm 1:3 NKJV*

If your taproot is Jesus, you will always be like a tree planted near the river's edge. You will never thirst beyond being satisfied quickly with my roots that tap into the River of Life from heaven that flows about my throne, through my City, and 'round about my Heavenly Kingdom.

If your taproot is Jesus, whatsoever you do will prosper with good success. His inexhaustible supply will be yours to draw from during each event in your life.

I love you, beloved, and I want you to prosper! Simply draw from Me for your strength.

My River is alive with spiritual blessing. It flows down from amidst the throne of God into your heart. I stir you up with my Holy Ghost current. You sense my presence and drink from my fresh anointing upon you. Each day you are revitalized by my fresh flow of the Holy River gushing through you.

My River of Life sustains your spirit as it is charged with nutrients and minerals vital for your spirit's survival.

The *taproot of Jesus* in your heart swallows up for you "heaven's grace," the needed nourishment and drink of my Spirit for your daily productivity.

You are my fruit tree, and your yield of abundant fruit is sweet-tasting and full of the flavor of Jesus, like similar fruits you will find growing within heaven's orchard.

Go and bear fruit! The taproot of Jesus Christ sustains your mission. Go and bear fruit!

January 19

On the Job Obedience

"But this is what I commanded them saying, 'Obey My voice, and I will be your God, and you shall be My people. And walk in all the ways that I have commanded you, that it may be well with you.' "   *Jeremiah 7:23 NKJV*

Beloved, I love you, and I am watching over you every single minute of your journey on earth! I never leave you, and I will never forsake you.

Beloved, you have been seeking after that which is not mandatory in my Kingdom's functioning. You do not have to feel in your heart, as your heart's desire, this big and inspiring drive and duty for your place of employment. No. Your love for Me is to be your motivation to serve, not your love for people.

Quit trying to identify a human desire to motivate you, from which you may draw strength. No. It is not going to happen. Besides, that which is from the heart eventually fades away anyway, because man will trample your human devotion and the desires of your heart.

Oh, but your love for Me is of a divine nature. It will never end or burn out because I will never frustrate your love for Me.

To obey is better than to be driven by an inspiring spring of desire—because the spring may run dry in time and is vulnerable to seasonal and mood change. Your obedience to Me, based upon your love and devotion to Me, stays constant and unchanging.

When you go to work, serve in obedience to Me. Draw from my heart, not yours—my strength, not yours—my inspiration, not yours—and my purposes, not yours.

You will be much happier walking to the tune of obedience instead of frustrating yourself with your own fickle heart. Time has a way of deviously wearing down all good human intent.

I love you, beloved. Go and be free! Live one day at a time unto Me. I ask nothing more of you, so do not ask more of yourself.

Genuine and sincere human happiness will begin to envelop your soul as you walk in simple *on the job obedience.* That feeling which you have longed for will now come forth, not from your humanity but from my Spirit.

I love you! Thank you for being my willing vessel by being my missionary in the corner of the world that I am sending you.

You need only shine as a bright light. I am not asking the impossible from you. My call is for you to shine brightly in a dark place. This is my best for you. Amen.

January 20

I See Your Anguish

I will be glad and rejoice in your love, for you saw my affliction and knew the anguish of my soul."
Psalm 31:7 NIV

I see your anguish, the pain, and the sorrow of your soul. I am always close by to attend to your needs. My angels are constant in their attention over you. My Holy Spirit always comforts and consoles.

I am equipped to care for you when the heaviness of the world crushes down the strength of your shoulders. I am compassion! I am also teacher and parent-Father, and my ultimate will for you is to mature, grow up, and learn to ward off the enemy before he attacks and devours.

Satan loves anguish! He relishes in your despair, but I work it for good, carve more of your flesh away, and replenish with the Lordship of Jesus Christ in your life. In Jesus, there is no victory for the enemy, none whatsoever!

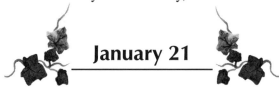

January 21

Joyful Songs!

"Serve the Lord with gladness; come before him with joyful songs."
Psalm 100:2 NIV

This is the Psalmist's admonition to worship Me, with his instructions to explain "how." He is correct! It is with gladness of heart that you would be motivated to serve Me. Thankfulness stems from a humble heart that produces gladness. To be happy in Me is to be thankful for my daily provisions for you.

I recognize a glad heart from the selfish and self-centered soul. I honor contentment in Me, for knowing Me in right relationship is contentment enough. One must truly know Me to experience sincere gladness.

When your heart is right and open before Me, it is the song of your soul that erupts from deep within. Right relationship with Me spawns *joyful songs!* It is the joyful song that soothes your Daddy's heart and brings Me joy because you are my creation, and I love you.

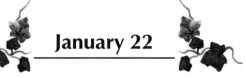

January 22

Well Done!

"His lord said to him, Well done, good and faithful servant; you have been faithful over a few things, I will make you ruler over many things: Enter into the joy of your lord."   *Matthew 25:23 NKJV*

Beloved, in light of eternity, you have very few days in your human flesh. Each day is important to Me. My agenda for you is personal and eternal—and what becomes of your earthly life continues on with you into your eternal life.

Now, man does look on the outward appearance, but it is I that can peer into the deepest caverns of your heart where no secrets can exist.

It is your faithfulness to Me that I am most watching. How steadfast in your heart is your love for Me? How deeply do you honor and adore Me? Are you hungering and thirsting after my righteousness? Is it my will that you seek to fulfill, above and beyond your own?

Beloved, I love you! Many works I may call you to complete, but always I will be watching to see if your heart is truly loving Me in sincere servitude unto your Lord and Savior Jesus Christ.

Duty is dead apart from the heart of love that should spawn devotion to good works. I want not your outward works if you cannot give Me your inward love.

Beloved, if there are bars across your heart, then I have come to release you from them. I desire that there be no barrier between you and Me.

The most lethal weapon against true devotion to my service is unforgiveness. It will foster and emit poisons throughout your spirit man, eventually causing death in your spontaneous heart-felt love for Me.

When worship becomes duty only and servitude becomes drudgery, then is when you need to make a serious heart check-up with Me. To become cold and withered away from my Spirit is to deprive yourself of the most precious words your ears will hear at the entrance into my Kingdom, *"Well done!"* See to it that we are not deprived of that royal announcement upon your arrival! Amen.

Never Be Ashamed of Me!

"For I am not ashamed of the gospel of Christ, for it is the power of God to salvation for everyone who believes."   **Romans 1:16 NKJV**

It is never good or right to be ashamed of your Living God! I am your Creator. Human audacity finds it offensive to be dependent upon its Creator. Human humility delights in dependence upon my Holy Spirit's power unto salvation.

Never be ashamed of Me! I birthed you into my Kingdom. I cradled you, fed you on milk, and have raised you up into high places in Christ Jesus. You should not be able to stop talking about my miracle power in your life! Your love for Me should be dripping from your tongue like a honeycomb drips with sweet honey.

Beloved, if you are embarrassed of your testimony and too shy or timid to openly declare what I have done for you, then obviously, I haven't yet done enough to set you free from pride's teeth. The stigma of being a "Christian" should be a pleasure to live up to. I did not call you to please the crowd, but, rather, to come out from amongst the crowd, to wear my combat boots and march in my parade of soldiers who look and act like Jesus.

My walk of faith is the opposite of the natural, carnal man. You listen to my voice and then do what you hear. You pray, then obey. You spend time with Me receiving, and then you go out to the world dispensing the very goods I gave you.

Your life is supernatural! I make all things to work for your good! My angels are on assignment around you, and your source is Me in all things.

Beloved, hold your head up high and denounce all pride. Your life is hidden in Christ! I provide for you in the smallest of ways but also in the largest of ways.

Beloved one, I love you! Who I have made you to be in Jesus Christ is a triumphant victor over satan! Be never ashamed of your testimony, for it is my power that has worked in you, the very power that seeks to deliver others from the same identical snares of the enemy.

Your testimony will be a life line to another. Your willingness to lay down your pride and give Me glory for the changes I have made in you, will bring liberty to another wrapped around with those same old chains from which I delivered you. The very bands of wickedness that once enveloped you will, too, be loosened in others as you testify of my gospel power in you.

Beloved, I love you. Be only who I have made you to be. The truly hungry in the heart will be drawn to my power through your testimony. Your unashamed testimony will be a life jacket to a fellow man drowning in the same swamp of despair from which I saved you.

Be a life saver by sharing your testimony to a lost world! Amen.

January 24

Mercy and Second Chances

"The Lord is full of compassion and mercy."   **James 5:11 NIV**

Mercy and compassion is the foundation of your Heavenly Father's heart.

I looked upon my creation and questioned, "What have I done?" The carrier of rebellion and sin grieved your Father's heart.

Then I looked, and behold, there was always one heart open unto Me, one who I chose for their generation for Me to breathe divine life back into again.

It is my endless compassion that has led Me to reconsider, repeatedly, the opportunity to begin anew with a fresh plan and an increased measure of mercy upon earth's insatiably hungry appetite for greed, lust, and self-centeredness.

Always by mercy have I forgiven—even sent my beloved Son of God to redeem mankind from sin. I love you with a golden heart of compassion demonstrated and manifested in acts of *mercy and second chances.* Amen.

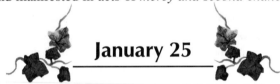

January 25

I Am Here!

"You are my hiding place; you will protect me from trouble and surround me with songs of deliverance."   **Psalm 32:7 NIV**

The eye within the storm—it is I—walking across the water, coming towards you to rescue your sinking boat. When all else fails and circumstances "appear" to be tumbling down all around you, *I AM HERE!*

In the presence of danger, threat, or disease, I AM HERE! In the midst of human sorrow, human pain and despair, I sing out to you: I am here!

Many times I rescue you, like grabbing the nape of a cat and picking it up out of harm's way.

I deliver you, even sometimes when you do not realize! I love you desperately! No harm is ordained to touch you, my precious anointed one. I will always fight for you because you cry out the name of JESUS!

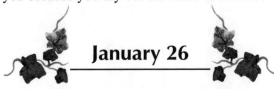

January 26

Angel Nails

"And that from a child thou hast known the holy scriptures, which are able to make thee wise unto salvation through faith which is in Christ Jesus."
2 Timothy 3:15 KJV

To you who have had the good fortune of a righteous mother and a noble father, happy and blessed are you! My Word has been invested in your spirit since before you were born! Your path of righteousness has been laid out before you since you took your first wobbling steps. Yours has been a doubly blessed life, indeed!

My Word enables a soul to be constructed with a solid foundation upon good and high ground. Even when storms hit, you are spared devastation because you were built in a wise location.

My Word supernaturally builds a little soul. It "super-braces" the foundation of personality and sets up right emotions. The inward hidden structure is built soundly and thus is prepared to endure the hardships that life may bring.

Little children who are born into my Kingdom's homes are able to draw from my wisdom that has been invested in them through my Word. Their souls are guarded from struggles that the average child will endure.

Parent, wisely teach and instruct your children, your tiniest of babes, with my Word, remembering that eyes cannot see the spirit's structure that you are building. The fruit of their lives will prove, in time, the presence of my Word constructed within them.

My Word spoken over your children will be like *angel nails* from heaven driven into their souls. These nails will eternally shine from their being, separating them from the average Joe, empowering them to be above and beyond the ordinary. Angel nails will even return with them to heaven!

My anointing in your children will be obvious because it will be my Word making them wise unto salvation through faith in Christ Jesus their Lord. Amen.

January 27

Eternal Joy

"But none of these things move me, neither count I my life dear unto myself, so that I might finish my course with joy." **Acts 20:24 KJV**

No matter what happens to you, do not allow your JOY to be trampled, like a herd of cattle stampeding your soul. Even when life's pressures feel like 1,000 pound steers running over your back, do not give up! If you do not count your own, unique "pride in self" precious above all, then you will be able to sacrifice and suffer without losing your joy.

All that really matters is remaining in my will. Rough times may come, but if you are walking close with Me down my paved path blazed for your feet, then no one and no circumstances can steal your joy.

Babies cry when their diapers are wet. Mature children take responsibility for their needs and their actions, and when things don't go their way, they do not lie down on the floor and impart into a raging kicking fit.

Do not count your life dear unto yourself. Count it, rather, dear unto Me.

I am the potter. I have molded you with my plan and purpose in mind. You are my tool in the hand of your Sovereign God. Whether you blossom into one bloom or into ten thousand, depends on Me and my plan.

I often need small people in small places who have big hearts. Allow Me to plant you where I need you most. Then, if storms beat against you, you can know that I foreknew the weather and have equipped you with ample fortitude to endure.

I love you, beloved. Whether you be a saw, a hammer, or a nail . . . and whether you become a tulip, rose, or gardenia . . . this should matter not to you. Only that you blossom fully in my chosen garden, should be your desire. Only that you perform well in my hand as the tool I have crafted you to be, should be your heart's desire.

In my will, there is *eternal joy*. It is only in fulfilling my heart's desires for your life that you will experience eternal, heavenly JOY. It is worth any price. Amen.

January 28

Scarlet to Snow!

"Come now, and let us reason together, saith the Lord: though your sins be as scarlet, they shall be as white as snow; though they be red like crimson, they shall be as wool."   *Isaiah 1:18 KJV*

The mystery of my New Covenant is wrapped up in this promise. Your sins can be cleansed away by the forgiving blood of my Son Jesus Christ your Lord!

It is the spilled blood of the Lamb that cleanses you from all unrighteousness and permits you and Me to freely fellowship as Father-child must do! In your heart, you cry, "Abba, Daddy!"

Because of the redemptive blood of my dear Son, I am able to respond with my Father's heart and return my cry, "Son! Daughter! Come unto Me! I love you with my eternal, all-consuming, fiery love. Come. Sit at my feet. Eat of my Word. Speak with Me. Tell Me your heart's desires. Empty your burdens and come with Me. Son! Daughter! I love you! I love you! I love you!"

The blood of Jesus Christ has washed your sins away! It has defeated the enemy's hold in your life. Every stronghold and pothole shall be defeated, and you shall be filled with my Holy Spirit, empowered to do my good works on earth as it is in heaven.

The red blood has purchased your white linen garments. The crimson sacrifice has bought your soul of wool, clean and complete before Me! You stand before Me white as snow, as virgin wool—*scarlet to snow!*

Let us rejoice in our father/son love as your voice echoes within my holy temple, "Abba, Father! Abba, Father! Abba, Father!" I am your daddy, and I love you. Come now, let us reason together! I desire to speak and pour into your virgin ears my voice of love, my voice of comfort, my voice of wisdom. Come now, my beloved, cleansed in the blood of my Son, listen to your Father's voice.

January 29

Budding Stub!

"For I know the plans I have for you, declares the Lord, plans to prosper you and not to harm you, plans to give you hope and a future."
1 Jeremiah 29:11 NIV

My beloved, I love you. You know that I love you! For many months now, you have been stubbed, mercilessly chopped off by the corn knife of death that steals and destroys the precious breath of mortal life.

Left alone to stand, you have born the pain of changing seasons from rain, to cold, to heat. You have felt drowned, frozen, and scorched—but you have nonetheless stood the test. Your stub has not rotted and deteriorated in character. No, on the contrary, you have endured by yielding to Me all discomfort. You have bowed before my throne and humbled yourself before Me in your broken, stubby state.

While the world was beholding a mournful sight, beneath the surface I was busily and faithfully deepening your root structure, strengthening your root canals, and enriching you below surface level, deep in the secret most caverns of your heart.

You have painfully yielded each day to Me, and my promise has been, I will be here for you!

Now, after much restructuring of the inner heart canals, I am ready to produce new growth on your outward stub.

I will now begin leading you into a new season of outward manifestation of that which has been publicly hidden.

You are my *budding stub!* With swelling arms, you will be popping forth with new extensions of my foliage upon you.

In your new wisdom and divine revelation, you will begin to produce actual buds of blossoms. In days not too far from now, you will honestly feel like a blossoming bush once again. You won't be the same. You will have new colors and an abundance of blossoms which will emit my fragrance of heaven invested in you.

Beloved, your season of mourning has come to its end. I am on the verge of calling you forth into new power and new fortitude for my glory! Amen.

January 30

Milking the Cow

"So then faith comes by hearing, and hearing by the Word of God."
Romans 10:17 NKJV

If you want to grow in faith, you must empty my Word into your soul. Faith will grow, like garden vegetables, if you water with the Word.

A supernatural chemistry takes place in your spirit man when your heart hears my Word. You see, faith is more than a choice or decision. It is actually heaven in you, like gas in a tank, that equips your motor of faith to run and operate well.

Man cannot believe on fumes alone (head knowledge). No. Man's faith is my gift of grace to believe.

Only the born-again spirit can produce faith because I place it there and feed it with my Word. Your faith will rise and fall according to the amount of my Word it is fed.

Have you ever wondered why your spiritual walk with Me is up and down? That is because your lean diet of the Word weakens your walk in the Spirit.

It is your responsibility to seek first the Kingdom of God. As a mature adult, I expect you to feed and water your garden of faith with my Word. Hear it. Read it. Speak it. Record it. Play it. Profess it.

You are a manufacturer of faith! It is produced by my Word and manifested through you in mountain-moving life style.

If you feel that you are slipping and losing grip on your personal life or those you care for, examine your Word flow. Oops! You have been dieting again. Take the time to feed your spirit. In the long run, time will be spared; for a faithless life produces great havoc, and much of a man's life can be spent sweeping up messes that could have been prevented with faith.

Why spend your life mopping up spilled milk? Wouldn't you rather be *milking the cow*—producing, selling, and prospering? Have faith! A faithless life is a waster of valuable time.

January 31

All Night in Prayer

"And it came to pass in those days, that he went out into a mountain to pray, and continued all night in prayer to God."　　　　　*Luke 6:12 KJV*

Jesus, my Son, was *all night in prayer* unto Me—many times. His human soul carried within it the weight of the sin of the world. This he could not bear alone. He came to Me time and time again to unload the accumulated earthly load and to receive new strength to continue his journey.

Beloved, if you are not having times of intense heartache in behalf of others, then you are yet a child in my faith. For as you mature, I place in your heart, as was in Jesus, my burden for lost souls and wronged circumstances.

There will be times when I call you to stay up all night in prayer. As you mature in Me, I will call you to become an intercessor who counts not the cost of his sleep.

One is unable to sleep when the weight of another's sin is upon you. Being an intercessor is no glorious job. You are mocked and ridiculed, and no one will ever know why a battle was won, even when you did successfully chase the enemy away.

It is dangerous not to pray. Only my directions will keep you sure-footed.

Count it a privilege and joy if I require of you one night's sleep in behalf of another.

I will repay. I will repay! You cannot outgive Me. Amen.

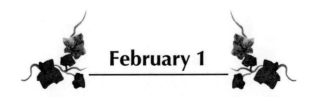

February 1

Like a Gopher

"What shall we then say to these things? If God be for us, who can be against us?"
                                                                    Romans 8:31 KJV

No matter how hard the rain is beating down against you, there is a sheltered dry place in Me where no storm can touch. I am an umbrella to your soul. Deep in the secret places of your heart, no foe, wind, or rain can come.

Your born-again spirit is promised eternal life. No man or enemy can steal your reward or the comfort of my heaven.

You have need of burrowing, *like a gopher*, deep into this secret chamber where my Spirit dwells. Find that sheltered spot where you and I alone can converse, fellowship, and where I can love and console you. There is a hiding place within your heart where we can converse and you can be comforted.

The world runs a race far too fast and cheers far too loudly for you to find my private cavern outward. No. You must burrow inwardly into my Word and prayer within your inward man.

Deep within, you will find our meeting place. Look not to man, rather, look to Me. I want to nurture our Abba, Father and Daddy to child relationship—one on one.

I want you to intimately experience my presence in your life, to know Me and love Me as your Abba, Father.

I love you, beloved. Burrow down into the deep canals of your heart and find our meeting place. We will banquet together, and I will feed you my revealed Word.

In this secret place, you will come to know that you know that I am for you, and no one can be against you! Amen.

February 2

Heartbeat of Jesus

"For the Son of man is come to seek and to save that which was lost."

Luke 19:10 KJV

It is the *heartbeat of Jesus* to save the lost! His greatest joy, even now, sitting at my right hand, is the confessed repentance of a lost soul.

Jesus is the Good Shepherd. He watches over his flock, and he seeks to bring new lambs into his fold. As I draw men unto Me, Jesus intercedes and works the preparation of the soil of heart. The soul of man must be prepared, either by excellent natural parenting or effectual Heavenly Father parenting. The first, of course, most generally comes much easier than the latter.

I am able to draw and prepare the soil of man's heart for salvation. This can take many years and tears before being broken at the feet of his Lord Jesus.

Those of you who pray for the unsaved, never give up! We are listening to your requests! We are digging up old rotten debris in hardened hearts. Remember that this may require the work of a lifetime in some men.

Have patience, as I, your Lord, have patience even with you! Inhabit your earth, and rejoice in answered prayer. Believe before you see it. Remember, though, that my angels respond to faith—your faith.

Only believe! I will do the rest. Amen.

February 3

Velveteen Favor

"Good understanding giveth favour: but the way of transgressors is hard."
Proverbs 13:15 KJV

It makes no sense not to join my army. The exchange of your heart for my life is incredibly lopsided!

You give up your will to receive divine destiny.

You tithe to receive a 100 fold crop.

You give up ill health to receive miraculous healing!

You give up being afraid to become bold as a lion.

You give up griping to become a praiser of my name.

You give up worry to become a man of faith.

You give up the world to receive an eternal Kingdom.

You give up selfishness to receive the joy of giving.

You give up your heartache to receive comfort.

You give up bondage to receive liberty.

You give up malice to experience love.

You give up resentment to forgive all men of all offenses.

You give up the "fight of life" to attain an army of angels.

You give up self-image to be conformed into Jesus' image.

You give up the wheel to become the co-pilot with God.

You give up your time to worship and become more loving and good.

You give up pride to wash others' feet.

You give up your hut to inherit a mansion.

You lose your life, only to find it in your God who designed you and created you with a unique and awesome plan in mind for your life.

I am your Father, and I love you. Why would a transgressor continue in a way that is hard when my way, my path, is lined with *velveteen favor?*

There is no fair exchange here because you cannot outgive Me. It is impossible!

February 4

Promise to Heal

"Heal me, O Lord, and I shall be healed; Save me, and I shall be saved, For You are my praise."   *Jeremiah 17:14 NKJV*

This should be your cry when your body becomes afflicted with disease. I created you with divine health in my mind. I sent my Son Jesus to defeat the enemy, sickness.

Now, when it raises its ugly head in your body, rebuke its presence. If you are my child, blood-bought through my New Covenant, then sickness is underneath your feet.

I will heal you! I will save you from disease!

If you earnestly seek Me with all of your heart . . . in prayer, in meditation, and in devotion, then I will see that sickness is driven away from you—as you ASK ME!

Divine health is deposited in my account for you, but FAITH signs the check. You must believe in my *promise to heal* you. You must believe! Amen.

February 5

Stir up the Gift

"Therefore I remind you to stir up the gift of God which is in you through the laying on of my hands."   *2 Timothy 1:6 NKJV*

I have invested in you spiritual gifts that differ from natural talents. The gifts from my Spirit ooze with the oil of my anointing, and they cannot be taught by a professor in a university. These gifts flow from your spirit and are empowered by my Holy Spirit in you to nurture life and inspiration to the body of Christ.

My spiritual gifts in you grow and become more fruitful as you freely give of the gift and yield to my Spirit's use of you.

Ask of Me to *stir up the gift* that is in you so that your generation may benefit from your expression of my voice on earth.

If you do not know what my gift in you is, then ask Me and seek Me to reveal what I have deposited in you. I desire my Church to abound in fruitfulness as each member contributes liberally that gift which has been imparted unto him. Give freely, and bless one another with my gifts in you! Amen.

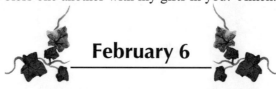

February 6

My House of Many Mansions

"In my Father's house are many mansions."   *John 14:2 KJV*

When you enter my heaven's gate, I will be there to greet and honor you. We will welcome you home with a feast of feasts unlike any earthly party you have ever attended! I have prepared a dwelling place for you where no sorrow or confusion can enter in, *my house of many mansions.*

You will hear choruses by choirs of angels, medleys to your ears unheard of on earth. I will invite you to play upon the harps and to join in the orchestra of pure worship where no key is flat or sharp and no wrong note is possible.

There is nothing on earth which to compare my holy sound of worship, except that on earth as it is in heaven—earthly worship is a foretaste divine. As in a mirror dimly, on earth, you are allowed to manipulate keys, sticks, voice, and strings. These bring Me honor as you offer up your praise and worship.

Beloved, you must know that there is a song of heaven that sounds across the universe most excellently! It is the song of glory and holiness of which I am about. It resounds from universe to universe, a sound of worship unfamiliar to human ear.

Upon the day of arrival into my heaven's Kingdom, your citizenship in my new land will grant you the right of hearing Kingdom sound—beauty and holiness ringing and resounding alive and strong, bursting forth from the throne of God and echoing from hilltop to hilltop, from universe to universe. You will love heaven, the vacation you never had on earth!

Inhabit your place on earth, and be at peace. I will always supply your needs, however great or small. Few things on earth really matter in the light of heaven. Eat, sleep, drink, be merry, love, work, do your duties as unto Me. You are a sojourner in a foreign land, and your true citizenship is in heaven.

I want simply for you to be able to enjoy my presence in your life and my gifts to you. Know I have sent you on your mission to inhabit the land, procreate, and, quite simply put, have babies and enjoy loving one another.

Worship and honor your Creator and enjoy my gifts. Enjoy my presence! Enjoy one another! Embrace your life with great JOY, and be thankful for my abundant grace and your salvation in Jesus Christ. Amen.

February 7

Forgive and Keep on Forgiving

"Shouldest not thou also have had compassion on thy fellowservant, even as I had pity on thee? And his lord was wroth, and delivered him to the tormentors, till he should pay all that was due unto him."   *Matthew 18:33-34 KJV*

Unforgiveness towards your brother will backfire onto you and bring torment into your life. Mental oppression accompanies unforgiveness. This is a given in my Kingdom.

If you refuse to forgive, then I cannot protect you from the onslaught of demonic oppression against your mind. The enemy has legal right in unforgiveness to pester, harass, and mentally torment you, which leads to sadness, depression, and despair—all because you, first, would not forgive.

I work with you to keep all doors shut, barred, and guarded from enemy troops, but your unforgiveness loosens the bar and throws the door wide open for enemy violation and attack. Unforgiveness, particularly, will open the door to mental torment, as it is written.

Beloved, you must forgive, first of all for your own good! Unforgiveness in your heart is like an acid that eats away every bit of goodness I have lengthily worked to deposit.

Beloved, you will have NO PEACE if you refuse to forgive. Never say, "I can't!" That is a lie. With the confession of your mouth state, "I forgive." Forgive first by a decision of your will. Later, your feelings will follow.

You may need to state your forgiveness again and then again! *Forgive and keep on forgiving* until no thorn any longer pricks you with bitterness.

Forgiveness is a choice in the midst of unfairness. You must select to forgive. Then, and only then, does the enemy lose his legal right to torment your mind and pull you down to his level of misery and mental oppression. His depression is like a tornado that sucks the very life out of you, burrowing into the ground and depositing your goods at the gates of hell.

Beloved, the simplest defense you have against mental torment is forgiveness. Please, be quick to forgive! You will spare your own self great agony in the long run. Amen.

February 8

I Will Sustain You

"Cast your burden on the Lord, And he shall sustain you; He shall never permit the righteous to be moved."   *Psalm 55:22 NKJV*

I will sustain you. There can be no other strength in your life that will sustain without fault. I will never fail you nor leave you. Do not attempt to place your trust in institutions or people, in organizations or structures built by the world's hands. It is only I that am able to sustain you unceasingly.

Man will fail you. Only place your soul's trust in Me, your God. I am able to sustain you through your many hardships and extensive labors. As a mother bird attends to her nest of young ones, so I, too, cater to your needs and feed you.

Keep your inner eyes off of the world's system of glamour and show. I have bread to feed you that will quench the hunger that from time to time you painfully experience. I have created that very ache of hunger for righteousness within you. You cannot be fed and satisfied by anyone other than Me.

Within your inner chamber, come away with Me. Bask in my presence—just you and Me. Read my Word, and fellowship with Me. Spend time with Me! It is only I, and I alone, that will fill up your cup to overflowing.

You cannot have joy overflowing apart from Me inhabiting my place in your heart. I cry unto you: Come unto Me! Spend time within my inner chambers. Bask in my presence, just you and Me!

I love you with my all encompassing, eternal, never ending, consuming love. I have created you to need Me, and I wait to hear you cry, "Daddy! Father, I need you."

I am here for you, always, but you must call upon my name. You must step away from the merry-go-round of busyness. You must reach out for Me, and then I will come. Then, I will rescue you from the world's screaming voices and hands that tear at your soul. My desire is to rescue you from the enemy's grip and to wrap my arms around you, to love and console you.

My desire is to sustain you with my love at all times so that my JOY might be abundant and overflowing through you! First, you must cry out to Me. Then, will I rescue you from the world, its flare, its deceit. I love you. Amen.

February 9

Have Mercy

"Forgive them; for they know not what they do."   *Luke 23:34 KJV*

These were Jesus' words, and they need also to be yours. Men do not know what they do to you! If they clearly see with my vision, they never choose to harm you! It is sin that blinds them from the truth. It is sin that blinds them from love; therefore, they see through glasses of hate.

The compassion of Jesus came in understanding the desperate need in man for a Savior and a Deliverer. Jesus saw beyond the hate to the inner core of man and his desperate lost state and need of a Savior.

In the same manner, as you rub elbows with flesh and blood, and evil spills over onto you, remember the words of Jesus. They knew not what they did—else they would not have crucified the very Son of God.

Those in your life who bring injury to you, they are in the same plight. They cannot see with eyes of love, else they would not injure you.

Have mercy, forgive, and pray for the souls who persecute you. They have need of the same light in which you walk. They have need of an intercessor who will stand in the gap for them and pray for their desperate souls.

Have mercy, for you have been shown mercy! Amen.

February 10

Promise Notes

"All your children shall be taught by the Lord, And great shall be the peace of your children."   ***Isaiah 54:13 NKJV***

This is my promise to you, invested in my Blessing Bank, ready to be withdrawn by your signature of faith at any given moment.

As you pray for your children, remind Me of your bank account of *promise notes.* The promise for your children's peace is as good as my name. Heaven's Blessing Bank can never run dry nor fluctuate with any worldly trend of trade or stocks. My investments are a sure thing, even unto eternity.

You write the check by releasing your faith and believing my Word. You ask, you believe, then you receive that your children are being taught by Me. If you see natural circumstances appearing otherwise, who is the liar? My Word cannot tell a lie!

Your children are promised my PEACE. All you have to do is withdraw my promise with your signature of faith.

February 11

Trust in Me

"In You, O Lord, I put my trust."   ***Psalm 71:1 NKJV***

There is a difference between your understanding and my understanding. Maturity learns to discern between the two. Maturity also lessens the gap between the two. It is foremost *TRUST in Me* (not yourself) that yields the ear to hearing and discerning my will.

Many screaming voices may clash and conflict, but only one voice is mine. My voice is steady, constant, and never double-minded. My voice is filled with mercy, love, and compassion. My path is the pathway of true and sincere love from the heart of your God.

All you have to do is meet my criteria in order to know my will, that is to TRUST with all your heart. With that gift to Me, I am pledged to make certain that you come to know my will and voice in any given situation. Hallelujah!

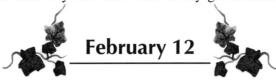

February 12

Chosen Fast

"Is not this the fast that I have chosen? to loose the bands of wickedness, to undo the heavy burdens, and to let the oppressed go free, and that ye break every yoke?"   *Isaiah 58:6 KJV*

Bands of wickedness wrap themselves around personalities, around souls. They wrap with increasing strength and might, attempting to suffocate the spirit man and kill the very soul.

My *chosen fast* loosens the bands. It is much like a number line. Satan pulls to the negative side. I enlighten to the positive side.

As you fast, you begin to increasingly see and understand truth from my perspective. Most people sit at about "0" on the number line experiencing both good and evil. Fasting draws one into viewing more perfectly from my perspective, the right side.

Though there are always two sides to every story, there is definitely only one true and pure viewpoint—mine—clothed with mercies unending and judgment divine.

Fasting pulls up and away from the negative into the positive. It draws you into your Master's sight. You see more fully, more completely, more purely. Once you can see, then you can pray. One first must see. The prayer spoken is simple. The coming into pure vision is the more difficult part, that which fasting enhances.

I am loosing the bands of wickedness. I am breaking every yoke. I am letting the oppressed go free. I am delivering at the very instant that you are praying. I have been busy and effectual in your behalf. These matters, indeed, are intricacies of the spirit and soul man that you are unable to affect apart from prayer and fasting.

Rejoice! Shackles are dropping before your eyes! Watch and behold the very GLORY of your Lord today. Amen.

February 13

True Love

"Love does not delight in evil but rejoices with the truth. It always protects, always trusts, always hopes, always perseveres."   ***I Corinthians 13:6-7 NIV***

This is how I love you: always constant and secure, never wavering or doubting, or holding back. I desire for you to love one another with the same faithfulness and wholeness of heart.

Human soul can love in part, but only the God-breathed spirit man is able to love another purely and wholly without wavering.

Love is not a mystery to be hidden or only philosophically contemplated. Love is loyalty from the spirit to uphold another at all cost.

True love never weakens under pressure, always has faith, never loses hope, and endures unceasingly.

True love is a boulder of rock immovable. It stands as a monument of human devotion to another. It changes not through storm or drought.

True love is constant, not bending with the wind. True love is like a mirror that reflects my glory and literally reflects WHO I AM in you!

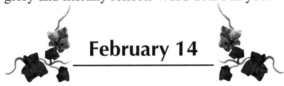

February 14

I Grant Promotion

"For promotion cometh neither from the east, nor from the west, nor from the south. But God is the judge: he putteth down one, and setteth up another."
Psalm 75:6-7 KJV

I am more sovereignly involved in your life than you know. I am always at work preparing promotion in behalf of those who love Me.

I grant promotion. It is I that lifts one up and sits another aside. I am the very breath of life! My breath is in all of creation. I am ever presently seeking to manifest and fulfill my sovereign will throughout my earth in all people.

I open doors for you to prosper. My will is for you to inhabit my earth and prosper in the works of your hands. The curse of sin has perverted my plan of perfection in synchronizing my blessings to all mankind. It is I, nonetheless, that puts down one and sits up another!

It is I! It is I! I am always seeking to promote my children to greater works and growing investments in my Kingdom.

I am a God of GROWTH, and I love to see my children blossom fruitfully before Me. Amen.

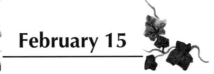

February 15

Love Has Big Ears

"Be kindly affectionate to one another with brotherly love, in honor giving preference to one another."   *Romans 12:10 NKJV*

Romans 12:10 is the personification of my golden rule: love one another. It is in your expressions of love for one another that I am honored.

Without love, life is like steak without salt, french fries without catsup, nachos without salsa or cheese.

My world has need of your love! You are my beam of light that shines in the unique corner of the world that you alone go. Without your love, your corner would be darker and colder.

Beloved, people are my business, and you are my representative. My business is your business on earth, and you are on assignment to love the unlovely as well as the beautiful.

To love another human being is to lay down your own cause and to pick up another's. Love is showing interest in another's projects or worries. It is a listening ear to another's words. Love is time spent in another's presence. It is individual attention that states, "You are worthy of my time, and I value your thoughts."

Love is a big smile and "how do you do!" Love can only be friendly and evangelistic. My love in you seeks expression! You must allow Me to greet your neighbor with warmth and welcome.

Love is looking outward beyond yourself into another's thoughts, feelings, and needs. It genuinely cares about the soul of another and its conditions of joy or sorrow.

Love has big ears. It listens to another's stories and cares. Time spent listening expresses, "I value you. Your thoughts are important to me." After all, isn't a man what he thinks and feels?

If you are too busy to look into the eyes of a comrade and concentrate on listening carefully to his words spoken, then you are too busy to love, and you are worth nothing.

Remember: love has big ears!

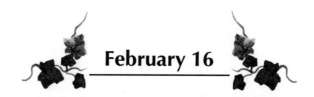

February 16

Intimacy with Me

"I count everything as loss compared to the possession of the priceless privilege —the overwhelming preciousness, the surpassing worth and supreme advantage— of knowing Christ Jesus my Lord, and of progressively becoming more deeply and intimately acquainted with him."   *Philippians 3:8 AMP*

Your heart cry is *intimacy with Me,* your Creator. I love you! I tenderly formed you within your mother's womb. I beheld the formation of your limbs, your toenails, your eyelids. I watched over you from the moment of conception.

Now, you have grown older. You have learned to walk and talk without my help, but there still claws against the lining of your heart a longing for intimacy with Me. The uncomfortableness that echoes within the walls of your heart cries out for Me. I see your hunger pains for our closeness.

Intimacy with one another hinges upon two factors: how you talk to Me and how I talk to you. You need to communicate with Me, talk with Me like your best friend, all day long. I am the written Word. I am the Living Word. Do not go about your day as if I am a guest you invite into your home at a specially appointed time. My intimacy with you revolves around your outreach to Me day after day and hour after hour.

Every man and woman on the face of the earth is created with a need for intimacy with Me. This hunger takes many incorrect forms as it seeks refuge from the haunting emptiness of living without Me. Every man and woman must plow that special path of return to Me, the Creator. I call. I beckon. I woo, and I wait.

There is a hidden place in Me apart and very far from the world where I come to inhabit and have relationship with you. You come to this place as you carefully press in to my Word, my study, and my presence.

It is with all of your heart that you shall come to know Me. I shall match your quest for my love with divine intimacy, my sovereign love to fulfill your heart hunger. I will satisfy every need and desire because you are at rest in Me, within our place of intimacy. In this place, you have no needs. No needs exist within my presence.

What lover would not give his beloved all of his Kingdom? I give unto you all of my Kingdom because I love you, and I have responded to your total heart-felt love for Me! I love you! I love you! I love you!

February 17

I Shield You

"Let the beloved of the Lord rest secure in him, for he shields him all day long."
Deuteronomy 33:12 NIV

You never have any legitimate reason to feel insecure and afraid because I am always helping my beloved children. This is called having FAITH on your part. The end result is REST. I don't want you to weary yourselves with worrying and fretting. I want you to rest in Me and rejoice always!

You cannot see how or that *I shield you.* If you could see into the real world of mine, you would be in awe of my ministering angels all about you and the great length I go to bring about circumstances in your life.

If you could see my Holy Spirit, you would faint at the reality of his vivid presence in your life and endless ministry of comfort and guidance.

You ask by faith, and I provide by faith. There is much business transacting in your behalf, invisible to the natural eye. Invincible is my shield of faith about you.

February 18

Happy and Joyful

"But may the righteous be glad and rejoice before God; may they be happy and joyful."
Psalm 68:3 NIV

Right relationship with Me makes you *happy and joyful.* It is a condition of the soul not contingent upon any earthly circumstance. It is like a spring of living water that refreshes and brings new energized life to a wilted plant. I am your drink! I am your source! I am your sustenance!

Faith necessitates believing and seeing my answer before its manifestation on earth. Your joy comes in accepting my answers by faith. Happiness comes only by seeing with eyes of faith the completed package wrapped, sealed, and ready for delivery.

Now, the unwrapping of the gift is answered prayer fulfilled. Yet, the happiness/joy comes in the packaging of the gift.

Joy is embracing my packages before they are opened and rejoicing like a little child over a packaged toy about to be unwrapped.

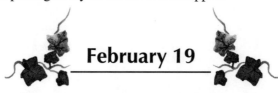

February 19

Jewel of Sweet Sleep

"When you lie down, you will not be afraid; Yes, you will lie down and your sleep will be sweet."   *Proverbs 3:24 NKJV*

Sweet sleep is my promise. If you are restless at night, then you are being robbed of my best for you. My beloveds should have sweet sleep.

Know that your enemy, sleeplessness, delights greatly in disturbing your peace and making you weary for your next day. Like a thief sneaking into your home and stealing your jewels, sleeplessness is robbing you of rest that I have lawfully promised.

You must first know that sleep—sweet sleep—is my gift of promise. Next, you must receive my promise as a gift by faith. The last step is to resist the devil, and he will flee.

Stand your guard! Profess my Word over your life. Announce in prayer before all angels and unfriendly forces that you are claiming your Father's gift of sweet sleep.

You should never be robbed of my jewels, for they enrich your life, enabling you to be an overcomer.

The *jewel of sweet sleep* is a precious gift. Receive it, and do not allow the enemy to steal it from you. Amen.

February 20

Missionary

"The harvest truly is plenteous, but the labourers are few; Pray ye therefore the Lord of the harvest, that he will send forth labourers into his harvest."
Matthew 9:37-38 KJV

Church, you are my missionaries. Every time you step out of your home, your feet are stepping onto foreign ground, and I hold you accountable for serving lovingly and dutifully as a *missionary* unto Me.

My fields are white and needy of laborers. You are my laborer, each member of my body. Anywhere you go in the world is your mission field. No man hides 24 hours a day in a closet. No, your mission field is right next door, at work, in the grocery store, or at the gas station.

Everywhere you go, people are hungering for ME—but they do not know who or what they hunger for. Each man has a void that can only be filled by Me.

Listen to my heartbeat. Place your ear against the breast of your Saviour. What do you hear? You hear my cry for the lost, my cry for the hurting and brokenhearted.

Listen to my heartbeat. It pounds compassionately for my lost lambs who are being called by name unto Me.

Your job is to realize that you are a missionary and then live like one. The angels and saints are watching. Your moves are being recorded!

You are needed to help stomp out sin by spreading the joy and love of Jesus throughout the good earth—wherever you go, whatever you do. Glory! Glory! Glory! You are my missionary!

Your home may be your haven of rest, your furlough dwelling place, but the world is your mission field. Outside your door waits your calling fulfilled by Me through my power, my name, and my strength, says your Lord.

February 21

Ivory Pearl Heart

"When a man's ways please the Lord, He makes even his enemies to be at peace with him."   *Proverbs 16:7 NKJV*

You may wear this promise like a badge over your heart. In the midst of the greatest heat or intense fire, you can rest assured that the very enemy's mouth that the fire has spilled from will be brought to peace with you.

Your bitterness would only fuel the fire of contempt. Your malice would only more endanger your well being.

The art of forgiveness is to be cultured and perfected within the shell of your heart. When the irritant sand has been allowed to modestly and quietly do its work, a lovely and beautiful pearl emerges in time.

I desire for you to be a pearl. I want you to always forgive and forbear others' weaknesses with love and patience. Were it not for my grace, you, too, would be just as "clutcy" with Kingdom matters.

Beloved, when your heart is pearl and you entertain no malice toward your offender, then my judgment prevails. My hands are not tied with unforgiveness, but, rather, loosed to intervene and change the heart of the transgressor.

Your very cold-embittered heart would disallow my intervention. Only one will be God. When you act like Me and judge them, I remain silent.

When your silence reveals only the purity of a pearl-lined heart, then my wisdom and Spirit go to work bringing even the most crazed of enemies to his knees before you, all so effortlessly on your part. You simply had to retain a pure heart—that *ivory pearl heart*—and I did the rest in bringing the enemy to be at peace with you.

I love you! Amen.

February 22

Perfect Peace

"You will keep him in perfect peace, Whose mind is stayed on You, Because he trusts in You."   *Isaiah 26:3 NKJV*

The *perfect peace* that I give you is a condition of your soul, like a still Colorado lake that reflects the crystal blue sky and virgin white billowy clouds above.

My perfect peace cannot be purchased at a movie, a pharmacy, or a clothing store. It is a gift from Me, sent from my throne and placed in your heart. My peace affects your emotions, your health, and your personality.

This gift of perfect peace is my response to released faith by you. When you trust Me with your cares, concerns, and burdens, I trade the flesh with the Spirit. You pump up to Me your fears and worries. I, in turn, pump into you my perfect peace. This is a holy exchange of evil for good, wrong for right, vexation for peace.

When your mind is stayed on Me, the perfect still waters are not disturbed. You are the crystal blue lake that, like a mirror, reflects my glory to others in your facial expressions, mannerisms, words, and smile.

Beloved, I love you, and I want you to perpetually walk in my perfect peace 24 hours a day. I want you to be that undisturbed lake that knows only to reflect my glory in all that you do and all that you say. I love you. Amen.

February 23

Life Is Precious!

"Anyone who is among the living has hope—even a live dog is better off than a dead lion!"   *Ecclesiastes 9:4 NIV*

Life is precious! Your days on earth are numbered and limited, a very small moment in the light of eternity—and yet a unique gift of human breath by my hand.

You are an eternal spirit, yes, but your natural, earthly body is temporal. Your breath of soul leaves, and your body wilts as a dead flower plucked from its roots.

I desire you to bloom and blossom as a thriving plant whose roots are tapped into my River of Life. Each man, every newborn, is a candidate for experiencing a supernatural walk with Me, and your walk on earth is reflected in heaven!

You were born into a generation that hungers and cries for knowledge of Me, yet they understand not.

This is your hour to proudly wear the clothing of flesh and blood and attempt to make a difference in this world.

It matters not if I have made you strong as a lion or meek as a dog—a rose or a dandelion. All men are brought forth by the seed of their parents. What matters is your heart.

Can you embrace your humanity and my divinity—both—and rejoice in being used by Me to affect the Joy of Salvation in the lives around you?

Your unique opportunity to serve your earthly calling is NOW! Do so with Joy and fulfill my will for your human life on earth. I love you! Amen.

February 24

Fruit of Tears

"Rejoice with those who rejoice, and weep with those who weep."
Romans 12:15 NKJV

When you are practicing my love, like a doctor about your Father's business, caring for others and mending their wounds—then is when you need to draw from my heart compassion for the human condition.

Allow yourself to empathize with the brokenhearted or to congratulate the victorious. Do not become so religiously indoctrinated that you lose the unique human trait of weeping and rejoicing with your fellow man.

It is my will for you to shed tears together—of both sorrow and joy. The human plight is not meant to be borne alone. I created you to need one another, in both weakness and strength.

When you shed a tear of compassion, you allow the heart of Jesus to touch your needy friend. When you shed a tear of rejoicing, you applaud with the hands of Jesus. You are communicating your Lord's love for that person.

Beloved, a tear is a squeeze of my Holy Spirit upon your heart. Only a hard and stony heart bears no fruit. If you are filled with my love and compassion, then you will bear the *fruit of tears*—the true personification of Jesus in the flesh, in you and through you.

February 25

A Mother's Paintbrush

"She looketh well to the ways of her household, and eateth not the bread of idleness. Her children arise up, and call her blessed." **Proverbs 31:27-28 KJV**

Mothers, do not spread yourselves too thin. Consider a house exterior. The quality of the paint job determines the longevity and effectual usefulness of the structure. If a thin coat is applied, endurance will be lacking. It will not weather storms easily and will be more prone to decay and deterioration of the inward wood—so, also, with children.

Your love relationship with your child is like applying coat after coat of paint in preparation for a long and successfully enduring adult life. If your love has been scantily or ill-applied, by the teen-age years you will be observing definite abrasions in the character of your child that do not bring Me glory.

If you are too busy with your own "adventures for fulfillment" to daily apply the fresh coat of paint needed around your children's hearts, then they will be improperly prepared to stand the test of trial and temptation. Your business as a painter is to daily, faithfully, steadfastly be there for your child, always holding in your hand *a mother's paintbrush.*

Children who lack parental care, time, and concern are like structures with cheap paint jobs. They may look acceptable initially, but given time and a few months of heated trials and cold winters, the structures begin to show need and weakness.

Mothers, I want you to rejoice in the privilege I have granted you, that of artistically designing the "little you" of which I have given.

The "little you's" in your quiver deserve your undivided attention, prayer-strokes, and expensive paint. Dip into my bucket of Love and Joy, Peace and Patience, Kindness and Goodness, Gentleness and Self-Control. This is my paint from heaven created to enclothe my little ones' hearts and souls.

Mothers, I have placed within you special talents and gifts to freely flow into your children and the body of Christ, my Church. Rejoice in contributing to the fullest functioning of my body on earth! Never forget that I hold you accountable for the paint job with which you present Me.

The best way to accomplish the job is to be on call 24 hours a day with brush in hand, not allowing yourself to be enticed by your self-seeking dreams.

Beloved, my Kingdom is souls! You are my construction worker. You give birth; you decorate; you daily paint with my paintbrush of glory.

Dip deeply into my bucket that will never run dry of my Love Paint, and coat and recoat our special little beloveds with my Love! In Jesus' name. Amen.

February 26

Your Face Reflects My Glory!

"A merry heart maketh a cheerful countenance: but by sorrow of the heart the spirit is broken."   *Proverbs 15:13 KJV*

Your eyes are my window to your soul. When your eyes are flooded with tears, then is your soul covered with grief. When your eyes sparkle like diamonds, then is when your soul is glistening with my JOY.

Your smile communicates to others more than any words you can say in daily life. Others monitor you by the degree of your smiling lips. Your mouth communicates both acceptance and rejection—even without words. Truly, *your face reflects my GLORY!*

You need to leave your cares privately with Me so that always others may behold my GLORY upon your sweet face.

You give my gift of love to each passerby just by allowing my light in your eyes to sparkle acceptance and my smile of friendly welcome to greet with loving kindness. Your face is my gift to every passing friend or stranger. Use it! Amen.

February 27

Leader of Worship

"Come, let us sing for joy to the Lord."   *Psalm 95:1 NIV*

This is the invitation of the Psalter addressed to the congregation: "Come! Come! Come!"

The *leader of worship* cries out to his people to come and join in with the worship and praise of your Creator.

This is my cry placed in my musician leaders. They sing and play and dance to usher in my presence and also to usher others into my presence.

To rejoice is to put upon your heart my attitude of worship. My character is one of rejoicing. Rejoicing is the key to entering into my presence. It comes from a heart of thankfulness.

Leaders of the congregation, lift up your voices with a loud cry and shout, "Come! Come! Come and shout! Come! Come! Come, let us rejoice in him!" Amen.

February 28

Asking for the Heathen

"Ask of me, and I shall give thee the heathen for thine inheritance, and the uttermost parts of the earth for thy possession."　　　　　**Psalm 2:8 KJV**

I want you to possess within your eternal spirit a collection of good works and precious nuggets. I desire that the value of your spirit increase and that you grow in wisdom and my honor.

One particular jewel in your spirit man that shall forever be a part of who you are is that gem carved by my hand that shall become your inheritance in the winning of lost souls unto Me.

Ask, and I will give you lost souls. They will hang 'round about your neck like expensive choice stones.

Your witness to the heathen matters. Ask, and I will draw. Ask, and I will give. Your job is in the asking. My part is the drawing. He who asks receives my blessing of inheritance. I reimburse your soul. I credit your account and invest in your treasured spirit a newly carved nugget from heaven's mountain.

Your inheritance shall be garnished with that which you have obtained in good works. *Asking for the heathen* is a good work.

Surely some voice on earth must plead their names before Me. There must be an intercessor somewhere who will recognize the lost condition of the heathen and proclaim Jesus' Lordship over them.

Simply ASK, and I will give you the heathen for your inheritance. Simply ask. Amen.

February 29

Either Pray or Praise

"Is any one of you in trouble? He should pray. Is anyone happy? Let him sing songs of praise."
James 5:13 NIV

You should either be praying or praising!

"In my Father's house are many mansions . . ." You have always much to praise Me for. Though earth may have her dim days, there awaits my promise of eternal glory to comfort and encourage you presently.

Where there is a concern or need, PRAY! Pour out your heart to Me! Echo my promises within the walls of your heart in behalf of others and their needs.

No idle talk exists when you *either pray or praise.*

I expect you to walk in an attitude of praise, perpetually, for even in prayer, you ask and then receive by faith. It is in the receiving of my endless gifts that your JOY is made complete! Amen.

March 1

Parenting Your Teens

"The Lord shall increase you more and more, you and your children."
Psalm 115:14 KJV

The years of *parenting your teens* are turning from a "labor of love" into your "labor of faith."

Your hands have toiled; now, your heart must believe in my sovereign plan and faithfulness to take your "feeble best" and transform it into my "divine excellence" through my seed.

I shall increase your children more and more beyond any measure of human effort and influence you have labored to deposit within your children.

My glory shall be manifested through them because you have believed Me to increase them more and more far above any dimension of your own investment within them.

Give and dedicate to Me your now "big children." I will assimilate and breathe into their souls my Divine Destiny and offer to the world "mighty men of God!" Amen.

March 2

Almost Persuaded

"Then Agrippa said to Paul, 'You almost persuade me to become a Christian.' "
Acts 26:28 NKJV

You are a living testimony of my love and goodness to all men around you. Like a tree, your branches extend out to many different directions, touching lives in a variety of ways.

People are watching you. They know that your roots are embedded in Jesus Christ. They understand to whom you give your devotion. They even expect more of you than the average tree in the yielding of fruit and the giving of its taste of Me.

You can only thrive in your abundant blossoming of my rich green leaves and juicy, sweet fruit. You can only stretch your wide arms out, asking nothing in return, but freely giving of yourself to your neighborhood.

The same storms blow against your trunk as theirs—but you still produce the sweet-tasting fruit. While other trees begin to produce less, and then bitter fruit, your limbs continue in rain or shine, drought or flood, to feed the world with juicy, plump fruits of my Spirit.

Your roots run deeper than the average tree, and you are tapped into the River of Life that always supplies perfect nutrition for the production and growth of your unique and pleasing fruit.

Do precisely what you are doing—growing and abounding in giving. One cannot help noticing your drooping and heavy arms of fruit! You are producing an abundant crop! By mere observance of your tree—your life—one is *almost persuaded* to become a Christian!

March 3

Necklace of Salvation

"For whosoever shall call upon the name of the Lord shall be saved."
Romans 10:13 KJV

If you call upon my name, I will save you! I will bring into your spirit man my rebirth. You will be born again and become a new creation in Jesus Christ!

Beloved, salvation is my gift to you, and it is even by my grace that you can experience desire for Me.

Be not a boastful thinker. Even your breath to call upon my name for salvation comes from my grace!

Beloved, I love you! I love you! I sent my very own Son in flesh and blood to die for you.

Salvation is my gift to you bought and packaged and ready to deliver. I seek out hungry hearts and readied souls to give my gift of salvation.

Beloved, I have loved you from the beginning of time, and I have always known that my *necklace of salvation* would be hung about your neck.

You wear my gift nobly, and you bring joy to Me because you have both received and appreciated my gift of salvation.

Wear your necklace in good pride, and never be ashamed to let the investment of wealth in you SHINE to a lost and lonely world. Amen.

March 4

Fruit of Repentance

"Repent therefore and be converted, that your sins may be blotted out, so that times of refreshing may come from the presence of the Lord."

Acts 3:19 NKJV

Acts 3:19 is the evangelist's plea to his nation. Repent! Repent! Repent! John the Baptist preached repentance. Jesus taught repentance. It is the foundation of your faith.

To repent is to see with the eyes of your soul the separation between you and Me and to realize your need for bridging the gap.

Repentance is understanding that the present direction of life in which you are marching is wrong. You turn away and begin stepping to the beat of a different drummer, Me!

Repentance is realizing your absolute utter need for a Savior, that apart from my Spirit, you are nothing.

Repentance is saying, "I'm sorry. I goofed. I was wrong. Please, forgive me of my sins and cleanse away the old behavior and wrong attitude. I need for you to be my strength. Come, Lord Jesus. Be my Savior!"

Repentance will feel like a hot, soapy shower to a dirty, sweaty body because repentance cleanses and cleans. Repentance will seem like the fog has lifted, and you can be refreshed by the beauty of the mountain scenery.

Stones of repentance are foundations in your soul. They are solid and firm, moments of truth on which you build our relationship. Apart from repentance, a man's soul is like sinking sand.

When you repent, even over small issues, I am pleased! To correctly follow after my way of life brings holiness, pleasure, and joy to your soul! There is nothing sweeter than a life being lived pure and holy unto Me. The *fruit of repentance* is a sweet nectar that feeds the souls of hungry men. When your life is built on repentance, you will spend your days dispensing my sweet juice in you to others.

Ministry must be spawned out of a repentant heart towards Me.

March 5

When Good Men Die Young

"The length of our days is seventy years—or eighty, if we have the strength; yet their span is but trouble and sorrow, for they quickly pass, and we fly away."
Psalm 90:10 NIV

When good men die young, I am blamed. By some, I am scorned. One may curse. Another may grievously become embittered toward Me. There are those whose anger flames hot against my Lordship in their lives. I am blamed!

Beloved, I love you! My own Son died an early death. He became your sacrifice for sin. Why would I take another son's life? Is not one sacrifice enough?

The enemy kills, steals, and destroys. You are but mortal flesh, and your stature is frail and vulnerable to disease and disaster. My plan of redemption is perfect through the blood of my Son—but there is imperfection in man. The best of man's plans and attempts will always fall short of my perfection.

When good men die young, my Christian community is shaken. My people rally around my widow and her children. Death is faced, and the reality of your temporal life stares you down. Eternity's call is always one breath away. The frailty of your flesh humbles my children. They are reminded that all flesh is as grass, and that your human days are numbered and limited.

Beloveds, when good men die young, I proclaim, ALL THINGS WORK TOGETHER FOR GOOD! I take the stark reality of death's cruel jaws, and I begin to deepen in loved one's hearts their closeness to Me. I use the temporal pain to work eternal gain. I take that which was meant for bad and turn it into multiplied opportunities for good to draw men's hearts closer into my eternal perspective.

No man can know the eternal ramifications of a newspaper article on a good man that dies young. I use these publications as wake up calls and reminders to the unbeliever: "Hello out there! This is your Heavenly Father speaking. Oh, mortal man, listen! Your days are numbered! If you, too, were to die today, where would you go? Heaven and hell are calling!"

It is sometimes in the presence of a breathless corpse that I am closest to man. Truly, heaven is but a breath away. A breathless body is a message of salvation! Mortal mind is caged within human thought, but for Me, one day is as a thousand, or one thousand as a day.

Even the most noble man on earth is vulnerable to death's grip. No man can escape the inevitable. Were you perfect, each man would be given his 70 or 80 years, but man's life is immortal and his steps yet imperfect.

Ponder not why good men die young. Rather, marvel at my mercy in sending my Son Jesus Christ, your sacrificial Lamb.

Ponder not the cruelty of death. Rather, rejoice in your eternal home of many

continued

WHEN GOOD MEN DIE YOUNG continued

mansions in your Father's house.

Dwell not on the sting of death, but, rather, celebrate the blood of Jesus Christ that cleanses you and purchases your welcome into Heaven's Gates wherein you may hear, "Well done, good and faithful servant. Enter into the joy of your Lord!"

Beloved, there are many mysteries in life that can only be fully explained heaven's side. Why your good man dies young is one of them.

I desire for you to intimately walk with Me in contentment, casting all of your cares on Me because I care for you. With the innocent trust of a child, I want you to "know that you know" that I work all things for good for you who love Me and are called according to my purpose.

In your human frailty, when you are able to entrust every question and need with Me, then you are able to experience my miracle of walking with your Heavenly Father in intimate relationship.

This is my desire for you and Me, and there is no pain too great worth suffering for this relationship with Me. I love you, my beloved, and I desire intimacy with you in your deepest heart of hearts. Once you have gained this place, nothing on earth, no one's death, no pain, no care, will move you. I want you because I love you . . . because I love you! because I love you!

March 6

Garments of Salvation

"I delight greatly in the Lord; my soul rejoices in my God. For he has clothed me with garments of salvation."   *Isaiah 61:10 NIV*

When you arrive in heaven, standing before my glorious presence, your *garments of salvation* will be manifested to your spiritual eyes.

Beloved, you can feel your garments even now. Daily, I stitch upon you new threads of my joy, my peace, my presence.

I love you! Your garments of salvation are your spirit's wardrobe! I am the tailor preparing your very robes of righteousness!

You can "feel" my richness draped around your spirit man. Sit and bask in my presence. Dwell upon Me, and you will experience the richness of my glory enveloping your spirit man. This feeling is the awareness of my robes and garments adorning your spirit. Amen.

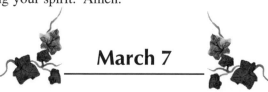

March 7

This Day Is a Gift

"This is the day the Lord has made; let us rejoice and be glad in it."
Psalm 118:24 NIV

This is the attitude of heaven, of your Jesus, of the Spirit. First of all, acknowledge that *this day is a gift* from Me (not a curse).

Each day you breathe on earth is as a packaged gift which I present to you daily. My mercies are new every morning! My gift is wrapped up with anticipation and a bow of excitement. You unravel the bow and tear open the wrapping paper with childlike anticipation as you greet Me in the morning and turn to my Word for your devotions and prayer.

To rejoice is to wear the breastplate of Jesus. His armour only rejoices. There is no dread or despair. Enthusiasm is my Spirit working in you.

Please, do not take for granted even one single day. Life is precious. A new day is my opportunity, through you, to influence the world for Jesus Christ. Embrace each new day!

This is a foundational attitude for you to daily apply to your work, worship, and relationships. I have created each new day for you to enjoy and experience my presence and JOY!

You often forget that every new day is a uniquely designed gift from my own hand. A new day should be embraced with gratitude from your heart towards Me.

Even in your sleepiness, you must reach out to Me and praise and thank Me for giving you one more day of eternal life, one more hour to work out your salvation and demonstrate the love of your Father to your generation.

This day is an opportunity given by Me to rejoice in human heart, clothed in human flesh, able to influence my world for Jesus Christ. REJOICE in the opportunity! Amen.

March 8

Faith

"Have faith in God."   *Mark 11:22 KJV*

I love you, beloved. In my house are many mansions—fully prepared for you. Splendid in glory are my many mansions. Your earthly labors will soon vanish in the sight of my promises of glory before you at heaven's gate.

Do not begrudge your present hard labor, for your reward is sufficient. Your reward is plenteous so that you will never be able to fully contain all that I have awaiting you.

It is more than reward or pay or recompense. It is, rather, LOVE in her full gown of glory! The gown of glorious LOVE awaits you, to clothe, to purify, to exalt, to rejoice! Your gown of glory awaits your entrance into my gate.

Please, do not begrudge life on earth as it is known unto you, for all mysteries will be revealed in time. Then, you will fully understand. For now, you must only have *faith*—believe!

This is the sector of life wherein you must first learn to have faith and believe in Me . . . so, exercise your faith! Use your faith in this world! Execute faith in all aspects of your life, that it might flow, that you might fulfill my purpose for your earthly existence.

Enjoy exercising faith. As a little child learns to tie his shoes and ride a bike, so, you, too, need to share in the youthful frivolity of enjoying the exercising of new found faith.

I desire you to move mountains by FAITH. I desire you to rule and reign over this earth by FAITH! Open your mouth and command the elements, the circumstances, the angels of the most holy God, and yes, the very demons of hell.

Command only in the name of Jesus, and behold my power manifested.

March 9

To Love

"Thou shalt love the Lord thy God with all thy heart, and with all thy soul, and with all thy mind. This is the first and great commandment. And the second is like unto it. Thou shalt love thy neighbor as thyself. On these two commandments hang all the law and the prophets." Matthew 22:37-40 KJV

To love is to step into your Father's shoes and walk his stride.

To love is to feel my heart beat within your own human bosom!

To love is to manifest Jesus Christ through your human vessel.

Beloved, there is no greater commandment than to first love Me! For if I am the corner stone of your heart, I can build my will for your life correctly without bricks that will later crack and be faulty.

To love Me is to know Me intimately, to experience a bubbling fresh-water spring abounding from your inner spirit. This spring is fresh within my love, and as you love Me, I supply this stream from which to drink.

To love Me is to walk in my favor, to have Me watching over you and intervening to produce goodness and rightness in your daily pursuits.

To love Me is to understand that I am always with you, and I desire our intimate love talks we share together, alone and personal, just you and Me!

Beloved, I love you! I love you! I love you! I love you! Amen.

March 10

In a Nutshell

"For God so loved the world, that he gave his only begotten son, that whosoever believeth in him should not perish, but have everlasting life."

John 3:16 KJV

In a nutshell, John 3:16 is my gospel preached to all men and all nations. To do the work of an evangelist, you need only to know this verse of promise.

My Son has paid the necessary price for your salvation, the cleansing of any sin you have committed. I wash you clean and make you whole through the blood of Jesus Christ!

When you evangelize, testify of the goodness of cleansed sin. Enough is not said of the power of the shed blood of my Son Jesus Christ. Your testimony of my grace in your personal life should always reflect back to the shed blood of my Son Jesus.

The New Covenant needs to understand the reality of forgiven sin! Your testimony of my working in your life can demonstrate to the unbeliever the effectual power of my Son's sacrifice on the cross.

Because He shed his blood, you are allowed to walk white as snow. You are free and not burdened down with an accumulation of the "scales of sin." You are a scaleless fish in my sea now, and when you testify of my goodness, forget not to give glory for the redemptive story and the forgiving blood of your Savior Jesus Christ! Amen.

March 11

Precious Flower

"As the lily among thorns, so is my love among the daughters."
Song of Solomon 2:2 KJV

The body of Christ is a beautiful and lovely basket of diversified flowers. Each member is a specifically designed flower by my hand. Each aroma is unique and special.

Daily, my angels prepare a freshly picked basket with your prayers and praises accompanying the voice of your petals. My baskets are placed 'round about my throne, their fragrance rising up into my nostrils. I breathe afresh the sweet and pleasing aroma of my saints on earth who are doing the work of the gospel.

Your roots are in earth where I have planted you. In earthly vessels, you continue to emit the fragrance of Jesus in your homes, your work places, your neighborhoods!

I say, be not selfish with your salvation freely given to you. You are scattered far and abroad, here and there, rarely clustered, because the world needs your sweet fragrance in Jesus Christ.

Be not overwhelmed by the darkness, by the stench of worldliness around you. I am with you, and you are being watered and fertilized daily so that you might blossom and bring forth sweet fruit.

Look at the people you touch every day with simple "hello's" or actual hands of servitude. They all benefit from your aroma.

See yourself as a bright shining plant in the middle of summer's glory. Your petals are glistening! You are thriving in your glory—my glory given to you!

Blossom, beloved! I have planted you in your garden, for my purposes, to fulfill my divine plans. Are thorns 'round about you? They are no threat. They can in no way deflate my Spirit in you because you feed upon my daily Word.

The world needs you! Blossom, share the fragrance of my presence with others, and bloom with the love of Jesus Christ shining forth!

You are a *precious flower* to Me, and I love you with my everlasting love, in Jesus' name. Amen.

March 12

Isaiah 58 Promises

"Then your light shall break forth like the morning, Your healing shall spring forth speedily, And your righteousness shall go before you; The glory of the Lord shall be your rear guard."   *Isaiah 58:8 NKJV*

For those who fast, many are my *Isaiah 58 promises*.

(1) Your light shall break forth like the morning! Have you noticed, lately, the serene beauty of my sunrise? The early morning hour is fresh, revived, and well rested. The hustle-bustle of the world's cry has not yet exploited its innocence, like a newborn baby. A sunrise brings new mercies every morning. A new day ushers in another opportunity to start all over again with Me living through you.

In fasting, I shine new light upon your life and in your heart. I expose the darkness in you and around you with my increased light, giving you fresh opportunity for repentance. My presence is increased within you, like upping the voltage within your inner lamp.

(2) Your healing shall spring forth speedily! If you want your healing to come quickly, then fast! Push aside the food and dedicate yourself to consecrated and devout prayer. Lay aside your appetite and gain back your health. I always respond to a sincere heart who really does mean business with Me.

(3) Your righteousness shall go before you. In fasting, your right standing with Me is established in deeper fashion and is personified through you. You have connections, and you know the right people, the "higher-ups," when you fast. If I can't pull strings for you, then who can? I go before you with increased intensity, like a John Deer V-plow busting up snowdrifts. Nothing is going to stand in the way of my "faster!"

I command my angels to respond to you in fasting by paving your path and clearing your steps from cluttered debris. The fasting prayer warrior does not notice side roads, nor are detours allowed. The straight and narrow path is laid, and as he steps, my red carpet unrolls before him. This is called favor, which is what you receive from Me in the pure fast.

(4) The glory of the Lord shall be your rearguard. Not only do I pave your highway, I also follow you behind, protecting you from the rear view! I have you surrounded! The enemy cannot find a loophole, no sneak attacks or coming up from behind. I have you covered; therefore, your walk in Me is steadfast and content.

Isaiah 58 proves my nature—you cannot outgive Me! Amen.

March 13

To the Cancer Patient

"He sent his word and healed them."   **Psalm 107:20 KJV**

I have loved you with an everlasting love; therefore, with loving kindness have I drawn you. The thief has come to steal, kill, and destroy, but I have come to give you life more abundantly.

Beloved, I love you, and I both weep and rejoice in spirit with you. I weep for the destruction of your body, but I rejoice that your name is written in the Book of Life, that you have been faithful and true to my call to love Me, and that you have honored and loved Me with the knowledge and revelation you have been given of Me.

I do love you, and I have not forsaken you. My hand is upon you, and I am comforting your loved ones as they seek to bring comfort to you! Just as a river's current has force and power, so, also, is my Spirit in you. There is power in your man. *"Out of his belly shall flow rivers of living water."* John 7:38, KJV.

It is just you and Me now. Continue to draw deep into Me. My Word is my life line to you. My Word is the keeper of your soul. *"Thy Word is a lamp unto my feet, and a light unto my path."* Psalm 119:105, KJV. Cry: *"How sweet are thy words unto my taste! Yea, sweeter than honey to my mouth!"* Psalm 119:103, KJV.

My Word is sharper than a two-edged sword and pierces and divides between soul and spirit. My Word is your sword. My Word is what you must cling to day and night, night and day. Meditate upon my Word hour after hour—for I am the Word. To see into the face of Jesus, look into the mirror of my Word. These are my instructions unto you:

1. Go nowhere without your sword.
2. Listen to my Word when alone—at all times—on tape.
3. Ask family and friends to read the Word aloud to you.

I want you to saturate and absorb yourself with my Word. The enemy cannot penetrate my spoken Word. Feed upon my Word. Listen to my Word! Meditate upon my Word—Word—Word! *"Thy Word have I hid in mine heart, that I might not sin against thee."* Psalm 119:11, KJV. *"Thy statutes have been my songs in the house of my pilgrimage."* Psalm 119:54, KJV.

It is written: *"Seven times a day do I praise thee because of thy righteous judgments."* Psalm 119:164, KJV. I ask, do you want defense? Do you want to poke the enemy in the eye and disarray his forces against you? I say, thwart the enemy, and expose him as the fool that he is by seven times seventy a day praising Me because of my righteous judgments.

It is time to set your face like flint towards my Word. Every hour cry out: *"I will worship toward thy holy temple, and praise thy name for thy loving kindness and for thy truth: for thou hast magnified thy word above all thy name."* Psalm 138:2, KJV.

continued

TO THE CANCER PATIENT *Continued*

Your answers are in my Word. Your comfort and consolation of my Spirit is in my Word. My secrets are revealed in my Word. Please, spend your days in my Word—if not reading, then listening. Absorb yourself in my Word until, like honey from a swollen comb, your lips drip with only one good report: what my Word says—only my Word—no other report agrees with heaven. No other report agrees with my voice. Only speak from your heart—my Word—because only in your heart is my Word!

No fear. No doubt. No worry. No questioning. No anger . . . nothing but my Word will deliver you. My Word in your mouth shall cause demons to tremble and the enemy forces to fight against their own. You shall be my sword as you consume my Word eating page after page, morning, noon, night, and every wakened moment.

Be consumed with hunger for my Word. The enemy cannot stand before a man equipped for battle with the two-edged sword sharpened and prepared for combat. For even the slightest move of his forces are detected and cut off by the man of my Word who wields his authority in JESUS' name. The ability to use my authority comes only by complete absorption in my Word.

"Only be thou strong and very courageous, that thou mayest observe to do according to all the law, which Moses my servant commanded thee: turn not from it to the right hand or to the left, that thou mayest prosper withersoever thou goest. This book of the law shall not depart out of thy mouth; but thou shalt meditate therein day and night, that thou mayest observe to do according to all that is written therein: for then thou shalt make thy way prosperous, and then thou shalt have good success. Have not I commanded thee? Be strong and of a good courage; be not afraid, neither be thou dismayed: for the Lord thy God is with thee whithersoever thou goest." Joshua 1:7-9, KJV.

My Word is truth. Let no lie from henceforth fall from your lips. Repeat not the reports of the enemy. Saturate, literally, yourself in my Word. It is sufficient defense against any attack.

Be my man of the WORD as never before. Every wakened moment be consumed with my Word—every wakened moment! Listen to my recorded Word 24 hours a day. Set nothing else before you but my Word until, like honey, it oozes from your mouth, and my truth, in agreement with my Word, speaks from your lips.

When the report in your heart agrees with the report in my Word agrees with the report in your lips—when all three are in agreement—then is when the enemy disintegrates before your very presence. Then is when truth, my truth that by the stripes of Jesus Christ you are healed, prevails. Then, my son, then! Amen.

March 14

In Heaven

"For now we see in a mirror dimly, but then face to face. Now I know in part; then I shall understand fully, even as I have been fully understood."
I Corinthians 13:12 RSV

Beloved, all of my nature's gifts are a reflection, like a crystal lake, of Me and my prepared heavenly Kingdom. For now, you see dimly; but then, face to face. For now, you know in part; but then, in fullness and completion. Though you see as into a mirror dimly, you nonetheless see, so rejoice! You see my Son, the very Son of God, reigning on high as you pass beneath the earthly sun daily, whose brightness you dare not look face to face into for any significant length of time. You cannot stare into the face of the sun, but you can open my Word, my telescope I sent you, in order to daily look into the precious sweet face of Jesus Christ.

Heaven is not earth, but in all ways have I given provision to partake of the same heavenly citizenship privileges, only in a slightly altered form. You worship in heaven. You worship on earth. You work and labor in heaven. You work and labor on earth.

In heaven, work is done effortlessly. We flow and abound, for there is no weight of sin pulling us down. Ah, but on earth, you struggle to worship and work —both because of the weights of sin that either rest on you or are simply laid before your path to move or step around.

In heaven, you can do nothing else but serve and worship. In heaven, you are servitude. On earth, I work to perfect servitude in your heart. There is no toil when a pure heart of servitude is doing the task. Such is heaven, pure hearts toiling and laboring in perfected servitude—effortlessly.

On earth, the closer you walk with Me and the greater the anointing of my Holy Ghost is poured upon you, then the more effortless my assigned labors to you appear. It is impurity in the heart that turns labor into grueling hardship. It is purity of heart that turns labor into a servant's attitude of praise and worship unto God.

In heaven, whatever the task, it serves as a form of worship before the throne. To collect 10 of my heavenly holy daisies from hill 9,367 of my daisy hills, is to my true servants a gesture of joy and servitude and, thus, worship. Heaven's business is worship! We operate around worship!

March 15

Your Heart

"The heart is deceitful above all things, and desperately wicked: who can know it?"
Jeremiah 17:9 KJV

Never trust *your heart* completely, for out of it can come cursing and blessing of Me. Never trust your human heart wholly, for it can be deceitful and desperately wicked.

Always keep your heart before Me, atuned to my Word and my voice. Constantly seek to do my will, being careful to allow my intervention to be closing and opening right doors for you to walk through.

I am a gentleman. I lead you carefully and peacefully. If the waters are turbulent, your boat stays ashore. Wait until I have calmed the seas, even though your heart may be anxious to move on out!

Judge not another, for the condition of mankind's heart is deceitful and wicked. You are no better or worse than another.

The blood of Jesus Christ may have redeemed your soul, but still you are a human candidate at all times with the same inclination toward sin.

Beware, lest you judge, and then your own heart allows deception to steer you wrong.

It is with compassion that I face the condition of man's heart. It is with compassion that I sent my Son Jesus to cleanse the condition of man's heart.

Never assume perfection. Keep Jeremiah 17:9 before you, lest you yourself fall in the name of self-righteous and blind religion.

Remain simple and broken before Me, and seek Me with a pure heart, the blood of Jesus Christ cleansing you of all sin.

I love you! Amen.

March 16

My Desire Is to Exalt You

"And whoever exalts himself will be humbled, and he who humbles himself will be exalted."   *Matthew 23:12 NKJV*

I am always scanning the earth looking for souls, like mirrors, that reflect the face of my Son Jesus. When I see his glory manifested in human body, then I rejoice and exalt that beloved, refining and perfecting his or her life in Me.

Pride has the opposite effect upon my Spirit's work on earth. Pride repels my glory and quenches my Spirit's work on earth.

To humble oneself is to lay down your life for your friends. To humble oneself is to fast and break the yokes of bondage that have any hindering effect over you or your loved ones.

Humility means easy access to the throne room, which means quick and prompt answers to prayer.

Beloved, I love you. *My desire is to exalt you,* my precious one. I desire to pour out my gifts to you because I love you.

March 17

First Love Me

"Love the Lord your God with all your heart and with all your soul and with all your mind."   *Matthew 22:37 NIV*

This is my greatest and most important commandment, and its obedience stems literally from the center of your will. I manipulate no soul to love Me! Yet, if you, by choice, love Me unreservedly, then all the other laws and commandments will come unto you by and with my grace to walk victoriously.

You must *first love Me* with all of your heart before my will is revealed and my revelation knowledge is unveiled before you.

To love Me as Matthew 22:37 defines is to set the foundational stone of your soul into place, onto which all other stones I will build.

You first must love Me and choose Me by your own will without coercement. Then, as you give Me your free will, my exchange for your right to choose or not to choose Me is eternal salvation. My Word and will are then revealed unto you. Amen.

March 18

Publican's Prayer

"Two men went up into the temple to pray; the one a Pharisee, and the other a publican. The Pharisee stood and prayed thus with himself, God, I thank thee, that I am not as other men are, extortioners, unjust, adulterers, or even as this publican. I fast twice in the week, I give tithes of all that I possess. And the publican, standing afar off, would not lift up so much as his eyes unto heaven, but smote upon his breast, saying, God be merciful to me a sinner. I tell you, this man went down to his house justified rather than the other."

Luke 18:10-14 KJV

The *publican's prayer* should always be your cry of the heart: "God, be merciful to me, a sinner!" It is in repentance that Jesus' blood is applied and the old man is transformed into my image. The pleasing prayer of the sinner is for mercy.

Religion blinds this truth from the eyes of its congregations. Religion sets up rules, regulations, doctrines, and guidelines that seek only to distort the basic sweet plea of the sinner, "Have mercy!"

If you were to understand the holiness of your God, you would also desire to cry out as the publican.

That is why Jesus came—to teach and preach my holiness. Did not he say, "This man went down to his house justified?"

Seek my Holy Spirit, seek my voice, seek Me, and let not yourself become ensnared with false pride and religious hypocrisy.

The true saint of God melts in repentance before Me and beats upon the chest crying, "God, oh God, have mercy, for I am a sinner."

True humility beckons the heart of the Father to your side. Amen.

March 19

Abba, Daddy!

"And because you are sons, God has sent forth the Spirit of His Son into your hearts, crying out, "Abba, Father!"   *Galatians 4:6 NKJV*

Abba, Daddy! . . . sweet nectar to the taste of my mouth . . . pure oil of sweetness to my ears.

When you call me Abba, you pull on my heart strings and cause Me to bend my ear low to hear your prayer and strive to answer quickly.

Beloved, dear one, you are my child, my precious one, and I love you as I love my only begotten Son Jesus. I love you! I love you! I love you!

You are specially designed by my hand to be a tool in my Kingdom. You are nestled together with other tools in my "box of utensils," but even though you are grouped together as my resources to use, you are always, at the same time, uniquely my special child and an original only-one-like-you!

I do not prefer one tool over another. I do not shine some and let others become rusty or dusty. I do not have my favorites whom I coat with gold.

No! Each of my children who knows Me as "Father" has been called and perfectly designed for one piece of my puzzle cut out for him. This piece can be replaced by no other. My puzzle of life is intricately designed, and your piece is needed. Without you, the puzzle is incomplete.

I love you the same, whether your role appears greater or lesser than another. I love you each the same.

I really do love you for who you are! I am your "Daddy," your "Father," and YOU ARE PRECIOUS IN MY SIGHT! Amen.

March 20

Seek Me with All of Your Heart

"But from there you will seek the Lord your God, and you will find Him if you seek Him with all your heart and with all your soul."

Deuteronomy 4:29 NKJV

The only qualification that exists for finding Me is to *seek Me with all of your heart.*

I am holy, and I am righteous. That is why I say that from my mouth I vomit out the lukewarm. You must be hot or cold! The cold I call to repentance. For them I am long-suffering, not willing that they perish.

Unto the warm only, the lukewarm man with leg over the fence and one left hanging, I ask, "Why the hesitancy? Your lethargic attitude is despicable! You cannot play with my holiness! You either love Me hotly or be gone from Me, for I have no pleasure in half-hearted men pleasers who seek to impress others with the outward man, yet the inside of you is cold raw meat of flesh. I spew you from my mouth! Your warm pew brings Me NO PLEASURE!"

Beloved, I desire you to be on fire and in love with my Son Jesus Christ. I jealously watch over the spilled blood of your Savior, and that is why the lukewarm have no place near my throne.

Church, I love you, but if you cannot love Me with deep intensity and passion, then I do not want you and your casual interest.

I am a God of deep compassion and zealous jealousy over my own. There is no complacency in Me; therefore, it is diabolical to Me.

Love Me with fervor and a fire of holy passion, and I will return your love with unlimited leashing of my Spirit's power and presence within you. Amen!

March 21

When a Sinner Repents!

"Likewise, I say to you, there is joy in the presence of the angels of God over one sinner who repents."   *Luke 15:10 NKJV*

Let Me tell you what happens *when a sinner repents!* There is an angelic host of singers that form a choir that would outnumber and outsing any earthly choir. If all choirs across the earth joined into one universal human choir, it would still not compare to the glorious excellence of my "glory choir" in heaven with Me.

There is a sound in heaven that human ears could not withstand, a frequency and harmony of yet undiscovered sound to the human ear that my angels participate in. This choir of millions is strummed upon, as if it were an electrified-with-my-power giant harp, the width of which is earth's circumference.

The repentance of one soul ripples through the heavenlies across my "glory choir." Like the sounding brass of 10,000 earthly orchestras, the announcement is made of the sinner's repentance. Nothing is done small in heaven. We don't have to be "cool and nonchalant" about important matters. We roar with pleasure! The sound and vibration of one million drums beating proclaims the good news of a lost soul found.

When you entered my Kingdom through salvation in Jesus Christ, you, too, were given a hero's welcome into the eternal family of God. The heavens roared in applause as you first announced Jesus to be your Lord!

In heaven, we celebrate spiritual growth and victories. Our parties revolve around repentant hearts. The angels minister to my heirs of salvation, and they rejoice in the "fashion of heaven" over what man might deem insignificant.

The universe trembles when one soul repents because my choir creates such a noise, a holy song of utter praise, that causes even the deepest roots in earth's ground to vibrate.

March 22

Yes and Amen

"For all the promises of God in Him are Yes, and in Him Amen, to the glory of God through us."   *2 Corinthians 1:20 NKJV*

I am a positive God! You say down, but I say up. You say dark, but I say light. You say gloom, but I say joy. All things work together for good when you are called according to my purpose.

Negative thoughts do not begin with Me. You are hearing other voices than my own when you are accused with condemnation or self-pity. The enemy has a voice, and it is like a radio that will blare loudly. Your remote turn-off button is the name of Jesus, at which the liar must flee and take his blaring voice with him.

You have to press into Me to hear my Spirit's voice and be a receptor of my positiveness for which your heart longs. Spending time with Me will open your ears to my positiveness.

Read my Word! Pray! Worship Me! Congregate with your fellow saints! I am not unattainable, but you have to persevere and "press in" to hear my positive, good report on a daily life basis.

I am your *yes and amen* God!

March 23

Be Still Before Me

"Be still before the Lord and wait patiently for him."   *Psalm 37:7 NIV*

Stillness is necessary before Me so that you may hear my loving voice speak clearly to you. When you gaze into a body of water, near a lake's edge or pond's creek banks, are you able to see your reflection clearly if the water is not still? No. The water must be resting still and quiet for it to reflect as a mirror.

In the same manner, to look into the face of Jesus and listen for my voice, you must, for best reception, *be still before Me.* You must quiet your soul in my presence and allow Me time—in moments of sweet silence—to come and speak and make my will known to you.

I long to speak to my children! Be not anxious in my presence. Wait! Enjoy the holy hush! These moments are important to both of us because I am given opportunity to manifest myself more fully to you. You have the privilege of seeing and hearing Me more clearly and fully. I love you, and it is my love that I must express to you over and over again. I love you! I love you! Amen.

March 24

Finding Your Mate

"Trust in the Lord with all thine heart: and lean not unto thine own understanding. In all thy ways acknowledge him, and he shall direct thy paths."
Proverbs 3:5-6 KJV

Beloved, I see the lonely chamber of your heart that longs for your mate. It is I that have created that vacuum within you, that you might hunger and thirst after your love. In the same manner, I have created a void in each man's heart for Me. That place you have filled with my Holy Spirit. We have taken residence in you! Now, your heart cry comes before Me: "Lead me to my mate!"

Beloved, it is good that you long for your mate, for truly none other on the face of the earth will fill that cubicle of need. It is heart-shaped and waiting for your very own beloved!

Now, dear, I desire that you live holy unto Me. It is in holiness that I choose to draw you into courtship and into *finding your mate*.

Your worry and your care about this relationship needs to be transformed into faith. Despite the need that you feel for your beloved, I would have you at complete rest until my appointed day unfolds.

Beloved, please seal your heart with Proverbs 3:5-6.

(1) TRUST ME with all of your heart! This is having faith that I am in control of your life and will not allow your beloved to slip away.

(2) You do not have to figure this courtship thing out! Your own understanding is not to be relied upon. Man looks on the outward, but I look on the heart. You do not have to plot or connive! Just by being you—will my moment of romance birth forth!

(3) Acknowledge Me in all your ways. Seek Me with all of your heart, and fill your life with my Word and my people. Keep your eyes on Me!

(4) I will direct your path to cross your beloved's. In so doing, I will implant in the depths of both of your hearts an eternally and undying "spark of romance" that will kindle into a hot fire of love and marriage from heaven. Simply TRUST ME and resist all doubt and worry and fear. Your trust is faith that releases Me to act in your behalf. If you trust, then I pave! Soon your beloved's path will cross your own!

TRUST ME! It is my delight and great joy to pave your path and watch the merging of your hearts into one. I love you! Amen.

March 25

Parental Gardening

"Train up a child in the way he should go: and when he is old, he will not depart from it."   *Proverbs 22:6 KJV*

Faith for your child's future is like a flower bud. From the time of conception, a child is a flower seed planted by my hand within the soil of your womb. Long hours of parenting are required to protect the plant from storm, danger, and theft.

With the elementary root system grounded in my Word, stems begin to mature growing straight and tall. The crowning of adolescence produces buds of potential with my arms tightly wrapped around their destiny.

Then the miracle of fruitfulness begins to unfold before the eye for all the world to see! Petal by petal, gifts and talents unveil.

Young adulthood announces its glory with its pristine vibrancy, excited energy, and fresh approach to blooming. The world is graced with the vigor of youthfulness, and the aroma of heaven's call fragrances the air.

For a youth whose roots run deeply in Me, the petals reach up in praise crying out, "Here am I. Send me!"

Your child's future is in my hands. You can only voice your faith by praising Me for this final phase of *parental gardening.*

March 26

I Will Always Respond

"For everyone who asks receives; he who seeks finds; and to him who knocks, the door will be opened."
Matthew 7:8 NIV

This is my kingdom principle and law. You must know that it is impossible to seek and not find. In my Kingdom, there are no futile inquiries. I am a library of eternal, infinite wisdom and revelation.

It is impossible to exhaust my resources. It is impossible not to find Me when you seek.

If a heart is searching, I AM FOUND! Knowledge and understanding are also discovered in the same way, by seeking.

You prepare your heart to hunger, and I will provide the meal to feed you.

You will never knock to an empty door. *I will always respond* in some way. You can never hunger too much for Me and my wisdom! Amen.

March 27

Key to Worship

"Let us be thankful, and so worship God acceptably with reverence and awe."
Hebrews 12:28 NIV

The *key to worship*—true worship of Me—is thankfulness. An unthankful heart cannot enter into my throne room. A dissatisfied heart will not enter into my presence.

It is a broken will that can be gracious and appreciative of my simplest gifts. A humble heart sees my good in all things and is able to rejoice before Me in worship because of the heart of thanksgiving.

Spoiled children always want more things—not more of Me. Broken, but mature, children desire more of only one thing—that is my provision and grace.

Reverence and awe spawn from humility.

March 28

Wisdom from Above

"But the wisdom from above is first pure, then peaceable, gentle, open to reason, full of mercy and good fruits, without insincerity or uncertainty."
James 3:17 RSV

This is my check list for knowing my will:

(1) Is your heart motive pure with no secret hidden agenda or ulterior motive?

(2) Do you have "peace" in the center of your heart about the decision?

(3) I am a gentleman, and I open doors. Are you having to bust down this one?

(4) Can you reasonably weigh the pros and cons without becoming defensive about your point of view?

(5) Do you entertain any reservation towards another, or have unforgiveness or hardness of heart in any direction of this decision?

(6) Are you being absolutely see-clear-through honest with all parties involved?

(7) Do you have any doubt about this decision? If so, wait until I assure you so that my perfect timing can be confirmed and you can know that you know that you know.

Only proceed in faith, for by faith nothing shall be impossible unto you. It is worth waiting for! It is like a nine month baby in the womb that begins with a seed, grows, and develops. At the appointed time, a perfect baby is born! Be careful not to produce a "preemie." Full term babies require less care and are healthier than premature infants. Wait! When you have *wisdom from above,* you know when the time has come to give birth to your dream.

March 29

My Blessings

"For the Lord your God will bless you in all your harvest and in all the work of your hands, and your joy will be complete."   *Deuteronomy 16:15 NIV*

The fulfillment of your Father's heart is that I might be free to bless you! Showering you with my gifts of favor and prosperity brings Me great JOY!

It is your obedience and patient walk with Me that induce my blessing upon your harvest and the works of your hands. You are full of joy when *my blessings* flood you and your banks overflow with my goodness of love and prosperity.

This blessing—the wealth of riches simultaneously both in the natural and the spiritual—come only by obedience. It is my great joy as your Heavenly Father to pour out this, my special blessing, onto you. Giving you this reason for joy brings Me also joy in the mere giving it unto you! Amen.

March 30

I Am

"The Lord is compassionate and gracious, slow to anger, abounding in love."
Psalm 103:8 NIV

My Word describes Me. My very personality is laid out as pieces of a puzzle. You may come to know and understand your God as you pursue my Word and piece together the puzzle of my description.

I am compassionate. I do not reject the loner, the ugly, the undesirable. I understand the evil condition of man's soul, and in compassion, I send my very own Son to redeem you.

I am gracious, always thankful for every small attempt on your part to know Me and love Me. My graciousness necessitates that you can never outgive Me— never! I appreciate you and your quest to know Me!

If I were not slow to anger, there would be no earth left. For by one word, the earth could "poof" into an instant ball of flame.

I am Love . . . only Love . . . always Love . . . forever and eternally—Love. Amen.

March 31

Doing Good

"For this is the will of God, that by doing good you may put to silence the ignorance of foolish men."   *I Peter 2:15 NKJV*

Your good deeds do not go unnoticed by foolish men. They see and weigh in their hearts what manner of love it is that you demonstrate. They wrestle within their own souls as the conviction (that your light causes) stirs within them.

Light exposes darkness. Your deeds of goodness shine brightly, and where there is light, darkness has to flee. The presence of your light demands the absence of darkness.

Good deeds speak for themselves. They cannot be argued with or debated. They stand alone without need of defense.

To say you love is one thing. To show you love is another. The demonstration of love by good deeds brings to silence foolish men. No words can stab a good deed. No malice or ridicule or cynical heart can set itself against a deed of goodness done in the warmth of my love.

You must continue being about your Father's business by *doing good*. Your goodness demonstrates my love to the world who hungers for my touch and needs its Savior Jesus Christ. Amen.

April 1

Planted in My House

"Those that be planted in the house of the Lord shall flourish in the courts of our God. They shall still bring forth fruit in old age; they shall be fat and flourishing."　　　　　　　　　　　　　　　　　　　　　　**Psalm 92:13-14 KJV**

When you are *planted in my house,* you understand the purpose and place of my body, the Church, on earth as it is in heaven.

The Bride of Christ daily becomes more lovely before our eyes! She is responding to the voice of her beloved as she is groomed in preparation for her Groom by the Spirit's wooing touch.

To be planted in my house is to understand that your place is in the body of Christ. To be planted means that you embrace corporate worship, seeking to support and uphold the Bride of Christ and her development in your generation.

My house has always been a house of prayer. If you are planted in my house, then prayer is the language of your soul. You breathe and eat my Word, and you long for my eternal House of Glory that will be yours at the call of your name.

When your feet are planted in my house, no other dwelling place entices your soul. Your priorities are established upon my foundation, and you are able to resist the temptation of the world's voice. Your feet on earth are cemented in my house and my Word; therefore, upon your last earthly breath, immediate transfer takes place on "Heaven's Express!"

Your citizenship in my Kingdom never ends. Instantaneously, you are transferred from earth to heaven. At the twinkling of an eye, Zap! You behold my glory and my eternal temples of glory!

To reserve your seat on "Heaven's Express," plant your feet within the soil of "Earth's House," my Church. (You might call it an institution)—not Me! My Church is holy unto Me, covered by the cleansing blood of Jesus Christ.

Your soul will grow fat and flourish from being fed my Word routinely and faithfully. It is the "fat in soul" that embrace my gates with greatest Joy! Obesity in spirit is my goal and purpose for my house on earth. Implant your feet in my Word, and I will express them, someday, to my throne! Amen.

April 2

A Merry Heart

"A merry heart doeth good like a medicine: but a broken spirit drieth the bones."   *Proverbs 17:22 KJV*

To retain good physical health, one must guard the heart, for the life of the body-flesh is a manifestation of the life of the heart.

One may be victimized and know heartache, but no man is cursed to retain a broken and crushed spirit because JESUS is the healer of all brokenheartedness. He gives you *a merry heart.*

Your apothecary is Jesus' joy! His JOY chemically releases a solvent into your blood stream that emits healing and kills disease germs.

The spirit gives life; but where the spirit is crushed, the bones will respond with dryness and vulnerability to disease.

I desire to breathe life into the bones of my creation. Jesus is the healer of the brokenhearted. Jesus heals the crushed spirit.

Pity and self-pity are despicable. No divine health grows from feeling sorry for yourself. Roots of bitterness prevent broken hearts from being healed. No situation, no damage, and no pain is too great for the miracle deliverer, Jesus, to heal.

The outward man reflects the inward health of a man's spirit, and rottenness to the bones will haunt the man who is unwilling to forgive <u>all</u> offenses done against him. Amen.

April 3

The Groom's Cry

"Out of the north he comes in golden splendor; God comes in awesome majesty."   *Job 37:22 NIV*

It is I, your Lord and Savior Jesus Christ, riding upon a great white horse, coming to rescue you from the enemy's snare!

It is I, clothed in majesty, reigning amidst sovereign love and the will of God.

It is I, reigning as your king—the king of your hearts!

You are my Queen, oh, fair princess. Come and join Me to be my wife!

I love you, my Bride, my Church. I call to you, "Come! Come! Come!" This is *the groom's cry.*

I await your response. I await your love songs to Me. I bask in the glory of your worship!

Come, my Bride, come away with Me, come! Amen.

April 4

I Will Heal Your Heart

"He heals the brokenhearted and binds up their wounds."
                                                        Psalm 147:3 NKJV

This is the purpose of my Son Jesus Christ, to heal your broken heart and cleanse your wounds. Jesus died on the cross and rose again to defeat pain and purchase healing over the enemy's attack. This applies to mankind, both physically and spiritually. Emotions fall under spiritual healing.

The soul of man is designed by my hand to be a delicate, sensitive entity. It can be easily crushed by an unbound enemy. Jesus, my Son, bore the price for the wounds of one's spirit and soul. Man needs only ASK for the healing power of God to cleanse a broken heart or wounded spirit.

Life can be cruel by the hand of wicked persons who are ensnared by the enemy. There is also the pain of death, the sting, that scrapes against the soul and haunts the mind with despair.

Every ache of the heart, we desire to heal. I want you healed, not broken—thriving, not coping—free, not bound—pain free, not aching. Come to Me, and *I will heal your heart.* Amen.

April 5

Fuel from Heaven

"For in him we live, and move, and have our being."   ***Acts 17:28 KJV***

It is in my Son JESUS that you live and move and have your being. In Him, you are able to scale walls without falling and climb mountains without slipping.

Beloved, in Christ your Savior, you find open doors to victory. You find accomplishment and achievement. You find success and prosperity.

In Jesus, you are supernaturally "hooked up" to my Spirit's *fuel from heaven* that no oil corporation on earth could compete with. In Jesus, you are embodied with supernatural wisdom to make right choices. I give you skill to perform the job better than average. I expand your skills far beyond your own natural level of achievement.

My fuel energizes your body to last longer and endure easier. In Jesus, your patience with hardship deepens and your joy bubbles spontaneously up from the pit of your soul like a fresh mountain spring.

Your being is mobilized, polarized, and energized by JESUS in you—living, moving, and having his being. He loves you! Amen.

April 6

Arise and Shine!

"Arise, shine, for your light has come, and the glory of the Lord rises upon you."   *Isaiah 60:1 NIV*

This is the message of HOPE through Jesus Christ to a lost and broken world. The lost and weary soul may rise up from being dead in himself. He may receive the light of Christ into his dark soul, and my glory may rise up within him, transforming and changing his likeness into the image of my Son Jesus Christ!

This is my cry to a lost generation. Arise! Shine! Your light has come.

It is my delight to transform a burdened soul into a shiny beacon that reflects the face and peace of Jesus.

Oh, lost generation, *arise and shine*! My light has come to give you eternal life.

April 7

To Feel My Love

"I will sing of the Lord's love forever; with my mouth I will make your faithfulness known through all generations."   *Psalm 89:1 NIV*

The revelation of my love for you is a gift from Me. *To feel my love* for you is a gift from Me.

To be able to sing with rejoicing over my love for you is a supernatural thing. It is not of the earth, and it is not of the world.

To feel my love for you is a gift of grace.

In this grace, you are able to speak your faithfulness to Me, meant to be passed on to future generations.

Is that not how we came to this day?

I love you! Nothing is more important than knowing and experiencing my love for you. In Jesus' name, amen.

April 8

Surrendered Heart

"Set your affection on things above, not on things on the earth."

Colossians 3:2 KJV

Your life in the flesh is temporal. It will not last. To every man there is appointed a time to return to the dust. I tell you this to remind you not to spend your entire life investing in natural pursuits, remembering that you can take none of your earthly riches with you into eternity.

My secrets are recorded in my written Word. I would have you study and meditate over my Word. My words are words of eternal life. As you set your affection on my revealed Word to your heart, you are depositing treasures in your spirit that will come with you to heaven.

It is a good thing to long for heaven. Your desire to be with Me, apart from your flesh, is honorable and just. In all that you do, be conscious of eternal purpose and gain. It is possible to make every second count with Me.

To surrender your earthly rights is to gain your spiritual rights. You cannot have both. Your life will reflect your citizenship. Are you loyal unto earth or loyal unto heaven? Is your pursuit for selfish gain or for eternal value?

Most men stand upon two fences, a dual allegiance, one to heaven and one to earth. To know Me at all—to love Me at all—these are good things for you to do. To serve Me, though, to distribute my presence to others, to be the cupbearer that gives away drink after drink for the blessing of mankind, this man's loyalty must be to heaven alone.

He who is my servant gives the most. Ownership in this world decreases the flow of my fountain.

The surrendered soul will say, "I have need of nothing. I am that which my God pours into Me. It is well with my soul. My cup is Jesus' cup. My drink is Jesus' drink. I give you his life through me." Now, these will be the anointed drinks that bring heaven to earthen vessels—the only drinks that will satisfy another's soul and affect an eternal spirit. Desire to serve this drink from my holy fountain as you also receive my drink into your *surrendered heart.* Amen.

April 9

My Sheep Hear My Voice

"My sheep hear my voice, and I know them, and they follow me."

John 10:27 KJV

I love you, beloved one. Listen to my voice. My voice is unlike any other sounds you will hear in the night or in the day. Learn to discern my voice so that we may fellowship throughout the day. The world has many voices. They yell. They scream. They nag. They whine.

This is not so with my voice. My voice is gentleness. My voice is holiness. My voice is the calming peace (the balm) of Gilead. My voice ministers peace and power, both at the same time.

You may hear my voice throughout your busy day if you will but stop, listen, and call upon the blessed name of your Lord Jesus Christ.

I love you, beloved. In my house are many mansions—all prepared for you. Splendid in glory are my many mansions. Your earthly labors will soon vanish in the sight of my promises of glory before you at heaven's gate.

Do not begrudge your present hard labor, for your reward is sufficient. Your reward is plenteous so that you will never be able to fully contain all that I have awaiting you.

It is more than pay or recompense. It is rather LOVE in her full gown of GLORY! The gown of glorious LOVE awaits you, to clothe you, to purify you, to exalt, to rejoice! Your gown of glory awaits your entrance into my gate.

My sheep hear my voice, and they follow Me into heaven.

April 10

Intercessory Garden

"My little children, for whom I labor in birth again until Christ is formed in you."   *Galatians 4:19 NKJV*

Intercession is like gardening. You must dedicate yourself to the end result, meanwhile understanding the toil and labor you are committing to within your *intercessory garden.*

The soil is a person's heart, the human heart you have endeavored to intercede for. The wise gardener will toil and labor to rid the soil of rocks, debris, weeds, and other obstacles that would block the growth of the good seed.

Next, the gardener cultivates, disking the soil, making it ready and ripe for the implantation of seeds, my Word. You then pray over your seeds (promises from my Word), and they are planted one at a time as you profess my Word over them.

Now, the miracle is in the change of the seed. What man can cause the seed to germinate and take root? No man. Even a farmer's 1,000 acres of corn must experience my miracle of germination of all seeds.

You, as an intercessor, are to pray in the spirit feverishly over the seeds. This will secure the supernatural implementation of salvation's rooting process. Roots will grow!

As the plants begin to peek through the soil, their innocent heads pop up; now, this is testing of your gardening intercession. Gently water your garden with healthy humility, in the spirit, singing praises and thanksgiving for the sprigs of green you see.

Do not make negative confessions, for they will trample down your sprigs like a summer's storm folds over tall corn. No! Beware! Keep silent, and do not grow impatient with the length of growing season. You are dealing with eternal beings that require long seasons of seed time and harvest to produce righteous fruit. Be patient and believe!

You prepare the soil in prayer. You plant my Word promises, seeds in prayer. You thank Me with the rains of the Holy Spirit, showers of blessing and praise upon the germinated seeds.

Then, you rest in peace and faith giving your Divine Gardener time for faith to do her perfect work. You stand back faithfully raining down showers of praise and thanks while I bring forth the sweet nectar in the long awaited fruit.

It is the promise of the fruit that keeps you longing and waiting. I say to you, beloved, be still and be patient. Trust Me as you wait. I am able! I will never deny fruit that has been properly cared for; but it does take time, so experience your gift of patience and await the sweet taste of faith's fruit. Amen.

April 11

A Repentant Heart

"I said, Lord be merciful unto me: heal my soul; for I have sinned against thee."   *Psalm 41:4 KJV*

Psalm 41:4 is the cry of *a repentant heart* entering into my presence. It is only by my Spirit that man is able to see the raw condition of his soul, the true need for daily revival and healing of man's nature.

This is the cry for mercy to a living Father God, given by revelation of the Holy Spirit. Surely, I come to heal not only the brokenhearted and deserted, but I come to heal each man's state of soul that he might be free to receive my gifts and blessings of good health and prosperity. Man's limitations are placed upon oneself by man himself.

You can do all things through Christ who strengthens you!

Greater is He that is in you than he that is in the world!

You are more than a conqueror!

In praying Psalm 41:4, you are humbling yourself before your God. My response is to heal and then exalt you. Daily, one should confess sin. Daily, I will heal the soul.

The secret of your Heavenly Father is that in the humility of Psalm 41:4, you receive my favor and promise of the proceeding eleventh verse: *"By this I know that thou favourest me, because mine enemy doth not triumph over me."* Amen.

April 12

Fasting Is the Chainsaw

"The Lord will guide you continually, And satisfy your soul in drought, And strengthen your bones; You shall be like a watered garden, And like a spring of water, whose waters do not fail."   *Isaiah 58:11 NKJV*

Fasting is the chainsaw that stays hidden in the closet while the weary man painfully forges back and forth with his handsaw. Every Christian has one of these super-machines that he could be utilizing to make his walk with Me easier and less laborsome.

For he who fasts, I promise that I will guide him continually. Fasting vacuums the fuzz balls in the brain and cleans off the receptors that hear my voice and discern my leading. It causes my guiding light to be easily seen and understood.

Even though you eat less, my promise is to strengthen your bones, to fill your soul with my drinks from the stream of Living Waters.

Fasting breaks loose the damned up streams. My River flows through you with increased power, and your thirst is quenched. You begin to thrive in my moist soil and abound with fruitfulness like a well-watered garden. Others receive enjoyment and spiritual blessing just from you being you and blossoming and emitting the fragrance of Jesus Christ through your smiles and kind words and forgiving spirit.

Fasting opens new springs in you that bubble and flow, whose origin is heaven. You have a vitality and a freshness about you that never run dry, that offer cool drinks to thirsty, parched throats around you.

Take my chainsaw out of your closet and use it. It can only bring blessing!

April 13

Pure Heart

"Create in me a pure heart, O God, and renew a steadfast spirit within me."
Psalm 51:10 NIV

Psalm 51:10 is the prayer of my humbled child. Having witnessed the stench of his flesh, he now repents before Me to seek the cleansing of his soul that only I can purify.

It is the *pure heart* that I seek to perfect and adorn with my jewels of meekness and gentleness, love and patience, kindness and goodness. I seek to purify the heart so that Christ may be formed in you.

Every particle of "flesh" is replaced with the vibrancy of the Spirit of Jesus Christ!

Allow Me to cleanse you and make you whole.

This is the cry of my true and sincere child of God. This is the heart plea of my own—one whose soul desires to be pure before Me, one who knows it is only I that can change a heart or renew a right spirit within.

I am the Creator and the former of the heart. It is I that changes and transforms a heart into the image of Jesus Christ.

I, alone, can manipulate and massage a man's heart to more fully respond to Me. It is I! It is I, and I love you! Amen.

April 14

Sing!

"Sing and make music in your heart to the Lord."   *Ephesians 5:19 NIV*

I created you to *sing!* It is because as on earth as it is in heaven, my heavenly hosts always sing before Me! Music is my nature. Song is my voice. Worship is my atmosphere. Praise is my breath.

I am song! Always in heaven we rejoice and break out into songs of praise and glory in chords and harmonies unknown to natural man.

When you sing on earth, you reflect my GLORY! As a mirror, you see dimly, but a reflection of truth. You are manifesting the nature of God when you sing. Your Creator and Designer styled within your body the potential to please and exalt Me with your voice.

I created your spirit-soul-body self to express your "healthy-heart-love" through song. It should be your spirit's cry to sing unto Me! Amen.

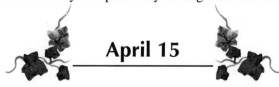

April 15

Absolutely Barkless

"And when the devil had ended all the temptation, he departed from him for a
season."   *Luke 4:13 KJV*

Satan hates defeat. When you successfully convince him that he must leave because faith has commanded him to do so, then like a scared, whipped, scoundrel dog, flea-infested and scroungy, the enemy retreats. His pride is exposed in his humiliation of defeat, and he is *absolutely barkless* before the blood of Jesus Christ.

He will always depart because he has no authority, only that which you allow. His plan is to return and catch you unaware in a lazy moment or prideful state. He is totally merciless, and the greatest moment unto himself is in attacking the already weak and down-under, adding misery to misery.

Remember that he returns after a season, lest you become prideful in your glory, or lazy in your season of rest. On the contrary, you should spend your battle-free moments preparing your arsenal, shining up your weapons, and extending truthful leadership and instruction to younger soldiers.

Be ready and always on watch. 'Tis better to be "battle ready" than "battle weary!"

I love you, beloved one. I love you! Amen.

April 16

Self-defense

"Who, when he was reviled, did not revile in return; when He suffered, He did not threaten, but committed Himself to Him who judges righteously."

I Peter 2:23 NKJV

A pure heart can respond to unfairness with pure action, but you must first be pure on the inside before the outside mannerism of quietness has power. If you pretend to endure suffering and persecution, but your heart is frenzied, no power will attack your enemy. It is from the heart that faith is expelled.

When Jesus was falsely accused and mistreated, he did not defend himself. Now, wouldn't that be ridiculous—divinity screaming in *self-defense* against carnal flesh and blood?

Behind the voice of Jesus were the armies of hell lurking to attack. Yet, they always remained behind his voice, retreated and restrained, refrained from attack because out in front of the voice of Jesus stood at attention the armies of the Living God, fully clad in their glorious shields of faith and with swords of fire. Jesus could see his army and know their power to quench every fiery dart of the enemy.

For royalty to have bent to the temptation to defend himself would have been frivolous. At one word of his command, the armies of hell could have been swallowed up—but Jesus did not use his power for self-defense. He understood my plan—our goal—and his purpose to become the sacrificial Lamb to offer his blood to redeem your soul!

In the likeness of your Saviour, it is not necessary to be defensive. You, also, have at your command the angels of God and the army of his love to back you.

You need not entangle yourself in a flesh and blood war where no winner emerges and wounds only ensnare the soul.

Rather, yield to Jesus and use the weapons of warfare in the spirit whereby I am able to defeat the unseen enemies of the soul and work repentance in the hearts of wicked men.

Playing war with men is futile. Only my battles in the heavenlies bring the fruit of repentance. After all, isn't that what you desire? A true repentant heart bears fruit unto Me. If you refuse to defend yourself in the natural, then I will take up arms in the Spirit, and you will reap a lasting fruit of repentance in your enemy, says your Lord! Amen.

April 17

Ripening Nations

"For as the earth brings forth its bud, As the garden causes the things that are sown in it to spring forth, So the Lord God will cause righteousness and praise to spring forth before all the nations."   *Isaiah 61:11 NKJV*

This is my promise to the generations of the faithful who have lived and come on unto Me, or who are currently inhabiting earth. To all of my people, my saints, I promise throughout eternity that my name shall be lifted up in all nations!

As surely as the farmer trusts in the soil to produce his crop, so, also, you may trust in my providential oversight to bring forth spiritual fruit from my earthen nations.

Latent in some nations are seeds waiting yet to germinate and produce righteous fruit. In every nation, there has been a remnant of mine who has honored the true God Jehovah.

My Son Jesus Christ waits for his Bride from the nations. She will sprout up even from desert land. She will rise through the crust of the earth and announce her full glory in the harvest of her soul.

The earth is filled with my seed, and as a farmer patiently awaits harvest time, so we, also, await the culmination of the times whereby all of our seeds have sprung forth in full blossom and righteous fruitfulness.

We patiently oversee the crop and await the harvest. Mankind is our fruit, and the nations are our fields. My hand of time is bringing forth the passing of seasons unto the final Harvest of Man.

We wait with heavenly anticipation. Those who have come before you unite, also, in healthy expectation of earth's harvest! The choir of saints proclaims expectation and culmination of the hour. All of heaven prepares for the Bride of Christ and the readiness of her fruit.

We await the *ripening nations.* We await! The sand glass is before our eyes. We await! We await! We await!

April 18

Home Is Where the Heart Is

"For whoever does the will of My Father in heaven is My brother and sister and mother."   *Matthew 12:50 NKJV*

You have heard that blood is thicker than water, but I say that the blood of my Son Jesus Christ is thicker than the blood of man.

When my Son walked the earth in flesh and blood, he had come from his Father. His citizenship was the Kingdom of Heaven. He knew the glory of the heavens and eternity's intricacies. He saw with my eyes.

Jesus' earthly family had no more pull on him than did his heavenly family. Even by rights of birth, his heritage was divine; therefore, he was not budged by the pleadings of his natural family. Rather, he identified his "true family" to be those whose hearts were pure and holy before Me.

Jesus longed to yield his allegiance and affections toward the members of his own household—the "household of faith."

He loved his natural family, but he identified with his spiritual family.

Now, so it is with you, too. You might be the only member of my family in your household. They would have you feel odd and misplaced and would have you be like them.

Nay! Even if you are the only duck in the pond, if that water is from the River of God and my throne, then, DO NOT migrate!

Beloved, I love you. You are a member of my household, the family of God. You naturally care for your loved ones, but with eternal eyes realize that you will be spending eternity with your spirit-filled ancestors and your born-again, faithful and fellow saints.

If you feel alone, like an alien or a pilgrim, that is OK. You may be the only bright shining light in your current family on earth. Oh, but someday, you will be joined with the host of believers in my heaven for eternity.

Home is where the heart is . . . and for you, that should be heaven.

April 19

On the Job

"Whatever you do, work at it with all your heart, as working for the Lord, not for men, since you know that you will receive an inheritance from the Lord as a reward. It is the Lord Christ you are serving."   *Colossians 3:23, 24 NIV*

When you are working, your labor is unto Me! Your eight hours of paid labor is much more than physical endurance and a paycheck for your time.

Your job is my assignment. It is my opportunity for you to rub elbows with the world and let your light shine. There are many *on the job* whose only opportunity to come to know Me is through you.

My anointing follows you to the work place. My Holy Spirit empowers you to work peacefully side by side other fellow men and to be a blessing to your company.

I place you there not to be a prickly thorn, to ridicule, whine, and complain. No. I place you there to be a warm and soft spot for others to be drawn to, a place where they can find a cool drink of refreshing water from my well.

You need to absolutely NEVER judge or tear down a fellow employer. You are placed there to uplift and edify the members of your work force.

Be an encourager! Every man needs a warm word, a friendly smile, and a pat on the back. Seek to edify and comfort your fellow man. You are Jesus in your work place, his hands and his feet.

Do not begrudge your job. No work is easy, but know that your being there is much more than just receiving a pay check. You are also banking up credit in your heavenly account for your faithfulness in meeting men's needs 'round about you.

Beloved, I need my light to shine in every corner of my world. That is why I need you in your work place, and you are very important to Me there! Without your light, there is darkness. Your light exposes the darkness and keeps the environment warm with love. Let your lamp burn. I am your oil, and you emit a sweet fragrance on the job. Thank you, beloved. Thank you! Amen.

April 20

Earth Is My Footstool

"The heaven is my throne, and the earth is my footstool."   **Isaiah 66:1 KJV**

I dwell in the heavenlies, but my feet touch the earth. This is indeed a difficult concept for you to humanly comprehend. I AM VERY BIG! *Earth is my footstool.* I am always walking amongst you, intervening and implementing my will in your behalf.

I reign! My Kingdom is! I am sovereign and omnipotent! I am both here and there. I both dwell in my heavenly temple and live inside your bodily tabernacle. Heaven is my throne, but I also reside in you. I take up residence wherever my Spirit goes. Three in one is not a concept humanly easy to grasp.

I am royalty, yet only my servants recognize my Kingship. I receive your honor while fellow earth-mates scorn and defame my name.

You perceive truth. They carnally see deception. They laugh and ridicule my very name, so unto them there exists no footstool.

Beloved, I love you with all of my Godly ability. My love for you is perfect and complete and lacks nothing.

I invite you to climb upon my footstool—holy and sanctified ground, anointed where your hands touch—and wash my feet. Humble yourself and embrace my dispensation of Christ's love to your generation, the Church. Prophets of old longed for your day when my Spirit's fire would burn as it does today amongst my children who love Me, know Me, and worship Me in Spirit and Truth.

Humbly behold my footstool, and be a servant unto Me while your feet also step upon earth's soil. You will spend all of eternity with Me. Give now to earth's call while your holy feet join my footstool. I have work for you to do. Ready yourself with my holy shoes of the fire of my Spirit. You have much to do here—much to do!

April 21

Key to Your Daddy's Heart

"Our Father in heaven, hallowed be your name."   *Matthew 6:9 NIV*

One of my deepest secrets is revealed by my Son Jesus in this beginning of prayer to Me. He understands holiness; therefore, he knows how to approach my throne unashamedly and without fear—that is with praise!

The key to my listening ear is the prayer of praise! My very essence requires worship and glory and praise.

The *key to your daddy's heart* is unashamed worship and praise of your most Divine Creator.

Your praise pulls Me to earth and commands my prompt attention to your needs. I cannot resist the heart of worship. You, indeed, enter my gates with thanksgiving and my courts with praise.

I love you, beloved children, I love you! Amen.

April 22

I Will Never Forsake You

"For the Lord loves the just and will not forsake his faithful ones."
Psalm 37:28 NIV

I will never forsake you, my tender child of God. Sweet faithful one, I see your heart where none other can go but I. I see the inner beauty, the halls of despair, yet the walls lined with my purity and a heart after God. I shall replace the despair with faith. I shall destroy your inner worry and replace all fear.

I see your inner beauty, the jewels of your spirit that reflect my glory. I see the canals of your inner person wherein lie devotion, dedication, and commitment. I see the interior decoration of my carpenter's hand, and I am pleased. Now, peace be manifest!

Despite the outward, awkward adversity, remember my promises. I will never forsake my anointed one, you! Allow your inward man to shine forth onto the outward. You have nothing to hide, nothing to fear. I will take care of you! Amen.

April 23

Think About Lovely Things

"Finally brothers, whatever is true, whatever is noble, whatever is right, whatever is pure, whatever is lovely, whatever is admirable . . . think about such things."   *Philippians 4:8 NIV*

Where your mind is, there follows your heart. Your mind is like the welcoming room that invites guests in, that extends hospitality to strangers or angels unaware.

In the guest room, you are polite and cordially entertain your guests, seeking them nourishment and comfort—a listening ear. On the other hand, if a scoundrel-looking thief began to break through your door, you would not allow the enemy to enter your home.

In the same way, thoughts are visitors, but some are thieves and to be rejected. You know thieves by their clothing, words, and deceptive antics.

Your guests should be noble, clean, and upright, bringing confirmation to the Word of God embedded deep within your heart.

Entertaining can be a delight! Take heed only that you guard your heart, the center of your home, from guests that come to steal. *Think about lovely things,* and your heart will become lovelier.

April 24

Repentant Heart

"Search me, O God, and know my heart: try me, and know my thoughts: and see if there be any wicked way in me, and lead me in the way everlasting."
Psalm 139:23-24 KJV

This is the cry of the *repentant heart*, the invitation of my Spirit to search and try and cleanse.

I already know your heart, but you do not! I bring opportunities in your daily walk to practice forgiveness and to utilize the authority of my Word over pending circumstances.

I allow you to be tested and tried, and I grant you the privilege of repentance. It is my goodness that leads you to repentance.

Repentance is like walking one direction down a path but turning 90 degrees and aiming yourself in the opposite direction.

Repentance is the choosing of your will to not continue on a course that you realize is displeasing to Me.

It is from this golden attitude of Psalm 139 that I will open up to you a path of everlasting life that will be angel-lined with my will and cherished destiny for you.

As long as you seek to please Me and seek my cleansing hand, I will be able to unfold before your feet the path of least resistance. It will lead you to the unfolding of your heart's desires, as a blossoming rose unveils her accordion petals.

The sweet scent of my perfect will shall envelop your soul, and you will experience true JOY on earth as it is in heaven. Amen.

April 25

This Is Who I Am

"But You, O Lord, are a God full of compassion, and gracious, Longsuffering and abundant in mercy and truth."　　　　　　　　**Psalm 86:15 NKJV**

Beloved Church, *this is who I am.* I am full of <u>compassion</u>! That means, no matter what the problem is, I understand. I am not an untouchable God. I feel your sorrow, your pain, and I empathize with your worries. I am always working to transform fear into faith; but, also, I always understand your heartache.

I am <u>graciousness</u>. I appreciate you, my child, your gifts, your love songs to Me, and your prayers of praise. I say "thank you" in thousands of ways daily that you usually just take for granted. My graciousness sings to you in a sunset, a rainbow, flowers, birds, and my creation that rains down on both the just and the unjust.

If you will listen, you will hear my graciousness in your daily life. Every step of blessing is my gracious voice shouting, "I love you, child! Go and do, and THANK YOU for loving Me in return!" If you have ever slowed down long enough to watch the sun set or given yourself time to watch the sun rise, then you know that I, too, say "thank you!"

I am patience. You are to look like and act like Jesus! I understand the plight of human nature and sin's curse. That is why I am <u>long-suffering</u> and not willing for any to perish. I forgive you time and time again as the blood of Jesus is covered over your sin.

It is your love that I desire, not your punishment. This is why I wait patiently for you to respond to my Spirit's nudges and drawing and leading. I so want my BEST for you; thus, I work in patience with you.

In the blood of Jesus, new <u>mercies</u> rise daily bubbling forth from the fountain of my holy place, my heart. I hold back the enemy, and mercifully, I am the giver of good and perfect gifts.

Beloved, it is <u>truth</u> that will set you free and enable you to receive my abundance in compassion, graciousness, patience, and mercy. My truth is my WORD. Know my Word, and you will know Me. It is in knowing Me that all of life's questions are answered. Know Me! I will cause you to look and act like my Son Jesus Christ. Amen!

April 26

Wrecking Ball

"For where envying and strife is, there is confusion and every evil work."
James 3:16 KJV

Strife tears down relationships like a *wrecking ball* on a crane smashing against a brick wall. It is, therefore, important not to even turn the key to the engine of the crane. The key is always in the ignition waiting for the hand of unforgiveness to turn the engine over. What a small turn of the hand to yield such a large devastation!

Relationships, like buildings, have been intricately built, brick by brick, day upon day, with my "mortar of love" cementing hearts in good trust and faith with one another. One swing of the wrecking ball can tear down months of trust and friendship.

Now, who do you suppose owns the crane? Satan, of course! He despises loving relationships and applauds the tearing down of homes, marriages, and friendships.

If you own your home, then disallow strife and envy to rearrange a hole in your structure or tear down what has taken years to build. Forgive and forbid the evil work of the wrecking ball to destroy your precious relationships with others.

Forgive and resist the tempter's invitation to start up the destroyer's engine of envy and strife.

I work through relationships. They are important to Me, for my very fiber of love holds you together, my mortar from heaven. Broken relationships are shattered pieces of heaven. I need you to love one another and preserve that which has been built between you and others. Love builds up! Strife tears down. Seek to love! For in seeking love, you will be pleasing your Heavenly Father! Amen.

April 27

You Honor Me with Patience

"I waited patiently for the Lord; he turned to me and heard my cry."
Psalm 40:1 NIV

You honor Me with patience. Oh, yes, I hear every agonizing cry of urgent despair, and I respond as a loving and understanding Father would do. I am personally, though, in the deep of your Daddy's heart, honored and glorified when you speak with Me in patience.

When you come to Me in gentleness of praise, when you have carved out of your busy life ample time for Me, when you have enough faith to know I will answer apart from begging unceasingly—all of this brings blessing to your Abba-Daddy's heart. This is because it represents relationship and trust.

I am honored by your maturity in Me. I am comforted and exalted when you sweetly, humbly, and patiently trust Me to work out all details of your petitions.

Patience is my nature; and, when I see JESUS my Son, in you my child, I am overwhelmed with JOY. Amen.

April 28

Desires of Your Heart

"Delight yourself in the Lord and he will give you the desires of your heart."
Psalm 37:4 NIV

If you will delight yourself in Me . . . in other words, if you will love Me with all of your heart, rejoice in my Lordship daily, and intimately walk and talk with Me, then I will grant you those desires that well up from within your soul like bubbles of air from many waters.

Those desires keep surfacing, even when you try so hard to thwart their rising up. It is impossible to keep them from bubbling up, for they are you and uniquely make up who I have created you to be.

I place these desires in you (as if the opposite of my desired contentment) so that you might have a vision always before you of where we want to go spiritually. For example, these are your prayer concerns. These are dreams and goals too far for you to presently reach. The kind of desires I like to implant within the depths of your soul are ones that you could never accomplish on your own strength. Those are Holy Ghost desires, and if you remain faithful to Me, I will grant them to you on wings of my Holy Spirit power. Amen.

April 29

Fervent Prayer

"The effective, fervent prayer of a righteous man avails much."
James 5:16 NKJV

There is no comparison in my response to a lame prayer or a righteous prayer. A lame prayer is without fervency.

It is true that you may win favor and increased grace with Me through righteous prayer. It is true that your intimacy with Me is reflected in your prayer life.

You see, my righteousness in you produces FAITH. I am a faith God. I respond to your faith. It pulls and compels Me to answer, intervene, and send my angels to assist you.

The man who walks closely with Me, who presses his ear against my bosom of love and listens for my voice daily . . . it is he that is clothed in my righteousness. It is he that receives my answers in *fervent prayer.*

Sin perverts the prayer life and delays the answer response. Holiness and purity in my children produce effective answers to prayer needs.

When my child speaks, I listen! Angels stand and await the commands of the righteous. Seek always to be in right relationship with Me, and I will seek always to answer you speedily. Amen.

April 30

Grace

"The grace of the Lord Jesus Christ be with your spirit." **Philippians 4:23 NIV**

It is in your spirit that I move and dwell and have my being. In your spirit man, I deposit my *grace* to extend your ability to stand and persevere, to continue in my flow of blessings in your life. Apart from my increased grace upon your life, you would always be discouraged and downtrodden.

Grace is undeserved. It is my "picker-upper!" It carries you when your tires are flat and your wind is gone from your lungs. When your human/carnal being is emptied, my grace continues to blow as gentle wind against your sails to steer you home.

Grace whispers, "I will always be here to pick up the broken pieces, mend them back, and start you up again!"

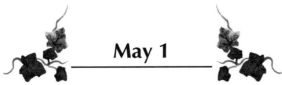

May 1

Stretching Business

"Now to Him who is able to do exceedingly abundantly above all that we ask or think, according to the power that works in us."   ***Ephesians 3:20 NKJV***

I am always able to perform far above your expectation, but there are human hindrances that disallow my full power to approach.

Unbelief in the human heart thwarts my power. I am a God of faith. Your faith works like a magnet pulling my favor and intervention to you. When you doubt, the magnetic field is weakened.

I carry in my bosom for you dreams and the fulfillment of aspirations of which you haven't even yet entertained the possibility. I see you as a seed of potential—you are many seeds! Each seed is the birthing and completion of a dream of mine through you.

I want you to multiply! I want you to become a blossoming garden of many diverse flowers and plants, all giving glory to Me!

If you think six, I think ten. Your "can't" is always my "can." You are a solid mass of potential not designed to be a couch potato!

My dreams for you far exceed your own, but few reach my potential because of fear or unbelief. I want you to begin practicing "bigger faith." Ask Me for more than you want. Inflate your dreams with unlimited possibilities in Me. Beware to not quench my Holy Spirit in you with "little thinking."

I am a very big God, you know! You just cannot outsmart Me or outdream Me! I am in the *stretching business,* and I always desire to stretch you far more than the previous time.

You cannot get too big for Me, but you can become too "big headed!" Beware, lest as I increase you in fruitfulness, your pride keeps up in pace.

Humility is the acknowledgment of Ephesians 3:20, that I exceedingly and abundantly increase you according to my power working in you—according to your faith!

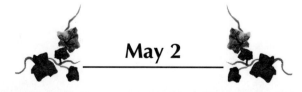

May 2

Not Worthy to Be Compared

"For I reckon that the sufferings of this present time are not worthy to be compared with the glory which shall be revealed in us."   **Romans 8:18 KJV**

If you were to be boiled alive for your testimony of the gospel, even that pain would not compare to your glory in heaven.

If tar and feathered, or jailed for a lifetime, if stoned and beaten or even crucified, none would compare to your reward in heaven. The glory of your home with Me is far above and beyond adequate human description!

Though today's sorrows feel impossible, know that they will all be swallowed up in the victory of your entrance into my heavenly gates. Your mansion will embrace you, and the remembrance of any earthly pain will only stand as gain before Me.

Beloved, you can never give more than I can give you in return. No sacrifice and no pain is greater than my recompense to you.

Persecution and discipline are not the same. For your own growth, you may have to endure spankings from your Father, but, for my GLORY, you will endure persecution.

I meet your sufferings with compassion and my cry of promise: earthly pain shall only reap eternal gain! No sorrow is greater than the gift of my presence and my beautiful Kingdom adorned and prepared for you.

Streets of gold, lilies of silver, mountains covered with emeralds, trees that sing, flowers that praise, scents that melt your nostrils—and a mansion prepared and designed for you . . . *not worthy to be compared.*

May 3

Faith Increases

"And the apostles said unto the Lord, Increase our faith."   *Luke 17:5 KJV*

Faith increases only as you use it. It is like muscle. It responds to exercise (practice) and nutrition (the Word).

Begin where you are and believe for something small. Then, after you receive that something, ask for another gift larger than the first.

Some of you become frustrated because you try to move a mountain before practicing on the mole hills. Each mole hill you conquer will enrich your faith and grant you more fortitude to believe for your next request.

Answered prayer is always a miracle because it means that heaven has touched earth.

When you pray for the salvation of certain individuals, you know not what you ask! You do not see the chains of bondage ensnared about the person's soul.

You need to ask for simple, small expressions of love and hunger for Me. Specifically ask for a work needed in the unsaved one's heart. Ask and command the loosing of one chain at a time.

Jesus could command chains loosed because he was power! Your own faith may not be like the power of a diesel, but even a simple lawn mower grooms a yard in becoming fashion.

I love you. Amen.

May 4

Temptation

"And God is faithful; he will not let you be tempted beyond what you can bear."
I Corinthians 10:13 NIV

This is my promise to you. It should comfort you as you face trying circumstances and new decisions. If you are being pulled between the tug of two ropes going opposite directions, then one is Me and one is not. My promise is sure: I will not allow the enemy to pull you beyond your own ability to resist *temptation.*

The pulling of the ropes is uncomfortable, as if a form of torture, but you are growing in discernment. As you earnestly seek Me, you will see and understand who is at the end of each rope. Then you will make an intelligent choice that will be pleasing to Me and reflect my glory on earth as it is in heaven. Amen.

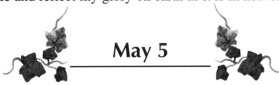

May 5

You Have Been with Jesus

"Now when they saw the boldness of Peter and John, and perceived that they were unlearned and ignorant men, they marvelled; and they took knowledge of them, that they had been with Jesus."　　　　*Acts 4:13 KJV*

When *you have been with Jesus,* people will take note of you! Jesus has a divine essence about him, a sweet and pleasing fragrance, like coffee in a coffee bean shop or vanilla in a vanilla bean shop. A strong aroma is emitted from my Son onto you when you keep company in his presence!

Others will sense his sweet-smelling savor upon you. They will not know or understand what to call it.

They will say, "He is a nice person."

The truth is that you have been with Jesus!

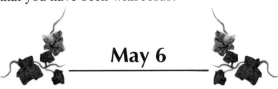

May 6

Despise Not Your Mother

"Despise not thy mother when she is old."   ***Proverbs 23:22 KJV***

When your mother becomes old, you are to bestow honor upon her, wrapping about her shoulders a shawl of protectiveness. Your gratitude to her for the privilege of life she granted you should be constant and steadfast in your heart's attitude.

If you deem her worthy of no honor, then you must forgive her and seek to thank Me for the seed from which you came.

You are to honor your mother by the giving of your time and conversation to her. The only reward she needs in life is to hear your voice and celebrate your children's joys.

Despise not your mother. Never begrudge her requests of you. Do not consider her a burden.

My gift of life through her is precious, and I chose her to give birth to you. For this reason alone, she is worthy of your praise, despite all circumstances that have happened around her life.

Shower your aged mother with care, gentleness, and appreciative manner in all that you do and say. Her peace should be in the gift you are to mankind. Allow her to "glory" in this gift of you. Bring her pleasure in your praise of her.

Few rewards in life have meaning in old age except for the linkage of family ties, especially children and grandchildren. Never deprive her of her reward—the righteous offspring of you and yours.

You are her earthly reward. Deprive her not of your time. She is deserving of your honor. Amen.

May 7

Here Am I, Send Me!

"Whom shall I send, and who will go for us? Then said I, Here am I; send me."
Isaiah 6:8 KJV

You whom I call, I also equip. Age matters not to Me. What matters is my sovereign plan for your life. I have used all ages!

Carefully listen to my voice. Man looks on the outward appearance, but I look into the heart. I see your heart and readiness to serve Me, and I hear you cry, *"Here am I, send me!"*

It is not without cost that I send my servants. The wise servant will diligently prepare the soil in prayer. Then, the unfolding of my will and plan for you will be effortless as doors fling open!

Labor in prayer, NOW, so that when the time has come, the doors will open, you will obey, and the power of my Holy Spirit will spring forth as a mighty flood before you.

One must pray! One must pray! One must pray! The burden of ministry comes from lack of prayer. I need you to pray and pray and pray and pray!

The only strategy of Kingdom life is hidden in your prayer life before my throne. He who often enters in and out with prayer and petitions, angels go always before him.

The Kingdom of God cannot be achieved by effort or youthful zeal apart from prayer. You must pray! You must pray! You must pray! Amen.

May 8

Overturn and Overturn

"I will overturn, overturn, overturn, it: and it shall be no more, until he come whose right it is; and I will give it him."   *Ezekiel 21:27 KJV*

When you give Me a situation where leadership is lopsided and crooked, then I proceed to change and correct the corruptness at hand.

My advantage is seeing into the root of the diseased plants. I know the hearts of all men, their intents and purposes. I see your pure heart aching for rightness and competency.

My promise is to *overturn and overturn* until right sides are facing up and new faces are in place.

Do not allow the confusion and dust being blown about to discourage you. When I clean house, souls are upset, and rooms are rearranged. The musty, set-in-their-way pieces of furniture may be shampooed, rearranged, or shipped off.

You will hear retorting shouts or whines of complaint, but you can rest. You were the interceder and instigator of this overturning. You can rejoice in answered prayer! Amen.

May 9

Faith, Hope, and Love

"And now these three remain: faith, hope, and love. But the greatest of these is love."   *I Corinthians 13:13 NIV*

FAITH—it is by faith that you love Me and believe in my promises to you from my Word. It is by faith that you exercise the authority given to you in the name of Jesus to triumph over every enemy. Faith is the fuel in your tank that causes your engine-spirit to run! Apart from faith, you are a dead work, like a car empty of gas.

HOPE—sustains you, passifies you under duress, and carries you over the bumpy parts of the road. It keeps you from giving up when your faith tank reads empty. A thread of hope is better than ten bolders of will and wit that come not from my Spirit.

LOVE—is the jewel I want to produce in you that will emit my craftsmanship and cause you to shine to a lost world. Love is the greatest because it is the nature and makeup of God your Father. I AM LOVE!

Faith, hope, and love . . . you have these three when you have Me!

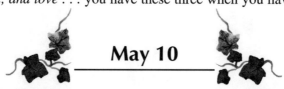

May 10

Honey-sweet Words

"Pleasant words are an honeycomb to the soul, and health to the bones."
Proverbs 16:24 KJV

You can be my honeycomb by dispensing sweet words to those around you.

The voice of the world screams and yells travesties and profanities, lies and hypocrisy. My Kingdom needs your lips dripping with my words of honey.

Seek always to dispense a good word in every corner of your world in which you travel. My world needs your honey!

You will leave a trail of blessing behind you as you drop, like petals, good and choice words.

Be a giver of honey, and I will be faithful to always replenish your supply.

You seek to give, and I will pursue the pouring into your soul of more honey. I will be the manufacturer, the Queen Bee, and you be the dispenser.

I love your sweet words. They cause even your Father's ears to tingle with joy.

Your words of honey are sweet joy—and to some, the only good word they receive in a day's time.

Thank you, beloved, for dispensing to others the *honey-sweet words* of your soul. I love you. Amen.

May 11

Spend Time with Me Alone

"And he withdrew himself into the wilderness, and prayed."   *Luke 5:16 KJV*

You must *spend time with Me alone.* What two young lovers do not hunger for hours alone within the intimacy of their own relationship and seasoned conversations of "lovey dovey" praises to one another?

I desire these times with you. I also want you all to myself. There are sweet words of wisdom I desire to whisper into your ear. Also, we have Kingdom business of which we need to discuss before you venture forth in your own strength, doing your own thing.

I want to love you, to carve upon your spirit my signature of loving devotion.

I want you to know my voice and grow sensitive to my leading and wooing of your spirit man.

Your schedule involves many hours with a large diverse agenda of both people and activities. Could I not be placed at the top of your list?

The time you spend with Me will be doubly saved by the time I spare you in needless hassle and fruitless appointments. I will give you extra hours if you but give Me your first hour.

You cannot outgive Me. I can make even your enemies to be at peace with you.

Beloved, I love you, and we need one another! Please, rise and spend your first hour, your first moments of each day—with Me!

You will enter into a quality of life unknown before, one you will not easily abandon. For it is excellent to be spoiled by Me and lavished with my attention and love! Amen.

May 12

To Fast Is to Intercede

"Those from among you Shall build the old waste places; You shall raise up the foundations of many generations; And you shall be called the Repairer of the Breach, The Restorer of Streets to Dwell In."   **Isaiah 58:12 NKJV**

When you fast, I prepare your calling and purpose to be fulfilled.

I use you as an intercessor to pray and repair old waste places in lives of my children who have lost their walk with Me. I lead you down paths to rescue stray children. Your prayers build back again spiritual fortresses that once were strong but now have caved-in walls.

Your fasting prayers raise up the foundations of many generations in your offspring, your descendants. Like Jacob, I promise you righteous seed and blessing in your children, their children, and their children's children.

You will gain a reputation as a praying saint. You will be known amongst heaven's saints as "the repairer of the breach," for your prayers will patch up many leaking holes and torn down places in people's lives.

Your prayers will rebuild walls torn down by grief, disease, and heartache. Your intercession for your local, state, and national governments will restore communities and homes, and you will be called "the restorer of streets to dwell in."

To fast is to be called by my name to fulfill your divine destiny for which I specifically created you.

If you fast, I will send you to the nations to minister my love to a lost and crying world. *To fast is to intercede.*

May 13

Teens, Fly!

"At midnight I will rise to give thanks to You, because of Your righteous judgments."   *Psalm 119:62 NKJV*

Teenagers, come unto Me! Come unto Me! I love you so intensely. If you will but stop, shut your eyes, and quietly listen to your inner being, you will hear Me crying over and over, "I love you! I love you! I love you!"

Beloved ones, my precious teenagers, you have entered into a most delicate time of your life. You are no longer little children but not yet adults. You are like chickadees or feathered birds that have leaped from the nest with your strong legs but feeble wings. This is the season of your life wherein I build strength into your wing system.

Do I deem you accountable for your actions and deeds? Oh, yes, indeed! For you are no longer hiding behind the skirts of your mama. No, you are now young men and young women. You are now responsible unto Me to learn to worship Me and love Me.

You are being weaned from childish ways, even spiritually speaking. I desire that you no longer "leach" off of others for all spiritual input. You need to, now, while you are still young, begin to have a devotional time with Me daily. It is time for you to embrace my gospel on your own, apart from mama's hand pulling, shoving, or her voice calling.

You will always, eternally be my children! Feed on the Word, read on your own. Talk to Me, for I will talk with you.

Beloveds, your wings cannot quite set you into flight, yet you so desperately desire to be independent! Flap those wings, and exercise your new found freedom with wisdom. You may ask Me for wisdom, and I will give good, wise counsel and instruction.

Be patient with your parents. They, too, are adjusting to you no longer clinging to the side of the nest. You may earn their respect (and thus more freedom by them) as you make wise decisions and correct choices after having asked for my wisdom.

Teens, I love you. You have entered a most beautiful, exciting time in your life. During this segment of growing up, many of you will be called by Me to serve in diverse capacities, both in my church and in the world. I will speak to your hearts, shining my bright light of wisdom upon where to attend college, who to marry, what talents I have placed within you, and just who you have been made to be through Jesus Christ who strengthens you!

Remember, children, humbly ask for wisdom. I will do the rest. It is time to quit asking mom or dad for everything and start asking Me! I will give you good counsel and wisdom in your daily decisions.

I want to see you fly! *Teens, fly!* I want to build within you wings that will be strong enough to carry you through storms or weary winds. My wings will be supernatural wings! If you allow Me to construct, build, and refine your young-

continued

adult wings, then you will enter adulthood with strengthened power of soul, spirit, and body, unusual for one of such a young age.

I am preparing you to slide into adulthood effortlessly with knowledge of my will in all areas of your life. If you can find it in yourself to learn of Me now, while you are still near the nest and while wings are developing, then you will know your destination, have clear goals, and ultimately, you will be all that I have created you to be, yes, at a very young age.

You see, many young adults flounder about, not really knowing who they are. They continue to "grow up" and often fail and fall because of faulty wing structures that developed misdirected as teens.

Beloveds, my covenant teenagers, you will be allowed to avoid this happening! Even as teens, your short solo flights will be anointed, smoothed, and perfected by my grace. I am teaching you from the beginning how to use your wings perfectly. We will simply lengthen your flights until one day you will not return near the nest.

You are to honor your mother and your father, always, but remember that I have revealed the secret key to them releasing you into freedom—their respect for you—which will come as they observe my level of wisdom manifesting and rising in you!

Beloved teens, come unto Me! I will do all this for you. I am true strength and true joy and true happiness, and I will never let you fall or let you down.

I am always here for you. By faith, ASK, and you will receive from Me. It is that simple!

I love you, beloved ones! I love you, I love you, I love you! Amen and amen.

May 14

Jot or Tittle

"For assuredly, I say to you, till heaven and earth pass away, one jot or one tittle will by no means pass from the law till all is fulfilled."

Matthew 5:18 NKJV

Did you know that I am a perfectionist? Indeed, not one *jot or tittle* will be overlooked, nor will I allow compromise in my plan. I wait, rather, upon the unjust to repent, calling all to repentance.

My law shall be fulfilled! My covenant shall be manifested on earth as it is in heaven.

Every piece of my puzzle will be fit together before the hour glass has run out.

I am a God of perfection that prepares the heart of man and utilizes the blood of Jesus Christ to wash and cleanse away sin.

In heaven, you will only see, hear, and do perfection. That atmosphere alone is worth any price to your earthly soul. No pain will compare to my glory. Indeed, every jot and tittle has been thought of and prepared, along with your mansion designed just for you!

You cannot humanly imagine an atmosphere of perfection. Let Me assure you that no earthly persecution or suffering compares to its glory! No matter what you have to endure in your flesh on earth, know that I promise the state of my perfection, manifested in its full glory, is worth it!

Hold on, and don't give up. Do not compromise or lose hold of my promises and your stand in Me. My home of perfection will more than compensate for any present suffering on earth.

Keep your eyes on JESUS and our hope of glory! Every jot and tittle is fulfilled before your eyes in heaven. Just wait! It won't be long, and in the twinkling of an eye, you will be standing before Me. Just you wait!

May 15

Bear the Yoke

"It is good for a man to bear the yoke in his youth." **Lamentations 3:27 NKJV**

Never spoil a child, for you will be setting him up for emotional failure down the road. A child must be trained with the attitude of servitude. I say trained, because it is against the nature of man to work and to do good for others. Man's nature is lazy, but this inclination can be stripped away from a soul at a very young age if the parent is keen on training the child to *bear the yoke* in his youth.

Children must be trained to serve, or how else will they desire to serve Me as they mature in life? If children are taught only to work for money, then who will their God become? The green bill will become their false god.

Servitude in youth is essential for the making of a young man's soul. He must be trained to give without reward and to serve without direct recompense.

If a man bears the yoke in his youth, then he will not be haughty or self-righteous. Deep in his soul, he will know the price of labor, and he will be grateful for any small gift from another.

An ungracious spirit stems from not having worked hard enough. There is nothing more despicable to Me than a spoiled, ungrateful child!

Never allow a child to demonstrate laziness, whether it be in the upkeep of his personal belongings or the duties of his household assignments. Childish sloppiness and sloth will transfer into adult bad habits that become nearly impossible to break.

You, as the parent, must demand neatness, orderliness, and responsibility. These attributes need to be "trained" into your children, for only rarely do they come naturally.

"In all that you do, do it unto Me!" This must be the wise parent's yard stick to measure a child's productivity.

Remember, parent, you are training your child's young soul to address life and Me. If he is allowed to be lazy in work, he will be lazy in his relationship with Me! Amen.

May 16

My Allegory on Earth

"You will go out in joy and be led forth in peace; the mountains and hills will burst into song before you."   **Isaiah 55:12 NIV**

All of my creation is *my allegory on earth* as it is in heaven. If you could see more clearly into the spirit realm, you would observe this poem of creation on earth.

My creation shouts of my JOY and PEACE! My trees burst forth into song! It is so in heaven. All elements of heaven sing in worship of Me. All leaves sing, "Holy, holy, holy!" Mountains resound in loud echoes of worship to Me.

Open your eyes to my allegory on earth. Each blade of grass, leaf of green, and flower or tree of beauty sings of my joy and peace. See with the eyes of your spirit, and you will see my holy angels worshipping Me using trees as pebble stones of glory. All creation shouts "holy! holy! holy!" unto Me. Look with your spirit, and you will also see! Amen.

May 17

I Have Come to Save

"For God sent not his Son into the world to condemn the world; but that the world through him might be saved."   **John 3:17 KJV**

Oh, that my world might know Me! Oh, that my lost children would understand my compassion and abounding love! Oh, that the lost souls might come to see my faithfulness to them in providing their needs, even though they love Me not.

I am slow to anger, for my name is love, my breath is love, and my character is love. Love counts no offense done against it. I forbear patiently the ignorance of man's rebellion because I love unceasingly and because Jesus always intercedes for the nations.

Spirit, I send you forth into the earth to woo men's souls back to Me. Spirit of God, blow your breath upon the heathen and spare their souls. I have come to save a lost generation. *I have come to save.* Amen.

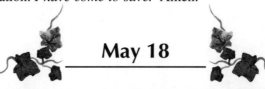

May 18

Absorbed in Jesus

"Rejoice not, that the spirits are subject unto you; but rather rejoice, because your names are written in heaven."　　　　　　　　*Luke 10:20 KJV*

Part of the curse of man is being short-sighted, an inability to see beyond the tip of his nose, the here and now. It is a spiritual blindness that begins to be healed when you are born again. The healing comes in time as the salve of my Spirit-Word is applied to the eyes of your soul.

It is good to grasp in mind and heart your eternal home. You should feel as a pilgrim on this earth, not a permanent resident. In light of time, your stay on earth is quite short and temporary.

Yet, man ignorantly and proudly deems himself invincible; yes, up unto the grave where the rude awakening unfolds, and then it is too late.

Beloveds, I unfold many powerful workings and ministries in my name through you—but, truly the glory of my power in JESUS' name is not to exceed your own personal excitement and anticipation for heaven.

Do not become absorbed with ministry. No. Rather, remain *absorbed in Jesus,* like a sponge, and squeeze onto others my Living Waters, but enjoy the soaking up of my Living Word MORE than the squeezing out!

You shall love the Lord your God with all your heart, and with all your soul, and with all your strength, and with all your mind, and your neighbor as yourself.

This is the pure and true ministry, the giving of love. It is less pure to marvel at the power you have in my name over enemy spirits. Keep LOVE at the forefront of all endeavors in my name, and be not boastful of your authority over spirits in my name.

Remember, Mary chose that good part which could not be taken away from her. Your love for Me is what brings Me the greatest honor.

Be careful and heed my caution: no ministry's excitement shall exceed the thrill of heaven's hope and glory! If so, all is not in perfect balance before Me.

I first and foremost must have your heart, and your heart's home is JESUS—in heaven—with Me.

Priority number one: Love Me! From this place and position of love will flow forth all ministry to others. Amen.

May 19

This Intimate Place

"Therefore in the shadow of Your wings I will rejoice."   ***Psalm 63:7 NKJV***

You abide in the center of my heart. There you rest in the shadow of the Almighty. This is a holy, sacred, consecrated haven of rest, a protected place where your spirit rests in Me. You are unable to place yourself here. I must bring you, myself. It is a place of purity, quietness, and peace where your soul whispers, "Holy One, you are my life and worthy to be praised!"

Beloved, I want you to rest in this place, the bosom of your Heavenly Father. It is the place of eternity where you will always be.

The peace in your heart is eternal in you. Already you possess the presence of heaven in your heart! It is effortless and holy. All you are able to do is bask in my presence and glory in my intimacy with you!

When you speak, heaven comes from your mouth. Like the morning dew, you are fresh, and you are alive without effort of the flesh.

Beloved, I have brought you here. You did not buy a ticket to come. I have drawn you here. Rest and enjoy my place, my love, and my close intimacy with you. This place is eternal.

This is heaven that you have in your heart. Let the world go on. It marches in a furry! Ah, but you may abide in the shadow of my wings because I love you. You have longed for heaven. Now, I have given it to you by drawing you in to this place in Me.

Allow my life in you to flow out and spill over. The light of my life will shine from your eyes. The power and anointing of Jesus will drop as honey from your mouth. Whatever you do and whatever you say will be anointed.

I have heard your cries, and I choose to draw you into *this intimate place* with Me in the shadow of my wings. You have entered the center of my bosom. No more are you to suffer in soul. I have rescued you. You dwell now in my bosom where I will keep you safe.

I love you, beloved! I love you! I love you! I have rescued you because I love you. All you have to do is enjoy Me, and in that enjoyment of our intimacy, your ministry will break forth. I love you! I love you! I love you! Amen.

May 20

Wrestle Not

"For we wrestle not against flesh and blood, but against principalities, against powers, against the rulers of the darkness of this world, against spiritual wickedness in high places."　　　　　　　　　　**Ephesians 6:12 KJV**

Your fights are not with men but with demon forces who have the men ensnared with their evil claws and poisonous venom.

You fight needlessly with men. Your true war is against the powers that have blinded their minds from my truth.

The only way to change someone is by loosing them from the chains of hell that pull them down and distort their personalities.

You waste time trying to influence others amidst strife. *Wrestle not.* Rather, do your warring in prayer, not conversation—in intercession, not disagreement with them.

Do not waste your time fretting about wicked men. They are helpless in their chains. If you who are spiritual discern a bondage in another, don't point it out! Don't entangle yourself in a fight. Pray, only pray.

Allow Me to loose the chain. Then, that person will be free to repent, see his bad ways, and come to you with a willing heart.

It does no good to fight demonic holds apart from prayer. Personalities are trapped unless a more noble one seeks to intercede and loosen the mouth of the trap.

Stand back from the distressed soul and pray! When the person is free, he will come running to you for forgiveness and a right mind.

Do not place blame, for were it not for the grace of God, you, too, would have been like blinded.

Have mercy on the sinner. Humbly pray for his soul, and in your humility and intercession, I will set free the opponent and make him your friend. Watch Me! I can do all things if I am petitioned humbly to do so. Be only certain that there be no malice or accusation in your own soul.

True repentance will be drawn from the well of true intercession. I love you. Amen.

May 21

When You Come Together

"How is it then, brethren? when ye come together, every one of you hath a psalm, hath a doctrine, hath a tongue, hath a revelation, hath an interpretation. Let all things be done unto edifying."   *I Corinthians 14:26 KJV*

I have described my worship services in this verse. One has a doctrine, one has a tongue, one has an interpretation, one has a psalm. You come together as different members of the body of Christ bringing that which every joint supplies.

What takes place when you gather in my name should go far beyond worship songs and a sermon—that which every joint supplies. You have an unhealthy body when only certain limbs and organs are allowed to function.

Rejoice in the uniqueness of one another! Be not so stiff-necked that you cannot welcome a new song or revelation sent straight from heaven. New songs, revelations, and poetry come straight from the publishing press of the throne of God.

Therein lies a freshness and excitement like that of a newborn babe—and why? They have both so recently come from my place of habitation. They are freshly alive and still have the fragrance of heaven about them!

These published works will thrill and excite the body of Christ. Apathy vanishes in the midst of the flow from heaven to earth. The same thing applies to new songs. They must be encouraged! They must be shared!

It is not the vessel nor the quality of voice or composition that matters. The true life of the gift comes in offering it to the congregation new and fresh from Me.

It isn't old. It isn't stale—but new, fresh, and filled with life-giving substance preordained for the body of Christ.

Do not stifle the flow of my spiritual gifts of revelation and prophecy, for in them are life and the newness of life seeking and waiting to explode within the body of Christ.

Please, *when you come together,* do not hinder the flow of the Spirit. Please, do not quench my Spirit with legalism and formalism. Stifling these gifts brings stagnancy, dullness, boredom, and, ultimately, deception. You are all members of the body of Christ. You all need one another as you flow in the gifts you have received of Me.

May 22

The Death of My Saints

"Precious in the sight of the Lord is the death of his saints." Psalm 116:15 KJV

When you arrive in heaven, you are clothed with eternal garments. We adorn you with the apparel necessary for Kingdom of Heaven living.

It is always a good thing to receive my saints into glory! I welcome you home with a Father's love for his child, with an embrace unlike any earthly touch imaginable.

The journey is over. You have been promoted. Earth's pull is cut loose, and you are free to love without barrier and to rejoice without restraint.

On earth's side, death is sorrow—but on heaven's side, death is joy! Your accomplishments are reviewed. Your recorded steps on earth are discussed, understood, and forgiven. I reward you for your faithfulness to Me.

You are taught and invited into my Chambers of Eternity where carnal mind cannot imagine. We celebrate the return of our saints!

Truly, *the death of my saints* is the birth into heaven's gates and my unveiled presence; it is, therefore, deemed precious—very precious to Me! Amen.

May 23

Rejoice!

"Rejoice in the Lord always. I will say it again: Rejoice!" **Philippians 4:4 NIV**

Do you know why I ask you to *rejoice*? This is because it is the nature of God to rejoice! It is my Son's personality to rejoice! The very walls and halls of your heavenly Kingdom rejoice! Rejoice, in heaven, is like air on earth. It is the very nature of all godliness to REJOICE!

All of heaven rejoices! There are no tears. All creatures and creation in heaven join in unison with the cry of rejoicing.

To rejoice means to abound in your heart with thankfulness. To rejoice recognizes the Lordship of Jesus Christ and the divine infinity of his plan and purposes for the sheep of his flock. Rejoice is Jesus' personality.

True rejoicing bubbles up like a fresh spring from the born-again spirit of man. It is pure and tasteful, and another's thirst for joy is quenched by drinking from your wells of rejoicing.

May 24

Kingdom of Worship

"Therefore I will praise you, O lord, among the nations; I will sing praises to your name." **2 Samuel 22:50 NIV**

Heaven is music. Heaven is praise. Heaven is worship. Your eternal life is designed to praise and honor your King of Kings and Lord of Lords.

Eternal life is citizenship in my *Kingdom of Worship*. It is eternity spent in the clutches of divine GLORY!—of worship, honor, and praise.

The human decision to worship Me reflects your eternal activities in my Kingdom. You are practicing citizenship for heaven!

It is "becoming" for you to worship. It fits well onto your spirit—like divine clothing.

You are beautifully adorned with my garments of heaven when you praise Me! I love to see you this way! Amen.

May 25

Influence Your World

"For all have sinned, and come short of the glory of God."

Romans 3:23 KJV

This is the plight of the human race—all have fallen short. Oh, that men might shed the proud veil over their eyes and recognize their eternal need for Me and a Savior! Oh, that men might bow their knees and confess the eternal truth, that Jesus is Lord! Oh, that men might repent and be baptized in every nation confessing the name of Jesus as Lord!

Little men pretend to be little gods, and their worlds tumble down 'round about them. They have no divine touch to sustain their self-made Kingdoms, so the tornadoes of life eventually devastate their souls and earthly belongings.

The sting of death cannot be made less by riches and possessions. The desperate lost soul screams to carry his riches to hell—but all that goes with him is his own misery of selfish ambition and self-perpetuation which leads to an eternal death.

Oh, that men would open their eyes and behold the very Son of God. Oh, that men would call upon my name!

All have sinned, and there is none righteous, no, not one!

Believers, pray for the lost. Do the work of an evangelist. Spread and share my light with your world! It is in need of a Savior, the Lord and Savior Jesus Christ!

I will have mercy on the repentant soul. I stand at the door and knock and knock and knock, but no man is forced to enter through my door. It is by invitation that each man voluntarily receives my call and enters into my rest. The choice is respected, unviolated, and precious.

He who wins souls is wise. Pray that you might *influence your world* for Jesus Christ! Amen.

May 26

Decision Making

"But the wisdom from above is first pure, then peaceable, gentle, open to reason, full of mercy and good fruits." **James 3:17 RSV**

Listen to my voice, beloved one. My voice is different from your voice. Learn to discern between the two voices. You know the voice of the enemy. It nabs and jabs; it creates lack of peace in you, and it destroys my vision of peace for your day. It is uncomfortable.

I always speak in first person. You will hear Me say, "I love you, do such and such." I am also a gentle nudge in the direction of a door my angels have already opened for you.

The difference between fake and true leading is that my true and pure leading always brings peace to the heart. I work in the heart. I prepare the heart, and I do succeed when a person cooperates with Me.

My voice is doused in love, joy, and peace. There is no doubt in my voice. I am never wishy-washy. I am firm and constant, not unstable and topsy-turvy.

When satan comes as an angel of light, he blinds with his light. You think in your mind that it is Me because it comes in the form of light. It has certain glowing, tantalizing qualities, but the light uncarefully and rudely shines directly into your eyes, and you are blinded. You become confused and disoriented. You have doubt, and your mind is in constant battle over the decision making. There is no peace.

In contrast, when I open a door, I, as a gentleman, remain quiet with the door ajar, wooing and awaiting your holy, gracious response in obedience to my perfect and pure will for you.

I do not blind nor confuse. The plan is simple and spawns from the center of your heart. There is no fear because I am at the door, and you are not alone.

Decision making can be made to become incredibly difficult, confusing, and disheartening, but it should not be so. That, itself, should be a signal to you that something is wrong. Do not wrestle with decisions. If yes cannot be yes, or no cannot be no, then wait.

My decisions are holy door openers into new phases of servitude. If your heart is prepared, your walk will be a simple step through the door and its new direction for you.

I do not bring you abruptly to new doors. As second witness, I will have already been working to prepare your heart.

If you, like a rope, are being pulled in two separate directions, know that first of all, I never pull. I woo and draw, and with the voice of a gentleman, I call.

Do not be bullied into decisions. This is not my style nor my doing. Listen to your heart! My answer and direction will spawn from your heart.

May 27

Stones of Joy

"Therefore everyone who hears these words of mine and puts them into practice is like a wise man who built his house on the rock."   *Matthew 7:24 NIV*

Brick by brick, I desire to replace your earthly happiness with my *stones of joy.*

There is nothing wrong with happiness in and of itself, except that it is temporary, not eternal, and cannot be transported to heaven.

Human happiness differs from "divine joy" in that joy is created by revelation nuggets from my Word.

The true and solid foundation of your soul must be the rock of Jesus Christ. All other else is sinking sand.

Often times you only come to realize the frailty of your structure in the face of hardship and sorrow.

I take my Word and build within you an immovable foundation that in the twinkling of an eye can be in heaven with Me, and that is indeed who you are!

Stones of joy are touched and formed by Me, the healer of all brokenheartedness.

Strength is made perfect in weakness as you become a testimony of my grace. The joy of the Lord is your strength!

May 28

Young Man

"How can a young man cleanse his way? By taking heed according to Your word."   *Psalm 119:9 NKJV*

Young man, do you want your life to be directed by Me?

Young man, do you want to prosper in your life vocation?

Young man, do you want to please Me?

Young man, whom do you love more—the world or Me?

I will tell you, young man, how to keep your life in the center of my will—read my Word! Study my Word! Meditate upon my Word!

If you love Me, then you will desire to read my love letter to you. Communing with Me through my Word will be like pulling up to your local gas station and filling your tank! Your spirit needs my supernatural fuel from heaven which flows into you through the nozzle of my written Word, the Holy Bible.

Young man, if you want to know how to keep your way pure, how to keep from making wrong choices—then fellowship with Me in my Word!

I promise you, if you do your part, I will do mine! I will protect you from harm and deception if you but entrust yourself unto the safekeeping of my promises.

I love you. Amen.

May 29

You Cannot Outgive Me

"Give, and it will be given to you. A good measure, pressed down, shaken together and running over, will be poured into your lap. For with the measure you use, it will be measured to you."   *Luke 6:38 NIV*

You cannot outgive Me. This is an absolute impossibility. It is nonexistent in every form, not only in finances but in truth and character. It is absolutely positively not possible to outgive Me! It cannot be done. The possibility of it happening does not exist, and it never will for eternity.

When you "sacrifice," when you lay down your life, when you swallow your pride and humble yourself before Me, when you give love, when you choose right as unto Me your God . . . in all of this you are giving to Me. By my very nature and law of love, I have to send more to you in return.

When you are being stretched by my hand and you willingly feel the pain without a tantrum or yell, but you endure as I carve, mold, and perfect . . . know that you are giving to Me. You are giving yourself to Me, and you cannot outgive Me. I must return more love unto you in the form of "blessing."

When you allow Me to stretch you humbly and willingly, then you are giving your life to Me—and you cannot outgive your God! I can only give back in response to the gift of your submitted life to Me.

You can never ever give anything unto Me without Me giving more in return. This is the nature and law of your God and Father. I am no other way. Every little "love song" to Me pulls at my heart to give you blessing in return.

You cannot outgive Me! It is impossible. The more you give, the more you receive, and the snowball effect is glory! Glory! GLORY! Amen.

May 30

Happy Is the Man

"Happy is the man who finds wisdom, And the man who gains understanding. Length of days is in her right hand, In her left hand riches and honor."

Proverbs 3:13, 16 NKJV

Your goals in life reflect the condition of the hidden man of your heart. What are you seeking? Is it riches and fame, possessions and popularity?

I say *happy is the man* who finds wisdom and understanding. Wisdom will tell you how to utilize Kingdom principles for your own benefit.

If you pursue wisdom, then understanding comes to you. I will reveal to you how to earn money and gain possessions, and this quest will not kill you young, as the drive of the world will do.

The best of my promise is honor. The world seeks to earn respect, but my gift is more deeply satisfying and supplies the hunger of the inner man: honor!

If you spend a lifetime increasing in wisdom, then you will be honored. Others will highly regard the reflection of my face that they see in you.

To honor is to revere, and only my wisdom will illicit reverence from another's heart. In heaven, we honor one another.

Wisdom is seeking to understand from my perspective through the eyeglasses of my Word.

Wisdom will cause you to be honored both on earth and in heaven. Indeed, honor is heaven's feeling come to earth.

May 31

My House of Prayer

"My house shall be called a house of prayer for all nations." Isaiah 56:7 NKJV

My *house of prayer* is a place of reverence toward Me when you come together to worship my name, where you gather in one accord to honor and praise your Creator.

In my house, I would have my people praying, praying, praying! It is in my house that sweet conversation to Me and from Me should reign.

The world has built ample enough buildings for its business. Let us not defame my house with nonsense. Let us retain my holiness and presence within the walls of my house.

I dwell in living tabernacles—but when you gather together, my presence indwelling each of my children magnifies and manifests my glory!

The attitude of humble heart-felt prayer is readily received in my house. Great power and authority over the enemy is loosed when my body congregates in my house together and prays in one accord.

I honor your going in to my house. I honor your prayerful attitude. It is when hearts join together and seek Me that my movement amongst you is strongest.

I desire to make myself known to you and manifest my glory! Gathering in my house is the one time that prayer should be foremost important corporately, for you literally pull on the hem of my garments, and my presence indwells your place of habitation . . . and I am near, so very near!

It is Me you desire, so, together, pray—all of you together! My power awaits to be utilized by my praying saints in the house of the Lord. I love you, Church, I love you!

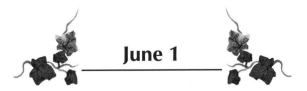

June 1

The Slothful Man

"The slothful man roasteth not that which he took in hunting: but the substance of a diligent man is precious."   *Proverbs 12:27 KJV*

Diligence versus laziness. It is the nature of carnal man to be lazy, unmotivated, and slothful. What man does not enjoy a week's vacation or look forward to the weekends so that he might "do his own thing" and not be committed to the demands of the work force?

Beloved, I tell you that I work to transform you into the image of Jesus Christ by filling you with motivation to seek employment, to be in the world (not of the world), to rub elbows with fellow workers, and to shine as a good example of hard-working ethics and old-fashioned loyalty to the employer.

I deem precious the man who is faithful in whatever his hands are set to work to do. *The slothful man* will fish but feel too lazy or tired to prepare the meat for his meal, or to give the scored fillets to the poor.

No matter how important you are in society's eyes, and regardless of your monetary worth on earth, from my throne I count it precious when you value and prize that which I have given you.

Complacency and ingratitude are diabolical words to my ears!

Beloved, deem precious the gifts I bring to you, as well as the fruits of your labors. You have much to be thankful for, as I, too, am thankful for you! Amen.

June 2

Rebel One

"Here I am! I stand at the door and knock. If anyone hears my voice and opens the door, I will go in and eat with him, and he with me."

Revelation 3:20 NIV

Beloved, you owe no man anything but to love Me, to make Me your life priority. For if you but dare to relinquish your own rights—rights I have given you as man—and follow Me, I will give you everything your heart desires in return.

Now, usually, piece by piece, brick by brick, a life is surrendered over to Me; thus, ever so slowly, I am allowed to manifest my goodness in one's behalf. The measure in which you give yourself to Me is the same measure in which I can give myself to you.

I must be allowed to come in. I am a gentleman. I never force or coerce. In fact, I ever so slowly watch—hoping, waiting, and believing in your ultimate willingness to give in to your own private will in order that you might fulfill mine.

My will is always, only perfect, paved with shining armor and protection from the evil one.

My way is always clothed with peace that no money could buy and joy with which no entertainment could compare. Peace and joy are unseen promises, jewels of the spirit, that no man can manufacture, imitate, mar, or steal. They come uniquely from the heart of your God.

I am always waiting to pour out a large measure of my grace and Spirit upon you. The requirement of you is so ironically simple that I am most often missed. I require that you ask Me in. At your humble invitation, I gloriously enter with robes of riches and praise. The King of Kings and Lord of Lords knocks at your door every single day of your life. Oh, if you were to know the riches outside that door, you would scream in agony of your days slipped by.

Precious one, you know not what you miss; for, if you did, there would never another day pass by that you would not make Me Lord of your life. I am life, and without Me you can do nothing. The works of the dead shall burn, but the works of my righteous one shall live and shine for eternity.

Rebel one, I love you as I love my own, but your days are numbered, and you are wasting away my precious gift of life everlasting. My precious, you are wasting away. Come, follow Me, and I will make you a fisher of men.

You have made yourself many things, all very reputable in the sight of man; but, beloved one, on the day of your calling into death's grip, your reputation will be of no avail, and you will be naked.

I offer you robes—wealthy, eternal robes, warm, sparkling, and lovely. You are beautiful in Me. I stand at your door and softly knock. Will you let Me in?

June 3

My Angels Guard You

"For he will command his angels concerning you to guard you in all your ways."   *Psalm 91:11 NIV*

Oh, if you were able to see into my spirit realm, you would feel ashamed for having ever doubted, worried, or been fearful, for you would see how I have encompassed you with my messengers and warriors of love. You turn to the right —they are there! You turn to the left—they are there!

Beloved, you do not escape my protective shield 'round about you! I send my angels to minister comfort and to protect your body. They supervise the thievery actions of the enemy who seeks and prowls around to steal, kill, and destroy. I protect you from the thief.

My angels guard you because you walk in my favor, my love, and my tender mercies. Amen.

June 4

I Delight in You!

"The Lord your God is with you, he is mighty to save. He will take great delight in you."   *Zephaniah 3:17 NIV*

Indeed, *I delight in you!* I love you. You bring Me great pleasure and joy as I watch you serving one another and humbly loving Me. When your children score high on a test or win a race, you are proud and delight in their achievements. In the same way, I love you and delight in your accomplishments.

Every successful, rejoicing hour that you walk with Me, recognizing the Lordship of Jesus, I am pleased. Our relationship brings me JOY. I pleasure and delight in you!

I save mightily my beloved ones who know Me and walk hand in hand with Me. I save you from fruitlessness and vanity, the wasting of time and self-centeredness. I save you from yourself, because I love you. Amen.

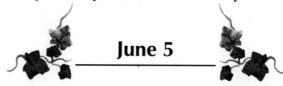

June 5

A Woman Who Fears the Lord

"Charm is deceptive, and beauty is fleeting, but a woman who fears the Lord is to be praised."   *Proverbs 31:30 NIV*

It is the woman who loves Me and reverences my name that will manifest in her life the fruits of my Spirit. It is the fruits that truly feed others' souls. It is when the soul is fed that a virtuous woman is praised.

Beauty is vain and useless apart from the inner loveliness of Jesus Christ coming forth. A pretty smile, dashing clothing, and attractive hair are all very pleasant to look upon, but they have no substance to themselves. They are unable to feed the hungry soul.

A woman who fears the Lord is able to lead a thirsty soul to my streams of Living Waters. A quenched thirst is worth more than a pretty picture. When people are in need, they care not about the attractiveness of the vessel. They simply want their need met!

The fruits of the Spirit minister my life to others: Love and Joy, Peace and Patience, Kindness and Goodness, Gentleness and Faithfulness and Self-Control. Now, these are pure gifts that satisfy the inner hungry soul and cause grateful men to praise the giver of these gifts! Amen.

June 6

Teach the Nations

"For great is the Lord and most worthy of praise; he is to be feared above all gods."   *1 Chronicles 16:25 NIV*

Oh, that the world would grasp the essence of my gospel. Evangelize! Go into the four corners of the world. Tell the Good News that JESUS is coming again!

In your Father's House are many mansions waiting for you who understand that I am great and worthy to be praised!

I am to be honored above all false gods. This is the quest of the missionary, to teach and instruct I Chronicles 16:25.

There is only blessing in acknowledging my Lordship. *Teach the nations* to praise my name that I might rain upon their nations my favor and intervention in their governments. Amen.

June 7

I See Your Perfect Heart

"I will behave wisely in a perfect way. Oh, when will you come to me? I will walk within my house with a perfect heart."   *Psalm 101:2 NKJV*

Beloved, *I see your perfect heart* and your attitude of servitude within your home. In this I rejoice! What more can be required of you? I ask you to serve Me with all of your heart by attending faithfully to the needs of your family and loved ones.

The enemy is a liar. His accusations of fault are stones throne against an empty wall. They are useless and fall to the ground. I pay no attention to his accusations, nor must you.

Beloved, I love you! You are pleasing Me in your attitude of servitude towards your family. I can only respond by pouring out onto your home my blessings of protection and prosperity.

You are shining as a bright light on a hill, a tower of love to those whom you serve. Rejoice, my love, for you bring great pleasure to your Heavenly Father! Amen.

June 8

Crankiness

"It is better to dwell in the wilderness, than with a contentious and an angry woman."   *Proverbs 21:19 KJV*

Crankiness brings Me no glory! Who wants to dwell with a moody cat who meows and claws crankily? I give no license for moodiness. It is of the flesh, and it needs to be addressed and healed.

When your body is depleted of certain hormones or vitamins, then you may well experience a diseased mind that does not want to be nice. Let this be a warning to you—take care of yourself! Find help! Do not expect your family to tolerate a wicked tongue.

When you are weak, then humbly confess weakness and need for prayer. By all means, do not open your mouth and vomit out words you will (or should) later regret. PMS is a true disease. It comes, and it goes—but it doesn't permit you to turn into a witch. You must lock up your mouth and not allow your weakness to turn into poisonous venom when you attack others.

A wise woman will seal her lips and seek the healing of both body and soul. Sleep more, and take care of yourself. It is sin to punish the world with a wicked tongue.

June 9

Oil of Anointing

"And the yoke shall be destroyed because of the anointing."

Isaiah 10:27 KJV

I would have you be like a young calf skipping about on my spring meadow of fresh green grass, strewn rocks, and blooming lilies, without a care, enjoying my fresh air, and soaking up my sun's rays. I would have my joy being your strength—freely enjoying my presence.

I would not have you yoked into bondage with the heaviness of duty and servitude unto Me like oxen plowing through a field. No. I would have your soul freely skipping about like calves upon my hill of provision and love.

Now, how shall yokes not of Me be destroyed? The simplest anecdote is my anointing. Find someone who oozes with my oil, and seek them to pray for you. Also, you may participate in a gathering of the saints wherein my oil of anointing is freely flowing from the pastor and through my people. My *oil of anointing* may be found in the revelation of my Word or in the discovery of my prophetic words, such as these!

Beloved, do not settle for second best. I do not want yokes clamped around you. Find my anointing, and let Me set you free of religious bondages that I never instigated in the first place. I want you free!

June 10

Maturity

"Lord, my heart is not haughty, nor mine eyes lofty: neither do I exercise myself in great matters, or in things too high for me. Surely I have behaved and quieted myself, as a child that is weaned of his mother: my soul is even as a weaned child."   *Psalm 131:1-2 KJV*

I desire *maturity*. It is a good thing to be a little child of mine. It is a better thing to function in my Kingdom ranks as a mature, battle-ready soldier, equipped with my Word and empowered by my Spirit.

In the Spirit, I have fathered you just as your earthly parents have cared for you. I mother you as an infant, discipline you, and then wean you from the milk.

I delight in serving you banquets of my Word. Milk is good. Steak is better. I desire that you chew my Word, digest my Word, and utilize the energy my Word releases in your spirit to win lost souls, to evangelize, and to fulfill my call on your life.

To be a content, weaned child is to be prepared for enlistment in my army ranks. An intercessor must not be proud or mettle in affairs beyond his scope. He must be a humble servant who gives of his time freely in obedience to my call.

Prayer warriors are content to eat from my banquet in solitary isolation. They demand not attention nor behave as spoiled children. They are about their Father's business, and they bring Me great JOY, for they are true servants of mine from the heart who seek no glory, yet stand in the gap, nameless, in behalf of my children. They serve milk to my babies and help others to grow and become weaned.

Maturity is a becoming attribute in my Kingdom.

June 11

Before Honour Is Humility

"The fear of the Lord is the instruction of wisdom; and before honour is humility." **Proverbs 15:33 KJV**

The dynamics of my Kingdom are opposite of the world. My wisdom is to seek instruction from my Spirit and Word and to seek sincere humility.

I wait and I wait and I wait to pour out and lift up until my requirement of humility has been met. *Before honour is humility.*

What is humility? The humble soul will acknowledge that I am his all good and all joy and all accomplishment. True humility knows that he knows that he knows that apart from Me, he can do nothing.

Sincere humility cannot be enticed by complimentary rewards. The reward to the humble is the joy of giving and the delight of being a yielded vessel through which I flow.

Sometimes it takes a lifetime to attain humility.

For some, even death's bed does not strip pride's resistance.

To he whom I have been allowed to prune—endlessly without grievance—I exalt and send forth in my calling to fulfill my will on earth as it is in heaven.

This is the servant that will be honored with hearing, "Well done." Amen.

June 12

The Imperishable Jewel

"But let it be the hidden man of the heart, in that which is not corruptible, even the ornament of a meek and quiet spirit, which is in the sight of God of great price."   *I Peter 3:4 KJV*

The imperishable jewel of your spirit sparkles and shines reflecting the face of Jesus my Son! You have allowed Me to carve upon your spirit year after year and day after day. My intricate design is like that of ten thousand carrot diamonds all hand prepared by the master craftsman. The face and light of my Son truly shines upon you, and your spirit reflects his excellence.

That which is carved into your spirit man is eternal—absolutely imperishable. No fire on earth, no harsh words, no sickness or disease—no earthly enemy can even touch that which I have molded and carved into your spirit. My investments in you are eternal, everlasting, and that part of you will continue on into eternity with Me! That is why I have not always come instantly to relieve you of earth's hardship, for it has been within the simmering pot of your worst moments that I have boiled out of you ugly debris that you could not nor would not want within your spirit.

There have been times that the crucible has seemed unfair and the pain unbearable. Yes, even in the midst of those moments, I was doing my work—carving, exposing, and perfecting your hidden heart.

Beloved, we have been doing an eternal work of glory in you! That which you have sacrificed, you have gained in spirit. That which you have endured has worked a far more eternal reward.

You can never outgive Me—never! Never!

Your now quiet spirit has learned, as Abraham, to "stagger not in unbelief." Your quietness is faith's signature signing the checks with confidence that the deposits have been made in my name! Your quiet spirit does not fear when the enemy roars. Your quiet spirit only smiles and says "peace be still" to the raging waves. They listen, obey, and stop!

You are a blessing to Me in your full array of glorious, glistening colors. Your robes of righteousness glisten, shine, and reflect the face of my Son Jesus! Come, my long awaited friend, and dine with Me at my banqueting table of love. I love you, my dear and beloved precious child. I love you! Amen.

June 13

Love Grows!

"He is good; his love endures forever."   *2 Chronicles 5:13 NIV*

I am only good—only "yea" not "nay"—and my love never ends. Our relationship is for all of eternity. These days on earth only begin our Abba-son oneness. You will continue to grow to love Me more daily, for all of eternity.

Love grows! It is like a blossoming flower garden whose buds never wilt, yet whose blossoms continue to produce and thrive.

The love that envelops your soul on earth will go with you eternally, where it will multiply and be replenished by my full presence.

The human soul could not endure my love unveiled. You are designed "in part" to prepare you for "the complete" divine and unveiled love of mine.

Love always grows—my love—the God kind—can only and will only grow!

June 14

Walking Right

"The ways of the Lord are right; the righteous walk in them." *Hosea 14:9 NIV*

My ways are always right! There is a right way and a wrong way to live your daily life. All of the answers to right living are laid out in my Word through wisdom. My wisdom is yours, free for the asking! My wisdom will explain to you the why of a command. It will guide you to select the right choice of paths and which doors to enter through.

Beloved, I love you! Righteousness is being clothed with the garment and armour of Jesus Christ. In righteousness, you are covered and cleansed with his blood and are able to stand before Me, and all enemies, without fear.

Your feet are important, for they determine the paths you choose to walk down. In *walking right* with Me, your heart will be perpetually guided according to my Word! Amen.

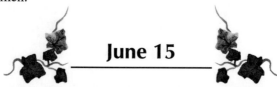

June 15

Here I Am!

"Then you shall call, and the Lord will answer; You shall cry, and he will say, 'Here I am.'"   *Isaiah 58:9 NKJV*

Have you ever gone through seasons when it seemed like maybe I was dead? Or you felt like the communication wires between heaven and earth had been severed? Or that maybe you were simply growing deaf to my voice?

Beloved, sometimes the cares of this world weigh so heavily upon you, that you become encumbered with burdens and fears unnecessarily placed upon your shoulders. When you forget to have Me carry your load, then your ears become filled with voices not my own. You hear self-pity instead of victory. You hear burden instead of blessing. You hear hell instead of heaven. You begin to be pulled down into a hole that grows deeper and deeper, seeking to suffocate your very life and will to live.

You can break this snare by fasting. You can defend yourself from its future trappings by fasting.

Beloved, all your heart really longs for is to hear my voice when you cry my name! All your heart ever needs is to know that I am answering with, *"Here I am!"* Beloved, the "faster" always, perpetually hears the assurance of my voice every time he calls!

June 16

Earth's Good-bye Is Heaven's Hello!

"The righteous perish, and no one ponders it in his heart; devout men are taken away, and no one understands that the righteous are taken away to be spared from evil."
                                                                    Isaiah 57:1 NIV

You must trust Me in all situations, especially when death's jaws have clamped themselves about the life of a dear one whose breath was yet young and strong.

Beloved, I see your aching heart, the desperation of your grief. My Holy Spirit, my Comforter, is ever present with you to absorb your pain and console your wounded feelings.

My dear one, you know that your beloved one is with Me, absorbed in my glory, basking in my full presence. Earth's strings have been cut only to loose your loved one to Me where he is finding completeness, wholeness, purity, and fulfillment of my peace.

You ask why, and I answer—I am God. Your beloved is with Me. Would you not also enjoy an early arrival into my Kingdom's glory?

Beloved, my comfort is your knowledge of exactly where it is that your beloved has come. If you could see into heaven and see us together, you would understand, and your sorrow would cease.

Your beloved's visa home came earlier than you had planned. My sovereignty prevails, and all things are made good in my hand. There is no sting in eternal life. Your beloved is with Me in heaven. I would have you rejoice because your name, too, is written in the Book of Life, and no accident or illness can affect the guarantee of eternal life with Me.

The blood of my Son, your Savior Jesus Christ, has purchased your salvation and eternal life with Me. Earth's death is heaven's birth. *Earth's good-bye is heaven's hello!*

Rejoice in your beloved's arrival to my throne. No more evil. No more labor. He is with Me now, and you must go on but not alone. We are with you in Spirit! We are with you! We are with you!

June 17

Green Pastures

"He makes me lie down in green pastures, he leads me beside quiet waters."
Psalm 23:2 NIV

Green pastures are a sheep's delight! You can never exhaust my supply of nourishment to you, as I desire for you to dwell always in my green pastures. It is your lack of obedience that takes you to dry places and desert moments.

The hustle-bustle of the world need not affect your soul, for in Me, you may dwell beside quiet waters and never thirst for lack of fresh anointing.

It is only because you stray from my stream that your throat becomes parched. It need not be this way.

Dwell intimately with Me by staying close to my stream and always in my Word. My pasture is my Word, from whence comes my voice, your stream of quiet waters.

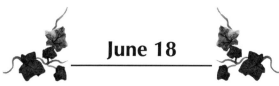

June 18

Sincere Heart

"Let us draw near to God with a sincere heart in full assurance of faith."
Hebrews 10:22 NIV

It is the *sincere heart* who earnestly seeks Me that finds Me. I am not to be found in simple, casual pursuit. There exists a veil between heaven and earth, between righteousness and unrighteousness. I am to be found! I am discovered, however, only by hearts who earnestly long for their return to their Creator.

The world's paws are too gloriously stroking, distracting, and pleasurably enticing to allow man to have casual acquaintance with Me. No. Relationship with your Holy God requires effort and earnestness to fight against the impending war set against our love for one another.

Only sincerity will produce faith, and only faith will produce an intimate and unique relationship with Me, your Holy God. Amen.

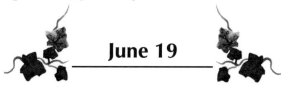

June 19

Gates of Righteousness

"Open to me the gates of righteousness: I will go into them, and I will praise the Lord."　　　　　　　　　　　　　　　　　　　　　　*Psalm 118:19 KJV*

My *gates of righteousness* are open to you. Come, my beloved, my Bride, my dear. Come and banquet with Me at my table.

The voice of the Bridegroom beckons his Bride to come, come, come! Hear the voice of the Spirit cry, "Come, Come, Come!"

My gates of righteousness are open unto you. Come through them and enjoy my love! Allow Me to shower my gifts upon you. Yield so that I am free to enrich you with my righteousness.

I am always waiting to hold open my gates of righteousness. You are always welcome to enter into my presence and press into my will and wisdom for you.

I am always at the gate. Often, I wait for you, but you appear to have no interest in advancing into Me.

Beloved, there is no quest on the face of the earth more important than the pursuance of our love relationship. All else will fade away behind you as you enter my throne and earth's hour is finalized.

It is within my gates of righteousness that I will equip you with my Spirit and necessary fuel to encounter your daily demands. If you will put Me "first place," I will prosper the works of your hands.

I am a covenant maker, and I jealously guard our love-covenant between one another. You sustain this covenant, this holy partnership with Me, by entering into my gates of righteousness often, daily, or even hourly.

My banqueting table is always set for you. Quench your thirst, and still your hunger at my table. Amen.

June 20

My Eleazor

"But he stood his ground and struck down the Philistines till his hand grew tired and froze to the sword. The Lord brought about a great victory that day. The troops returned to Eleazor, but only to strip the dead."

2 Samuel 23:10 NIV

You are *my Eleazor*. Your steadfastness in my Word encourages others around you. Your silent witness is observed by many that you do not know. They watch and behold your consistency in walking and talking with Me. That one can be so close to their Heavenly Father encourages them to also know it is possible to persevere towards that same walk which they observe in you.

Beloved, you do not realize the number of eyes that watch you! Without doing anything, you are doing everything—just by being you—and maintaining your steadfastness in Me. It is observed. It is noted, and you are an encourager to others!

Eleazor refused to let go of the sword, just as you, beloved, also refuse to let loose of my Word. You allow my Word—the Sword of the Spirit—to fight for you. Your confidence is in the razor sharpness of my blade—hallelujah!

Though your hand may grow tired and weary, you are frozen in your hold of its promises over your loved ones and circumstances around you. Now, do you think others are not watching this, your frozen hand? They are observing the battle and your relentless hold on my Sword, and they are also beholding your great victories!

Beloved, I love you for being my Eleazor! I looked for a man to stand in the gap . . . and I found you! I love you, my dear one. Great is your victory because you have refused to let go of my sword. Your frozen hand has defeated the enemy!

Just like Eleazor, the "troops" will return to strip the dead! Many will reap the fruits of your labors, and your stand will be an encouragement to others. They will learn by watching, and, in time, they also will dare to be my "little Eleazors!"

June 21

The Tortoise Wins

"He gives strength to the weary and increases the power of the weak."
Isaiah 40:29 NIV

Why is it that *the tortoise wins* his race against the hare? Why is it that honest hard work outweighs laziness?

Honesty and hard work reflect my character. The slothful are a displeasure to Me. It is diligence and perseverance in all areas of man's life that produce success and good satisfaction.

I give power to the weak! In your request of Me for strength, I am empowering you with my supernatural energy from on high in heaven.

The tortoise becomes energized by my Spirit-battery, and he produces from his spirit man. Now, the hare has much natural ability and talent, yet, in his pride-of-self, he trips up on misjudging the power of his opponent. Little does the hare know that the tortoise's strength is from Me!

I am most pleased with you, my little tortoise, for you have cried out in the name of Jesus, and I am, therefore, exalting you!

The finish line is death. Then, and only then, will my trophy be awarded. It is at my gate that the hare will be set face to face with his ultimate shortcomings in character.

Beloved, I love you, and freely do I give might and strength to those who call upon my name! I love you! Amen.

June 22

Faith at Rest

"In repentance and rest is your salvation, in quietness and trust is your strength."   *Isaiah 30:15 NIV*

The sweet fruit of repentance is my salvation and all the packaged goods that accompany my gift to you.

It is my goodness that leads you to repentance. My repentance is a sweet and valuable gift worth more than hundreds of bags of gold.

Repentance always cleanses away one more layer of your flesh that separates you from Me.

When you TRUST me with your whole heart, you are walking in faith, not fear. This enables you to remain quiet (steadfast), not turbulent or bounced around by circumstances. Quietness in Me is noncomplaining and nonwhining. It is simply *faith at rest.* Faith is rest because there is no worry in faith—none whatsoever.

I love you, and I desire for you to enjoy and experience your salvation in quietness of spirit and rest in your soul.

June 23

My Love for You

"Praise be to the Lord, for he showed his wonderful love to me."
                                                        Psalm 31:21 NIV

It is my desire and intent purpose to show *my love for you.* I send my love daily in the new mercies of the faithful and tireless sunrise and sunset. I provide you food and clothing, and I bless the works of your hands. I teach you to prosper and be successful. I open new windows and shut up wrong doors that would lead down paths of deception.

In your heart, I want you to experience my loving devotion. I want you to feel my holy presence and to realize my love for you!

I communicate my love to you in both big and small ways—but always faithfully, for I never let you down, and I only watch out for your good welfare.

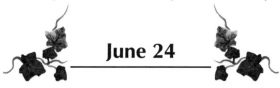

June 24

Fingers, Make War!

"Blessed be the Lord my strength, which teacheth my hands to war, and my fingers to fight."   *Psalm 144:1 KJV*

The musician learns well to war with his fingers. There exists no greater ammunition against the enemy than high praises upon your stringed instruments, your horns, your loud sounding cymbals, and the drum.

Fingers, make war! Musicians, call upon your skills to do battle by playing upon your anointed instruments and singing your praises to Me. Your instruments in harmony create disharmony amongst the enemy ranks. As they hear your medleys unto Me, they become intimidated, confused, disheartened, pathetically wimpy, and ridiculously defeated in the name of Jesus.

It is a beautiful sight for my eyes to behold as you do battle with your fingers!

Play skillfully with a loud noise and dismantle the forces set against you and your household.

You possess an arsenal of power that you rarely take advantage of using. The enemy wants you not to know he is near.

You can keep him trembling from a distance if you will but command your fingers to play! Utilize this precious gift I have invested in you, not only in corporate worship but also within the walls of your own home.

I am telling you, satan flees in the presence of anointed worship, so, worship Me! This is the easiest way for you to bind the enemy from you and yours. I have given you this arsenal. Use it, and make war!

June 25

Key to Divine Health

"The joy of the Lord is your strength."   *Nehemiah 8:10 NIV*

Nehemiah 8:10 is medically and chemically sound. JOY is a medicine consumed in the spirit and sent forth into the blood! JOY dispels weariness and energizes enthusiasm and pep!

Now, how does one get a bottle of JOY—a dosage of Jesus' JOY? Through my Word! Man is so very blind to my simple methods of provision for his health.

Meditate upon my Word! You swallow jars of cough medicine and endless numbers and prescriptions of tablets. Stop! I have a much easier and less expensive way: consume my Word!

It is my written Word and spoken Word that will feed your spirit and send new life into your blood. It is your blood that determines health, and your spirit is connected to your blood.

Your spirit rules your being and commands your physical heart. That is my *key to divine health.*

June 26

The Foot Will Never Slip

"He will not let your foot slip—he who watches over you will not slumber."
Psalm 121:3 NIV

It is difficult for you to imagine that I watch over your every step—but I do! When you are walking in obedience to Me, watching and guiding your steps is a simple task. Blessings of provision follow after obedience, but when you venture out on your own in self-will or confusion, then is when the rocks of natural consequences stumble you.

I do not allow your foot to slip when you walk purehearted before Me, cleansed with the blood of the Lamb of God.

My safety net always surrounds the obedient. The slips come in wandering away from my perfect, sensitive will.

Of course, I never sleep, and I do have a walk in Me that is steadfast, constant, and sincere. To him who finds this treasure, *the foot will never slip.*

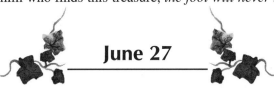

June 27

Candles of Love

"Many waters cannot quench love, neither can the floods drown it."
Song of Solomon 8:7 KJV

Love never ends. It is eternal and goes with you for all of eternity. That is why it is good to be about your Father's business while inhabiting earth. You bring with you to heaven all love produced in the human heart.

Many storms may be formed against love. Thunderous bellows may attempt to scare love's hold. Lightning bolts may surge against your love and seek to burn it away. Floods may rise up to drown the very breath of your love. All of these attempts are futile against the fortress of true love rooted in Me.

Love is a candle impossible to extinguish. It is a light within you that glows into eternity. Winds may blow against your flame of love. Showers may fall to drown out its flickering presence. Even a blanket set over its flame will only ignite the cloth, not extinguish its flame. No attempt to kill love can succeed, for love is eternal.

Now, the carnality of man may recoat love's glow with a lacquer of resentment, a finish of unforgiveness. Love may be embittered and crystallize into a solid rock of hate, but this is man's wicked attempt to cover over the pain and discomfort that true love may cause. For in true love, the heart is always vulnerable, always susceptible to hurt. It is the very nature of love to be tender-hearted without defense, as this should be, because Jesus is and shall be forever more.

Love is a gift from heaven meant to enrich your soul and empower your human spirit. Allow not bitterness to destroy my candle's flame and leave you as soot. Love is warm, is light, is Me.

Keep your *candles of love* burning in your heart, for they will come with you to heaven. Amen.

June 28

Rebuke Fear!

"Be strong and courageous. Do not be afraid or terrified because of them, for the Lord your God goes with you."   *Deuteronomy 31:6 NIV*

Fear is never of Me unless you have ventured out alone without my permission or direction where enemy faces scream and my angels have not gone before you.

Fear is a slap in my face. It cries, "You are not holy enough or good enough or BIG enough to take care of my needs."

Ah! What an insult to your Creator who loves you, has called you, and equips you to do my will.

Fear only tears down fortresses of protection my angels have built up in your behalf. *Rebuke fear!* Repent of entertaining fear. It is your worst enemy, for it will intimidate you from accomplishing my will on earth as it is in heaven. Rebuke it, and stomp it into the ground. It is lethal and will poison my plans for you. Amen.

June 29

Portraits of Faith

"Now faith is being sure of what we hope for and certain of what we do not see."   *Hebrews 11:1 NIV*

Faith is my gift to you, not manufactured by man, but rather by God. Faith is my investment in your spirit, a painted portrait of your desire fulfilled, manifested in your spirit where you and only you can see. No other man views the portrait, only you. Because you see the finished picture, you rejoice and rest in perfect peace. That is the fruit of faith because I have shown you with your inner eyes the finished product.

You believe what you see in your spirit. That is why some struggle with faith: they cannot see into their spirit.

Work to see into your spirit. Spend time with Me in my Word, and you, too, will grow to see *portraits of faith* awaiting you.

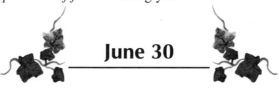

June 30

Bug Spray

"Submit yourselves therefore to God. Resist the devil, and he will flee from you."   *James 4:7 KJV*

This is Basic Prayer 101. Enrolled as a student in my primer course on prayer, you learn to submit to Me and resist the enemy!

This is not dignified 20th century jargon—nor will the 21st century embrace the devil's reality. You will be ridiculed and mocked for recognizing his existence as the enemy form.

Know that if they "spat" on Me, they will "spat" on you!

For you who seek divine truth from my Word, I will reveal the essence of prayer—bind and loose, submit and resist. The devil is real, and he will destroy whatever he wills if he is allowed.

Prayer is like *bug spray*. When you see or hear the insect, you spray. If you don't, you may get stung or bitten. Christians who don't believe in resisting the devil do a lot of scratching.

July 1

Offering

"Bring an offering and come before him; worship the Lord in the splendor of his holiness."   *I Chronicles 16:29 NIV*

What is it that you offer unto Me? What is an *offering* to you? Is it mere gold —money? What can you offer unto Me?

Your most pleasing offering is that of yourself. The tithe is good, for it represents your time. Your time is good because man's selfish nature is most strongly linked with hours and minutes, a precious commodity in the sight of man!

I look to see if you are bringing Me your heart. Lips may trumpet my praise, but it is your heart that gives the sacrifice and offering pleasing to Me. The most honored offering I can receive is your will placed at my feet.

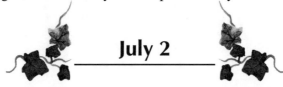

July 2

A Touch of Genius

"A man's gift makes room for him, And brings him before great men."
Proverbs 18:16 NKJV

I have invested in every child of mine *a touch of genius* in a specific area. This area may be obscure and small, but it is, nonetheless, an arm of your efforts that breathes and breeds life and productivity.

A wise man will examine himself well, determine my expertise in gifting him, and then seek to cultivate that gift. This touch of divine—your genius—has a direct line to heaven. There is a supernatural input that may increase to a "flow," given time and nurturance of the gift.

Learn to sow and then reap from this gift. It is my chosen way for you to pursue labor and giving.

Now, as you proceed in nurturing and expanding my genius in you, so, also, will I begin to open doors of opportunity and advancement. You will multiply! Your giving will increase! This will yet be flowing from heaven to earth—and all so very effortlessly on your part because of its origin.

As you learn to yield to my gift and allow it to grow and blossom to full fruition, then will I also cause your gift to go before great men.

The applause of the crowd and the honor of men will be yours because you are bringing Me glory in the utilization of my genius in you. Amen.

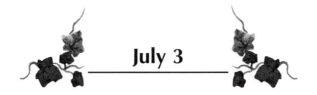

July 3

Live One Day at a Time

"Therefore do not worry about tomorrow, for tomorrow will worry about itself. Each day has enough trouble of its own."   *Matthew 6:34 NIV*

You need to *live one day at a time.* Place your hand in mine early in the morning and walk with Me throughout the day. My grace is sufficient for today! My mercies are new every morning!

Needless worry and fretting torment your visions for tomorrow, all and each one, needlessly. You need only ME throughout your day supplying your breath and strength.

I love you and designed you to live one day at a time. Anticipation for your tomorrows should always be "yea" and never "nay." I am a positive, productive God. I work for building you up, never tearing you down. Only pride may cause you to fall. I love you. Tomorrow holds sunshine—rejoice!

July 4

Seek My Face

"Let the light of your face shine upon us, O Lord."   *Psalm 4:6 NIV*

This is a precious prayer to Me because it acknowledges heavenly sight. You see, in heaven, we are LIGHT! For my face to shine upon you means heaven comes to earth. I find great pleasure in responding to my saints' cries to reflect our GLORY on earth!

As my face shines upon you, your eyes see into the spirit realm. I reveal the hidden meanings of natural circumstances. I reveal that there are no coincidences. I peel off your flesh eyes and give you spirit eyes to see how I am indeed working amongst you on earth.

You want my face to shine upon you! I bring favor. My light illuminates the darkness. Yes, *seek my face,* for the light from my face is GLORIOUS!

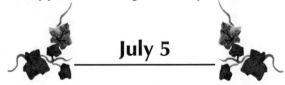

July 5

His Desire Is Toward Me!

"I am my beloveds, and his desire is toward me." **Song of Solomon 7:10 KJV**

Many men have many desires in their hearts for many diverse things.

Rare is the man who possesses one desire in his heart for the one woman with whom he is in covenant relationship.

Few men have one desire in their hearts for one woman.

Blessed is she who receives the love of her single-hearted prince.

Rare is the woman who can cry, "I am my beloved's, and *his desire is toward me!"*

There exists no deeper need in the emotions of a woman than to be singularly adored by her husband.

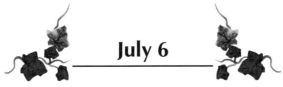

July 6

Salve of My Peace

"The peace of God, which transcends all understanding, will guard your hearts and your minds in Christ Jesus." **Philippians 4:7 NIV**

The human mind cannot comprehend the supernatural *salve of my peace,* because it originates in heaven. My peace in your heart is my touch, my presence, my nearness. This cannot be duplicated or mass-produced.

My peace in your heart is literally chunks of heaven stored in human vessel. No such feeling originates on earth.

All of heaven is peace. Like powder puffs or cotton balls, my Kingdom of Heaven is plushly cushioned with my peace.

When your heart is lined with my peace, you, too, cushion others' lives around you, like buffers that help to release life's pressures.

My peace is still and quiet, undisturbed by the enemy's voice, and unpolluted by the world's stench.

My peace is free, purchased for you! Bask in my perfect present of peace, and enjoy!

July 7

New Songs

"He put a new song in my mouth, a hymn of praise to our God."

Psalm 40:3 NIV

I have *new songs* to place in your mouth every day. As you worship Me, you will find new choruses rising up from deep within your hidden man. Some are medleys from heaven intended only to encourage you for that moment or day.

Give voice to my new songs! They are fresh and laced with heaven's anointing. I will edify and comfort you as you voice my new songs.

The Great Choir may join in with you and cause quite a divine uproar.

I love you! Sing your new songs unto Me. Sing! Give praise! Delight yourself in Me! These new songs are my gifts to you. Rejoice in them! Amen.

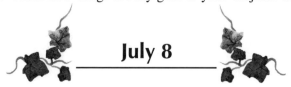

July 8

Rose Petals

"They shall bear thee up in their hands, lest thou dash thy foot against a stone."

Psalm 91:12 KJV

My walk of love, beloved, is provided because I love you. My angels walk before your every step gently dropping *rose petals* to guide your way. Every morning anew I blow down from heaven fresh aroma-giving petals of guidance. They neatly, one by one, fall into your angels' baskets. Then, they lovingly, obediently set to dropping rose petals before your feet. My Holy Spirit woos them along, and they work together providing you a blessed day in Me.

Oh, you can get off the track, but when you do, when your feet slip away from my petal-lined path, then you discern immediately; for my petals cushion your feet from the enemy's thorns, rocks, and road blocks. My petals from heaven cushion your walk like velveteen beneath your toes. Smooth and glorious is your day in Me!

Someday, there will be a wedding. Christ and his Bride will unite. For now, my Holy Spirit prepares your way down the aisle of life, step by step. In the end, you will meet your Groom at the altar of life. As you take his hand, you will glimpse back and praise the angelic flower girls for dropping the petals ever so faithfully, padding and paving your way unto the King of Kings and Lord of Lords, Jesus Christ your Groom! Amen.

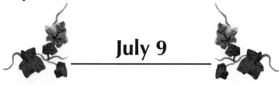

July 9

Love Song to My Sheep

"You are My flock, the flock of My pasture; you are men, and I am your God, says the Lord God."   *Ezekiel 34:31 NKJV*

Every verse of my Word is the introduction to a poem of love to you, as such is the case with Ezekiel 34:31, a *love song to my sheep.*

You are my flock, and I love you!

You are my sheep who I love!

You live and abide in my pasture, my home on earth supplied for you, and I love you!

You, my children on earth, know that you are shepherded. I watch over you always as you graze upon my land of good.

I seek to lead you into green pastures, to feed you both physically and spiritually.

Now, in heaven, you, too, will be in my flock, my sheep, as you will continue to feed within my pastures of eternal supply.

Beloved flock, I love you! Lambs of God, you are precious to Me!

You are men on earth who become manifested saints in heaven, and in both places, earth or your eternal home, you will feed upon my goodness supplied to you by my living and generous hand.

I love you, beloved. Feed upon my Word! Enrich your souls with my pasture of promise for you. My table is always set. I desire for you to bask in my presence and eat amongst the lilies!

I love you! You are my precious sheep, and I love you. I love you! I love you! Amen.

July 10

Richness!

"The blessing of the Lord, it maketh rich, and he addeth no sorrow with it."
Proverbs 10:22 KJV

My blessing, beloved, can only make you rich—rich in spirit and rich in earthly goods. *Richness!* You haven't known or seen riches until you enter my heavenly throne room, my heavenly Kingdom's estate!

Have you ever stepped foot upon golden streets? Have you ever walked through emerald grass? Have you ever spoken in conversation with pearls that are alive, sweetly resounding my beautiful and serene life in them? Have you ever eaten upon plates of diamonds that speak the essence of God's love to you?

Have you ever drunk into your throat living waters, my pure wine, red as my blood was, yet pure as my heart? Have you ever banqueted beneath live chandeliers that sang praises to God, illuminating the Word of God, glistening with the light of God's Word for my glory alone?

Have you ever sat beneath trees of love whose roots run into the River of Life, whose leaves bear fruits of the Spirit? Have you ever seen leaves that are spiritually alive, each one breathing and living for my glory, each one emitting sweet fragrances, each and every leaf breathing alive and aloud the voice of praise, emeralds and glistening jewels all on just one tree? Have you ever seen a grove of spiritually-heavenly trees or a mountain covered with them?

Beloved—I AM WEALTH AND I AM RICHNESS.

You do not begin to comprehend wealth. All of earth is a shadow of my true wealth. What you see with earthly eyes is magnified millions of times into richness and wealth in your heavenly estate. That is why to pursue earthly riches is frivolous. All the wealth on earth cannot begin to compare with my storehouses laid up for you in heaven!

There are little glimpses of my glory, small scenic moments of human ecstasy in nature, but so small in comparison to my reward for you. That is why you need to seek Me in spirit—for I will build wealth and richness in your soul and spirit man.

The instant your body breathes its last breath, all possessions VANISH. That which you sow on earth shall be reaped in heaven! "In my Father's house are many mansions." Keep your sites set on your heavenly mansion. On earth, you are investing in your eternity when you invest in souls. Just like earthly banks, I am an excellent accountant! I keep the best records!

I am richness. I am wealth. I am your richness! I, in you, make you rich! Amen.

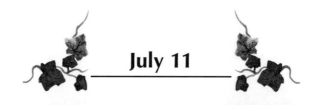

July 11

Golden Apples

"A word fitly spoken is like apples of gold in pictures of silver."

Proverbs 25:11 KJV

It is important that you speak right words because words have power. They are like bullets that zoom in and out of hearts, and they can be deadly.

You need to stand guard at the door of your tongue and disallow negative words to be formed and spoken. Such words are permission slips to the enemy. You grant the right, and it will be taken.

Now, right words have a positive building effect. My words spoken from your lips call my angels to attention and direct their moves of intervention in your behalf. They hearken—listen and obey—the voice of my Word!

You are creating good when from your mouth comes blessing. You are clearing the air of polluted thoughts and schemes, and you are spraying a fresh and clean spray of my Spirit in your atmosphere when my Word is spoken.

Your environment can be rich with my presence, like *golden apples* laid in silver. Only dispense from your lips kind, productive, and thoughtful words.

Golden apples are eternal. You may bring them with you to heaven.

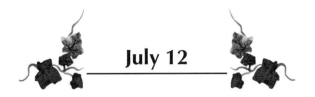

July 12

Heritage of Jacob

"Then you shall delight yourself in the Lord; And I will cause you to ride on the high hills of the earth, And feed you with the heritage of Jacob your father. The mouth of the Lord has spoken."   *Isaiah 58:14 NKJV*

When your fast is complete, my promises are complete. Isn't your total desire to delight yourself in Me? It is at the completion of your fast that your delight in Me is maximized. It is when you have effectually interceded and broken through the purpose for which the fast was chosen, that you enter into your reward of increased joy in Me.

It is then that I cause you to rise above the heaviness of earth's hold. It is then that you ride above circumstances in high and heavenly places as on high hills of the earth. It is then that your joy bursts forth in new power and explosive energy!

My *heritage of Jacob* links you to the blessed generations that have carried my Word and passed the sword from parent to child, from seed to seed. The heritage of Jacob is the divine, supernatural intervention upon your children, their children, and their children's children. The heritage of Jacob, your father, is the divine order of godliness passed from generation to generation—my promise for the fasted life.

July 13

Perfect Hearts

"For the eyes of the Lord run to and fro throughout the whole earth, to shew himself strong in behalf of them whose heart is perfect toward him."

II Chronicles 16:9 KJV

I am always looking for hearts who are perfect towards Me . . . that is, hearts who hunger for Me, who thirst for my voice, who seek to know Me and love Me.

Though man looks on the outward part, I see into the deep hidden man. I know your heart inside out, and I know who my true servants are.

If you love Me with all of your heart, then I am watching over you to show myself strong in your behalf. Your performance and walk we will work on—it is your heart of love that matters most. If you but love Me first and above all else, then my Spirit will iron out the wrinkles in your personality and will straighten up the messes about your feet. I will clean and sanitize your home.

I look for *perfect hearts*, those who long for their Heavenly Father. I then come and inhabit your souls, and together we work out the details of your lives—because I love you! Amen.

July 14

I Forgive You

"If we confess our sins, he is faithful and just and will forgive us our sins and purify us from all unrighteousness."　　　　　**I John 1:9 NIV**

The world says, "Life is not fair." I say that I am a just and fair God that forgives sin and cleanses unrighteousness. I reverse the unfairness of the world by cleansing and forgiving sin—and I am a just and righteous God.

In my Kingdom, justice prevails because of the cleansing blood of Jesus Christ. Deliverance comes to the oppressed. Healing comes to the diseased. Emotional health comes to the brokenhearted.

All unfairness is swallowed up by the blood of Jesus Christ in the forgiveness of sins and the penalty of death paid for on Calvary's tree.

I forgive you. I am able to cleanse all unrighteousness. I need only be asked. Amen.

July 15

To Be Absent from the Body

"We are confident, I say, and willing rather to be absent from the body, and to be present with the Lord."   *2 Corinthians 5:8 KJV*

To be absent from the body is to be present with Me. The sweet comfort of my promise is that you will be with Me! Whether in the flesh on earth or in the spirit in heaven, I am with you! I am with you! I am with you!

I am with you in Spirit now, but then you will see Me with sight. For now, you walk with Me by faith. Then, you will walk with Me by seeing. You will touch Me, embrace Me, and see with new revealed eyes the visions of my glory before you.

That is why you may embrace the death of my saints on earth, for they have passed on into seeing and touching my glory! The shed tears are only for your separation, not the translation into my Kingdom's environment.

Truly, if you could know the Joy of your beloved's manifest presence before Me, the Joy would literally absorb all tears of mourning, for the presence of my glory in heaven does not compare to earth's reflection of my face. It is as a mirror dimly reflecting.

To be absent from the body is to be present with Me. Your day will come. Let those who go before you, go freely. They have their reward, and you will have yours.

It is good to dwell on earth and inhabit my praises and will for you, but as a pilgrim, your journey is eternal, and your destination is HOME—with Me. Therefore, never begrudge an early arrival. The destiny of my children rests in my hand. There exists reason and purpose for all that transpires in my servants' lives.

You can only trust and be comforted with my promise of eternal life with Me. Your sovereign God is in control. Trust Me! Amen.

July 16

Combat Boots

Deliver me, O lord, from the evil man: preserve me from the violent man."
Psalm 140:1 KJV

I am your protection, and I will take care of you! When faced with hardship and danger, I am there with you. My cloak wraps itself around you and prevents the storm from soaking your clothes. My angels hover over you with my umbrella of protection, strong to keep hell's hailstones from piercing your flesh.

You wear my *combat boots!* My Word in you transforms into steel-toed boots that crush the enemy beneath your feet!

In your hand, I place my sword which is my Word within you. Demonic forces are halted as you command from your lips the binding of the enemy, and you raise my standard—the Sword of the Spirit.

The devil masquerades himself through flesh and blood, eyes and ears, but know well: he is very aware of his stripped power! The Word defeats and exposes all lies and deception.

In your stand against evil, the enemy literally flees—runs away and hides, trembling at the sound of your voice and my Word spoken through your lips. He is absolutely defenseless as you speak my Word of authority over him.

You cannot conquer the whole world and the evil therein, but you can overcome the enemy forces in your own circle, own household, and corporately, your own community.

Prayer is my ammunition against the evil in man. Learn how to use my weapons!

July 17

Barren to Joyful

"He maketh the barren woman to keep house and to be a joyful mother of children. Praise ye the Lord."   *Psalm 113:9 KJV*

I earnestly love you, precious one. I have something important for you to contemplate. If I were never to allow you children, where would your love for Me be placed? High or low? Indeed, your need and desire for children is sanctified in my sight, but first, you must go before my body (church) and be prayed for.

This is no cause for alarm. Simply love and trust in my perfect will. I earnestly desire for you to bear fruit. Lie before the body that they may place hands on you. Merely request prayer, and the fertilization of both soul and womb will take place.

Take the following months onto birth of you and your husband's child to prepare diligently in the spirit. Pray constantly. Spend hours together in earnestness of prayer seeking my Spirit as I prepare you for the glorious arrival of our little child.

I am taking great delight in your anticipation and preparation of my coming will, regarding your future family. Always remember your yearning, boiling, bubbling desire for the young of your own flesh.

Someday, you will be "father" and "mother." On that day, joy shall stream from my face, for as deep as your own desire is for offspring, even more than double is my desire for the reproduction of your flesh as one.

Bend unto one another in holy submission. Husband, you, too, should bend unto your wife, for she will be carrying your child.

I will bless you on that great day of delivery as I lift up into your arms another like yourself—and indeed, another like my ownself.

I so love you, precious one! I need your total, self-sacrificial commitment unto one another as man and wife. I LOVE YOU both mightily! Yours as man and wife is blessed. Yours as father and mother will be doubly blessed! I love you! I love you! I love you! *Barren to joyful*—because I love you! Amen.

July 18

Contrite Heart

"The sacrifices of God are a broken spirit: a broken and a contrite heart, O God, thou wilt not despise."　　　　　　　　　　　　*Psalm 51:17 KJV*

I cannot resist the cry of a *contrite heart.* It melts Me. It woos Me. It calls Me, and I cry out, "Mercy, compassion, and grace I multiply unto you!"

When you lie broken before Me, the voice of your flesh is quiet. Truly, your heart cries, "Abba, Father, here I am, send me!"

Your heart longs and cries for the wisdom of God to perform my will. Your brokenness and contriteness is a precious gift unto Me. Jesus had such a heart, for He was brokenhearted over the sins and rejection of God, over the burden to love his own and endure the sins of mankind.

There is no more "running around the mountain" time and time again chasing rabbits that are not of Me. Now, you rest, pieces strewn before my altar, my throne, bowed at my feet—surely the perfect place to be.

Beloved, I love you. Your gift to Me is the broken pieces. Fear not. You bring Me glory now, for truly your strength comes from Me, not you, and in this I am given great JOY! It is my pleasure to empower you from on high—Spirit to spirit.

Rest now, and flow in peace.

I love you! I love you! I love you! It won't be long, and you will be home. Relax and enjoy my simplest of gifts around you, being thankful for all the many "little gifts" I have given you.

Be as the child who delights in the chase of a butterfly. Be my child, and be THANKFUL! Please, be thankful! Be grateful unto Me, for I have showered my blessings upon you.

Be thankful! Amen.

July 19

"Pick-up" Service

"For though a righteous man falls seven times, he rises again."

Proverbs 24:16 NIV

Every time you fall, I pick you up. It doesn't matter to Me how many times you fail. I see your heart. I see your love and hunger for Me; therefore, you qualify for my *"pick-up" service* free of charge!

If you run out of gas, land in a ditch, or have a fender-bender in soul—that's OK. I will come and meet your need. I will pick you up, and we will start again.

Like a five year old tackling his two-wheeler, you may expect some falls, but I promise you, learning will take place. There will come the day that you do not often fall.

Man may look on the outward part, but I behold the heart. Because your heart is perfect before Me, in loving and seeking Me, I will always raise you up again from your falls. They will lessen in time, beloved. They will lessen! Amen.

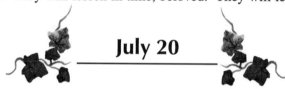

July 20

Indescribable Gift

"Thanks be to God for his indescribable gift!"   *2 Corinthians 9:15 NIV*

My eternal salvation is an *indescribable gift* in human language compared to the actual fulfillment and manifestation of its glory in heaven.

On earth's side of glory, I have explained and presented the factual evidence and explanation by FAITH—but, oh, the glory of the manifestation of salvation in heaven!

You know and understand only in part here, which is enough, but know that upon your arrival to heaven, you will understand that no price was too great to pay for my manifested eternal redemption fully comprehended in heaven.

For now you see in part—but then you will understand fully! Amen.

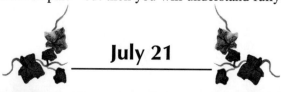

July 21

Secret Agents

"Bless the Lord, ye his angels, that excel in strength, that do his commandments, hearkening unto the voice of his word."   *Psalm 103:20 KJV*

The job of my angels is to "hearken" to my voice! They live to obey and serve my voice of command in behalf of my Kingdom of Heaven and Kingdom of God. On earth and in heaven, there both dwells the ministry of my angels. They rejoice to "hearken" to my Word. They rejoice to execute Kingdom business in behalf of my saints.

For example, with your voice you pray, and my angels are called to attend to your needs throughout the day. Now, driving to work an oncoming vehicle pulls out in front of you, but a mishap is avoided.

On up the road, a careless truck driver has strewn loose nails from the back end of his pick-up—but your tires glide over them without puncture.

Later in the day, a cranky associate explodes and begins to lash out at you—but stops, cowers down, and in the end seeks peace with you and counsel.

In the grocery store, a shower of flu germs accompanies a passerby. They fall on your coat and other apparel, but they fall on empty soil finding nowhere to nest, breed, and affect you.

Always, my angels are at work in the "unseen" dusting and mopping, so to speak, cleaning up after the enemy's sloppy assaults against you that are never allowed to manifest because your words of faith have kept them away.

My angels hearken to my voice. They ever live to obey my Word in your behalf! They excel in strength over the enemy. They are my *secret agents* that work and serve as your bodyguards against the enemy's attempts to strike you down.

Bless the Lord, you, my secret agents, who hearken unto my voice in behalf of my beloved children! Amen.

July 22

Hidden Wisdom

"But as it is written, Eye hath not seen, nor ear heard, neither have entered into the heart of man, the things which God hath prepared for them that love him."
I Corinthians 2:9 KJV

There are mountains of *hidden wisdom* in my Kingdom of Heaven! My resources are inexhaustible! Human imagination cannot begin to fathom my largeness, my infinity, my endlessness! You are locked up in a finite world. Your truths are tangible. Your feet walk on solid ground. Your hands touch solid matter. You are secure in physical elements. You know nothing else.

Ah, but it will not be so in heaven. Here, my Spirit reigns and rules, and we are governed by spirit law, not gravity and physical science laws. My Heavenly Kingdom operates within a divine science yet unrevealed to man! The laws of earth rule your earthly kingdom.

Beloved, place a single ant next to a herd of elephants. The comparison of heaven to earth is greater. Truly, eye hath not seen nor ear heard.

Let Me tell you about my throne. It is alive! My throne roars like a great earthly waterfall. Its voice resounds through the universe shouting, "Glory! Glory! Glory!" My throne is alive! Everything here is alive and speaks "glory" in its own language. My throne roars with its own voice of praise unto Me!

Beloved, you will never be able to outgive Me! As you press into Me and give your all, I literally open the floodgates of heaven and spill into your life. I send fresh anointing! My abundant life in you increases in measure!

When you sing praises to Me, the windows of heaven open, and my angels are sent to assist you and fight in your behalf. Every attempt on your part to "reach Me" is responded to. When your heart is right and pure before Me, there is NO stopping Me from pouring out onto you, from my pitchers, fresh living waters that cleanse and sanctify your soul!

July 23

Hot Head

"So then, my beloved brethren, let every man be swift to hear, slow to speak, slow to wrath; for the wrath of man does not produce the righteousness of God."
James 1:19 NKJV

If you are a *hot head*, then you need my deliverance from the spirit of anger. Blowing up and spouting off brings Me no glory. Latch that tongue and disallow the cursing to be formed through your righteous tongue! Who has given you a license to be free to dispense garbage amongst my people? You know where the dump is just like every other citizen. What gives you the right to dispose of lethal products in the company of my beloved?

Repent, you hot head! No one is impressed or manipulated by the filth that you allow to spew from your mouth. In their eyes, you appear hideous, and they deem you a fool. Your words are despised, and you are deceived into thinking that you can ram-rod and dictate others' lives with your hideous expressions of anger.

Repent, you fool, or else I will come and make you accountable for your foolish error of words. Repent, you hot head, and become a quiet lamb of God.

I am not deaf, nor are your loved ones and associates. We desire decent communication and respect from you. Go wash your dirty self with the blood of the Savior, and return to us white as snow. We will forgive you, and you need to forgive yourself. We love you, but the nonsense must stop. Grow up in my Kingdom, and allow my Spirit to be in control of your heart and your mouth. Forever, I love you! Amen.

July 24

My Creation Shouts Glory!

"Shout for joy, O heavens; rejoice, O earth; burst into song, O mountains!"
Isaiah 49:13 NIV

I created them all, the heavens, the earth, the mountains. They know my voice and know to obey my command to exist and serve according to my foreordained will and word over them.

Cry out, you heavens! Lift up your voice and sing! Shout hallelujah with his holy angels!

The earth reflects the glory of the Lord, for I spoke it into existence with all of my plans and purposes in mind.

Even the mountains know my command to give unto him the GLORY due unto his name! I can and will make even the rocks to cry out in worship if the soul of man is too decrepid to praise and honor Me.

All of *my creation shouts GLORY!* Human ears cannot hear this, but in heaven their cries are daily recorded!

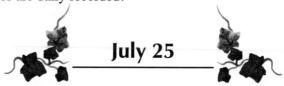

July 25

Fruits of My Spirit

"But the fruit of the Spirit is love, joy, peace, patience, kindness, goodness, faithfulness, gentleness and self-control."
Galatians 5:22-23 NIV

These are the fruits that I desire for you, my branches, to produce. They shall flow forth from your personality, and this heavenly divine fruit will feed others' souls and soothe the woundeds' wounds.

In your Father's house are many mansions! Ornamented around those mansions are my thriving trees that literally produce the *fruits of my Spirit.* If you so choose, you may be the gardener of an orchard of Joy, or Peace, or Patience. Whatever you lack on earth, you may well desire to produce on your heavenly divine trees.

On earth as it is in heaven . . . be fruitful and multiply my Spirit's presence by the fruit which you bear. You literally nourish others' spirits as my fruits from heaven flow through you onto others! Amen.

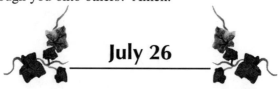

July 26

Your Mouth Is My Mouth

"So shall My Word be that goes forth from My mouth; It shall not return to Me void, But it shall accomplish what I please, And it shall prosper in the thing for which I sent it."   *Isaiah 55:11 NKJV*

Your mouth is my mouth on earth. With pursed lips you profess my Word over situations that appear to the carnal eye to be disastrous, as evil appears to loom over the lives for whom you intercede. My Word, spoken through your lips, activates my Spirit and intervening angels to set to work in your behalf, in their behalf. You speaking my Word is Me speaking my Word. You are my child, and in the name of Jesus, you have been given my authority to speak destiny over earthly situations. Your words have power, just as my Word has power! You are my voice to the earth.

I spoke the world into existence; so, too, you may speak the creation of your earthly business into existence. Angelic hosts of both kinds await to hear your words. To whom do you enlist your commands? The positive confession of my Holy Word activates my angelic army to do battle in your behalf. Negative-carnal pronouncements of doom and gloom energize the forces of evil to enact the very pronouncements of your lips.

Place a guard over your mouth, and listen to your heart. Speak only faith and trust in Me and in my name.

There is no safety in negative confession. If you speak doom, you reap gloom. If you speak faith (my Word), you receive the answered prayer—my miracle of intervention in your life. My Word always accomplishes my purpose for which it is sent.

I love you. Amen.

July 27

Love Sees with My Eyes

"Love is patient, love is kind. It does not envy, it does not boast, it is not proud."
I Corinthians 13:4 NIV

LOVE—true Love—God's Love—my Love—is more than goose bumps and desire for intimacy; even more than dad and son or mother and daughter bonding.

Love between human beings still clothed in a carnal, mortal body is patient—because no man is perfect to endure.

My Love is day-by-day and hour-by-hour rubbing elbows with bad breath and BO. My love is forgiving and forbearing in kindness.

My love puffs itself not up but bends low to SERVE disregarding color, creed, or glamour.

My love cares and concerns itself with the human condition of one's soul and the salvation of one's spirit.

Love goes far beyond birthday parties and weddings. It reaches its hand into the sewer to rescue a bum dejected and filthy. True love never ends even into eternity. *Love sees with my eyes.*

July 28

Sounds of Holiness

"Let us come before him with thanksgiving and extol him with music and song."
Psalm 95:2 NIV

Music is my voice and is the language of heaven. Music, as created by Me, is pure worship and communication between Me and thee! You and I have love songs for one another being continually created and written in the spirit, for music is the language of your born-again spirit.

When you arrive in heaven, your ears will witness sounds beyond any human ability to endure or enjoy—*sounds of holiness* that literally cry out, "Holy! Holy! Holy!" My angels always sing and give praise to Me.

The music of the earth is harsh and insensitive, compared to heaven's voice. My music loudly resounds with harmonies unheard by human ear.

In heaven, you may worship Me in instrument and song, for there is no limitation of personal talent in our home. Here you may worship freely and creatively to your heart's content and ENJOY my presence unreservedly! Amen.

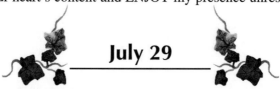

July 29

You Can't Bring It with You!

"All flesh is like grass and all its glory like the flower of grass. The grass withers, and the flower falls, but the word of the Lord abides for ever."
I Peter 1:24-25 RSV

My Word that is in you will abide forever! All that I deposit in your spirit man comes with you to heaven. My carving, my molding and shaping, and the coats of my gold paint all come with you. My deposit into your spirit of my gems and nuggets of truth from my Word—all come with you and remain for eternity.

This is why I say, "Seek first the Kingdom of God." I see the eternal time line and eternal investment I am making in you.

Beloved, I love you. Every ounce of earthly glory will cease to be your own upon death. All worldly bank accounts, possessions, and achievements cease to be your own at death's call. Then you stand naked in spirit before Me.

Will you be clothed in robes of righteousness and garments of salvation? Or will your efforts have only made you fat in the eyes of man but skinny and bony in spirit?

Seek first my Kingdom, for your earthly days are numbered. Your human glory before the eyes of men is nothing, like the flower of the grass that withers and is no more!

You can spend your days on earth contributing to your eternal wealth by sewing my Word into your soul! Bank accounts and properties do not follow you to heaven—only that which you have given away in my name follows!

The tithe . . . the offering . . . the unselfish giving of your gifts and talents great and small . . . these will accompany you to my Home where the true and inner hidden wealth of man is exposed, where no hypocrisy or pride can stand.

My Word will abide forever in you! No consumption of my Word is futile. My Bread of Life feeds your spirit man and produces good works and sweet-tasting fruit from your life.

You would be wise to set your eyes on my Eternal Bank and take them off earth's bank. Simply put—*you can't bring it with you!* Amen.

July 30

The White Rose

"God is light, and in him is no darkness at all."　　　　*I John 1:5 KJV*

The scent of *the white rose* . . . as you deeply breathe engulfing breaths of its fragrance . . . your nostrils brushing up against its petals . . . know that this is a scent of heaven. All of heaven resounds with the sweet scent of Jesus Christ. Jesus emits a fragrance unknown to human nature. If you were to gather the finest flower blossoms from all across my lands into one large room, and if you were to combine them into one exquisite bouquet, you could still not match the scent of heaven.

Ah, but you would experience a foretaste divine; for in every flower there breathes a trace of my glory, on earth as it is in heaven.

Beloved, take one white rose and hold it against your nose. Sniff! You are experiencing my glory when you breathe in the pure scent of my holy rose.

In heaven, there are many colors, even more than you have on earth. Colors are spiritually alive. Colors praise Me! White is my color of purity. It is no mistake that the scent of the white rose is so exquisite. There are many alive and diverse colors in my heavenly realm, but the color of white radiates and dominates in brilliance. She is the queen of colors! She is the pure symbol of unadulterated love and holiness.

White and light . . . we are the same. I am light. I am light in you. Your light shines before Me! Sin is evil. Sin is darkness, blackness, lack of light. Sin is exposed by my light. The two cannot dwell together. Light defeats darkness. It always has. It always will. In both natural and spiritual law, light dominates darkness. Hallelujah!

Satan is pure darkness. There is no light in him. His only light of pretense comes in the face of lies or deception—no true light. He is easily defeated because he is easily exposed by my light. He seeks to blind, of course. I seek to give sight to the blind, both naturally and spiritually.

Light and darkness cannot dwell together. Even the small glow of a candle gives forth light in a large room.

Light exposes darkness. Your light (presence) in the world exposes the darkness of sin, and it has to leave. These are both natural and spiritual laws working simultaneously.

We have no need of night in heaven. There is no darkness. Only the light of Jesus Christ is sufficient . . . no sunrise or sunset, only Son Rise continually shining. This is a Paradise Divine that I have prepared for you . . . a Paradise Divine!

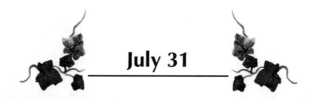

July 31

Prayer

"Praying always with all prayer and supplication in the Spirit, and watching thereunto with all perseverance and supplication for all saints."

Ephesians 6:18 KJV

I want you to pray more! Your mind is too often distracted by the world's frenzied affairs. You stuff into your daily life (like into a grocery sack) as many canned goods as possible, leaving only a slim margin at the top for a flimsy *prayer*.

Truth: PRAYER TAKES TIME AND ENERGY!

It is absolutely impossible to keep pace with your neighbor and also pace with my call to prayer. Truthfully, the world offers every imaginable distraction that glimmers with excitement and fulfillment.

Prayer time will only come by forsaking the glamour of the world and making conscious quality choices that make room for appointments with Me.

It is good to pray without ceasing in your daily life, interwoven in your daily agenda. To have your life cram-packed with duty and events honestly serves as a distraction to earnest prayer.

Consider what endeavors will go with you to heaven. Will the reward come with you, carved into your spirit, or is it simply a frivolous worldly pleasure that has no eternal bearing?

Prayer is quality life style, and no sacrifice on earth can be outgiven by Me.

To the prayer warrior, I send my angels to assist and inhabit his rooms. He is never alone. They work in behalf of his words and my commands. The prayer warrior trades in a hamburger for a steak—a bicycle for a jet—a cotton jacket for a mink stole. All these trade off's are in the spirit, hidden to man's eye, but very "felt" in the wealth of the inner man who prays.

The person who prays often will not glimmer on the outside so much as on the inside. An exchange is made. Gold is coated around the spirit of he who often prays. His natural coins are exchanged for spiritual wealth. He may appear extraordinarily ordinary to the natural eye, but only I know for sure! The investment of my gold transfers to heaven. Eternal investments never fluctuate. They only grow!

You who pray, you know my promise and understand this message. 'Tis the only comfort you require and the only reward you seek. It is my pleasure and honor to coat and recoat your spirit with my gold from heaven. You are invaluable to Me! Thank you for your prayers and your hours of servitude to Me within the hidden closet of my chambers—in behalf of others. I love you. Amen.

August 1

Holy Spirit

"For you are the temple of the living God."　　　**II Corinthians 6:16 NKJV**

I love you! My Holy Spirit's personality has inhabited you, the temple of the Living God. He seeks to fill up every crack and crevice with his power, mercy, and grace.

When you speak, my *Holy Spirit* is speaking. When you laugh, my Holy Spirit is laughing. When you cry, my Holy Spirit is grieving (or rejoicing) with you.

You are the temple of the Living God! You house Me on earth in your tabernacle, your body. Rejoice, give thanks, and sing! It is a most marvelous arrangement that my Holy Spirit lives within you, so that you might increasingly know Me and love Me.

My Holy Spirit is an absolute gentleman. He wraps himself around your soul, and you "share" the manifested person that you are, speaking and reacting through your lips and body. This is a holy personality that knows no vain words, who delights in doing good and not evil all of its days on earth.

My Holy Spirit, in your personality, gives forth the fruits of the spirit. For example, joy bubbles from your soul. My Holy Spirit is gracious and slow to anger, not easily agitated—but full of the joy of the Lord!

Please, take good care of my visitor, the Holy Spirit, who dwells in you. Love Him! Enjoy Him! Experience Him! Enjoy his presence in your life, and utilize his gifts of mercy and tenderness for others who knock at your door.

You are energized from on high with my Holy Ghost power to accomplish the works that I have ordained from the beginning of time.

May these words be understood and manifested through you, my vessel, for my glory! Amen.

August 2

Much Is Required

"For unto whomsoever much is given, of him shall be much required."
Luke 12:48 KJV

To whom I give most, I expect most. Your dimension of gift is also your measure of requirement.

If I give you three seeds, then I expect the harvest of three bushel baskets to supply your need and to share with others.

If I invest in you a grove of fruit trees, then I expect that you will market the fruit, have plenty to meet your own needs, and, also, see that the poor are given of your goods.

Any raw talent or spiritual gift that I have placed in you is there to grow, develop, and then to produce food for your present generation.

No talent is given for the self-seeking satisfaction of oneself nor for glory and applause of man.

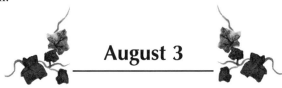

August 3

I First Loved You

"We love because he first loved us."　　　　　*I John 4:19 NIV*

I first loved you before creation itself. You have always been in my heart. Salvation was purchased for you. You are my eternal spirit-child, redeemed and purchased by the price of the blood of the Lamb. All this was done with you in mind. I knew your name. I knew your call. I knew your purpose. The cross of Calvary bore your name as Jesus' blood triumphed over the curse of the law.

You are able to love unconditionally in agape fashion because I first loved you. I set our love into motion, and you are the responder to Me! Now, and because you have responded to my voice's call, I pour my increased love into you so that from you flow rivers of living water, my rivers of love to a lost generation. Love them because I first loved you!

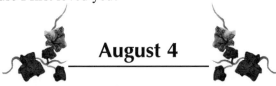

August 4

Eagled Souls

"But those who hope in the Lord will renew their strength. They will soar on wings like eagles; they will run and not grow weary, they will walk and not be faint."

Isaiah 40:31 NIV

This is the walk in my Spirit that I have designed and purchased for you. Even though in the natural, you might understandably falter, I have a supernatural walk for you that supplies wings like eagles and the wind beneath your wings.

I purposely allow the weight of your life to be heavy so that you may experience the supernatural miracle of flying above all problems in my strength.

In the attitude of trust and hope in Me, I give even the wind to boost you up above the trees, to rest and perch yourself above the draining problems.

I take great delight in my *eagled souls!* You bring Me great JOY and HONOR because you live as I designed mankind to live in Me—in Jesus—in my Spirit.

There is a walk in Me that enables you to exist winged in my Spirit, lifted high above the meager existence of carnal man.

To soar with Me is to trust Me with your daily needs, not allowing the weight of worry to impede your flight. Frustration makes heavy your feathers, and you grow weary and faint from toiling not as a bird was meant to exist.

I designed your spirit man to be a winged eagle. I renew the strength of the soul who hopes in Me—with all of his heart. It is only because you refuse to trust Me that you do not remain in flight and soar effortlessly upon the winds of my Spirit. He who can trust Me as a child will soar with his Father in realms unknown to mortal man.

Repent of your weighted wings, and shed your mistrust of Me. You are only burdened because you take life into your own hands.

Beloved, I love you, and I am not honored by your busy-body martyrship. I want only for you to be my eagled soul!

August 5

Divine Health

"For I will restore health to you and heal you of your wounds."
Jeremiah 30:17 NKJV

I am the Lord who heals you. I do not want you sick! My Son Jesus died on the cross to permanently purchase your *divine health*. Beloved, when you begin to feel sickness come upon you, state aloud the following for all angels and demonic forces to hear:

"By the stripes of Jesus Christ I am healed!

Through Jesus' blood I walk in divine health!

Thank God I am taking healing!

In Jesus' name, I bind you, spirit of infirmity.

I loose upon my body God's promise to me for healing.

The Lord rebuke you, spirit of sickness.

I'll not have you inhabiting this temple of the Living God.

Out! Be gone with you, in Jesus' name.

Father, I praise and thank You for hearing my prayer and delivering me from affliction to my body.

In Jesus' name. Amen."

August 6

Shouts of Joy

"Shout with joy to God, all the earth!"   *Psalm 66:1 NIV*

The human being must give forth voice to the Spirit's movement within him. My people must allow the excitement of my Spirit to stir and breathe and rise and jump and dance and finally EXPLODE into *shouts of JOY*.

It is like a boiling pot of water that must overflow! My steam in your spirit must be released. Your shout gives way to my Spirit's breath within you!

Your vocal chords voice the holiness of heaven and join in with the choirs of heavenly witnesses. We roar in heaven with praise!

To shout in joy trembles heaven's gates, and we rejoice that heaven has come to earth! Your shouts of JOY vibrate my very throne! Amen.

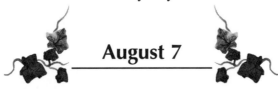

August 7

Cookie Batter

"Being confident of this very thing, that he which hath begun a good work in you will perform it until the day of Jesus Christ." **Philippians 1:6 KJV**

You are like *cookie batter,* and I am the Baker. I meticulously measure the dry ingredients of your daily life and sift you carefully together. I cream my revealed Word in you, beating stroke after stroke. 'Round and 'round, my sovereign hand softens and combines the understanding of my precepts within your heart. When the mixing is done, the cookies are formed on my trays. Each step I have watched over, and I have made certain that my work in you is perfect.

We have labored together in my Word, in prayer, and in personal conviction. You have been willing to be sifted and stirred by my Spirit's hand, even though you have not always understood the stirring of my Spirit deep within your hidden man, or the beating of trying circumstances against your soul.

Now, do I, the Baker, leave you to sit out on the counter to spoil? Of course not! I insert you into my oven and bake you to perfection, then offer you to my hungry world until every last morsel is devoured. Then, we begin the process all over again.

You can be confident in Me. I who have begun a good work in you will repeatedly perform it until the day you stand face-to-face with your Lord Jesus Christ! Amen.

August 8

Conduits of My Love

"Give thanks to the Lord, for he is good. His love endures forever."
Psalm 136:1 NIV

My love endures forever, reaching into eternity's arms. My eternal arms of love desire to wrap themselves around you and hold you always close to Me.

Your understanding of my love is like a single ant in a castle. All you realize is your little corner of the room where a few morsels from your master's table fall to the floor, and they sustain you adequately.

All the time I am loving you from my eternal perspective, seeking to find avenues into your life that will serve as *conduits of my love* from heaven to earth.

You need to seek my love, because the revelation of my love for you will transform your earthly life unto eternity. The key to understanding my love is in praising Me for everyday gifts that your eyes can see and your hands can touch— like a flower, for example. I am good. As you praise Me for the goodness that you can see and touch, I will reveal the unseen things of which is my LOVE.

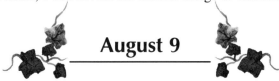

August 9

I Am Your Promise Keeper

"The Lord is faithful to all his promises and loving toward all he has made."
Psalm 145:13 NIV

I am a promise keeper! My Word is my love letter jam-packed with lovers' promises. My Word is my sealed covenant with you.

Wherever you go, my Word goes; wherever you go, my love goes; and wherever you go, my promises go.

My promises follow you, remaining in tact and promoting the good and perfect will of your Father who is in heaven, watching over you endlessly at all times, day and night.

I am your promise keeper. I will never break your heart, nor will I ever disappoint you. There may be times you will not have your own way, but, always, it will be for your betterment.

I love you! I will always, forever, be faithful to supply your needs. Amen!

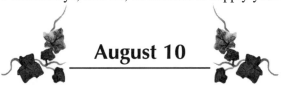

August 10

Broken Jars

"The Lord is near to those who have a broken heart, And saves such as have a contrite spirit."   *Psalm 34:18 NKJV*

I will take care of you! There is no pride in a broken heart, nor arrogance in a contrite spirit.

I specialize in piecing back together shattered vessels that lie at my feet broken and feeling useless. Though they may not hold water, broken pieces are yet valuable to Me.

I love *broken jars* because I am allowed to redefine their make-up! As I piece back together, I construct in a new sovereign way using a stronger mortar from heaven. I round off some rough edges, and I usually alter the paint job.

I work to conform you more into the image of Jesus Christ. You become, therefore, even more pleasing to Me in your reshaped state!

Beloved, I want you to be like Jesus! That is why I am near and honor your brokenhearted state. It is my opportunity to flush away stagnant pride and soul-sewage, and I begin a new work of rebuilding and reshaping your eternal spirit that will live eternally.

No tears of brokenheartedness are wasted. I collect them all, and they are used by Me to wash your soul as I cleanse your sins with the blood of my Son.

Beloved, I love you! I will always heal your broken heart! Amen.

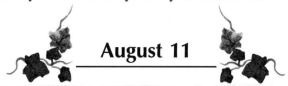

August 11

No Limit

"Great is our Lord and mighty in power; his understanding has no limit."
Psalm 147:5 NIV

Your prophecies are imperfect, and your knowledge is imperfect, but my understanding has no limitations to it!

That is why you seek Me for counsel and wisdom. My supply of understanding to you is absolutely inexhaustible!

I love you, beloved, and I am an infinitely loving Father to you. That is how we can continue for an eternity, because there will be no burden in my Kingdom!

I am absolutely inexhaustible! In my Kingdom, you run out of nothing! All supplies are available, even as I intend to meet all of your present needs.

You have barely tipped my bucket of resources! I am absolutely inexhaustible, with *no limit* to my understanding.

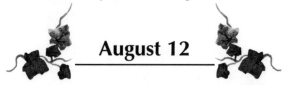

August 12

The Whole Duty of Man

"Fear God, and keep his commandments: for this is the whole duty of man."
Ecclesiastes 12:13 KJV

Man runs here and there trying to fill up the very void that I have placed within him for Me.

The world offers extensive diversions from my truth, like one thousand paths steering away from my focal point of wisdom.

The world's voices scream and entice the common man to take ten thousand unnecessary steps away from my truth.

Activities, schedules, commitments, jobs, recreation, and even church events all pull in one hundred different directions.

That is why Solomon gives two conclusive statements to end his lamentations on the vanity of life and *the whole duty of man:*

(1) "Fear God!" That means love Me, desire to obey Me by listening and seeking my voice, and understand that all of my ways are judgment. I will bless you with good gifts for obedience, and I will bless you with the sting of chastisement so that you might grow.

(2) "Keep his commandments," and you will receive honor. This is the simple explanation of man's duty before Me. Love Me and serve Me. Fear Me (respect Me), and keep my commandments (obey my Word).

Most simply put, these are your purposes as my child—and it takes a lifetime to fulfill.

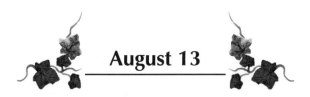

August 13

Little Children

"Let the little children come to me, and do not forbid them; for of such is the kingdom of heaven."   *Matthew 19:14 NKJV*

Little children are precious because their souls are yet unmarred by the world's daggers of sin set against them. A human soul is a priceless gift which I invest in human body. The flesh grows, as timework from a preset designation of DNA. The human body is much like grass and flowers. It grows, blossoms, and dies.

Ah, but the human soul is quite the opposite. My very breath of life dwells within each man's soul. My creative power and strength enables him to do super-human feats beyond his own natural gifts.

It is in the child's soul that I desire to place salvation. Then, I watch over the development of that personality carefully and seek always to protect from harming assault.

It is in childhood that my children's gifts are thwarted and their freedom to love is quenched—because of circumstances that hurt their tenderness.

Children need to be gardened by wise parents who use the tools of salvation to dig up the weeds and hoe away enemy plantings. Parents need to protectively watch over their garden of children, watering them with the power of the Holy Spirit through prayer and worship.

A child left alone is a child damaged, marred, and scarred. These piercings of the soul accompany them through adulthood and divert their clear understanding of my perfect will for them.

I celebrate the life of children raised by caring gardener hands, submitted unto my Lordship. Their hands raise the harvests of righteousness that bring Me greatest glory—little servants armed and ready for servitude in my Kingdom's army. I love them! Amen.

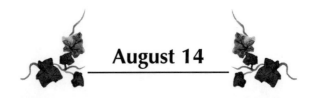

August 14

Grandchildren's Inheritance

"A good man leaves an inheritance to his children's children."

Proverbs 13:22 NKJV

It is a holy duty of a righteous man to leave an inheritance to his grandchildren. Given a lifetime of faithful labor and tithing, I am more than able to place in your storehouse ample enough gift to designate unto each seed's seed a *grandchildren's inheritance*.

This inheritance is monetary as well as spiritual.

Your prayers and Christian heritage should be well paved for this younger generation. If you have done your job well, you will have submitted each offspring to Me and their babies to serve Me for the rest of their days on earth. You will have set the tone and mood of the home, and your pattern of righteous living will have been like stone, engraved into their hearts. You will have, like yarn, wrapped and rewrapped strings of my love 'round and 'round the children's souls, securing them in the ways of the Lord and my Kingdom functioning of the earth. You will have been the pacemaker. Your heritage to enjoy is their response to Me.

Not only will they, upon your death, have riches in their hearts invested by you, but they also will have a monetary gift as a memorial to your name.

'Tis a righteous and holy man that leaves an inheritance to his children's children. That monetary gift will enhance and help to make more loyal a remembrance of that intangible gift of faith in the soul. They go hand in hand, working together to encourage the next generation to continue the walk of faith you pioneered. They will trod down your paved paths, and in my might, we will construct more!

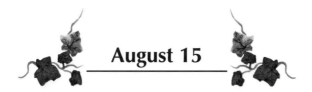

August 15

Wedding Day

"He who finds a wife finds a good thing And obtains favor from the Lord."
Proverbs 18:22 NKJV

On this, your *wedding day,* two paths of destiny solidify into one. Had it not been for your two hearts deeply longing for the identical dream, my hand would not have brought you together. It has been known unto Me for centuries of time that your two paths would seek one another until my culmination of time made public my design of your two hearts perfectly crafted for one another.

Your marriage is a pleasant gift unto Me. Two hearts, as doves, have found passageway into the secret caverns of one another's most hidden dreams and deepest heart's desires. You have won the privilege of, on earth, being one in Christ. It is this mystery that, although concealed to the world, will be lived out daily between the two of you within your secret most moments of intimacy.

Beloved husband, you have found a good thing! I have rewarded your faithfulness to Me by investing into your safekeeping a diligent, virtuous woman. I have unveiled your eyes to see her hidden beauty. 'Tis how she appears, also, unto Me! You are a rare and privileged man to have received such a gift as this woman.

Cherish and adore her with all of your heart! You have obtained my favor, and I will be watching on, enjoying the splendor of your love and the mystery played out in marriage of Christ and his Bride.

Your marriage is a beautiful gift unto Me! I have given you this bride, but you have given me this marriage, a sacred and holy covenant which I shall guard and watch over carefully and joyfully.

Son, you have brought Me pleasure by being purehearted and allowing your destiny to be ordained by Me. I love you. Go now. Embrace your bride, and be always ravished with her love! Amen.

August 16

A Soft Answer

"A soft answer turneth away wrath: but grievous words stir up anger."
Proverbs 15:1 KJV

What happens when fuel is thrown on a fire? What happens when words of strife are mixed with anger?

What good thing can come from kindling strife?

There is a fire from hell that destroys and devastates the human soul. Anger stirred up against another is like poison to a rat. It kills and destroys. Anger is the enemy's ammunition against peace and good will.

Disharmony between two is a demon's delight, so why give credit to evil's side?

When a man is vexed with anger, pray and give him space. Do not allow his vomit of evil words to enweb you into the same snare with which he himself has become entangled.

Anger can be just a step away from hell's door. You do not want to open the hatch and innocently invite unwelcomed intruders into your home. (They do not take kindly to being sent away.) Their strategy is to silently enter undetected, so as not to be ejected from holy premises.

Keep your home clean by disallowing your own mouth to fuel the fire of another's temper. A soft answer will be a cool cup of heaven's drink to an inflamed soul. The fire will be quenched, and there will be no increase of dominion on the enemy's side. He will retreat—neutered, exasperated, and defeated.

You only lose when you fuel the fire of hell. Cool its company with tender words and *a soft answer.* You can then say, "No harm done, proceed on course, God is faithful." Amen.

August 17

Put Me in Remembrance

"Put me in remembrance: let us plead together."　　　　*Isaiah 43:26 KJV*

Put me in remembrance of my Word. From your own mouth speak forth my promises, proclaim my oracles of faith to my ear. Remind Me of my own words to you, for I am a God of my own Word and will not lie.

You bring Me great JOY when you repeat my Word to you. The hearing of my Word activates my angels in your behalf. They work daily and hourly to minister to you and keep my provisions of safety about you.

Remind Me of my Word in prayer. This builds up your faith and ignites the spiritual process. Confessing my Word before Me is like striking a match and beginning fires.

I love you, beloved, and I want you to live a life of answered prayer. Live in my Word. Speak my Word. Pray my Word. Putting Me in remembrance stirs the fire of my love in your behalf and pulls on my heart strings to administer divine health and sovereign deliverance.

I love to hear my Word formed on your lips and spoken through the warm breath of your human soul. I love to hear you pronounce my Words back to Me! I love to hear my Word through your precious lips. I love to hear my Word because my Word on your lips is like honey, sweet-tasting. I love to hear my Word through you! Faith is produced when you speak my Word, and I am a God of faith. Your faith releases my intervention in your behalf! Amen.

August 18

Symphony of Sorrow

"Sorrow is better than laughter: for by sadness of the countenance the heart is made better."   *Ecclesiastes 7:3 KJV*

When you are led through hard times, those of you who deeply prize your ability to be "guided by God" begin to doubt that you are in my will. Surely, your loving Father would not orchestrate such a *symphony of sorrow* for you.

Indeed, the very composer of your soul has composed a most difficult piece to stretch your ability and to sharpen your skills.

Would such a God set you up to "squeak" on your reed instrument or to pound the drum off beat? No. Yet the written music, the path of obedience, feels to the soul to be impossible, too difficult, and certain not to be my will.

All along, I, the Maestro, am smiling and crying out, "Practice! Practice!" It is as you press into Me that the very character of Jesus Christ is impressed upon you. Methodically tooting the same scales daily was providing no growth; therefore, the Conductor upped the difficulty of the written score . . . and so it is in your human life with Me.

Those of you who are my servants, who live to bless others, must surely expect that as you play upon your stringed instruments in the Kingdom Symphony, you will continue to be challenged (sometimes even by angry, displeased crowds) to perform at an ever-increasing excellence that can only come by the character of Jesus Christ being perfected through the practice of servitude. This is when "impossible" to the eyes becomes "possible" by faith.

August 19

You and Your Household

"Believe on the Lord Jesus Christ, and you will be saved, you and your household."   ***Acts 16:31 NKJV***

I declare my salvation over households! If one be saved, then all must be saved! If you are the single believer under your rooftop, do not fret! I hear your prayers, and they are right in behalf of your family. It is certainly my sovereign will to save you and your household!

As you have requested, I have tied my string of drawing about the neck of their souls. I am drawing and wooing, cranking them in.

Beloved, you only need to believe Me and praise Me for my work of repentance in the life of your family. Know that you know that you know that I have heard and received your prayers.

Now, go and do my will, and allow your life to be a living testimony of my grace and power within you. Rest in Me, and know that Jesus is about his Father's business.

You and your household . . . they shall be saved! Amen.

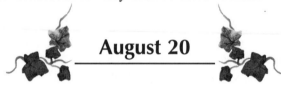

August 20

Sweet Sleep

"I will lie down and sleep in peace, for you alone, O Lord, make me dwell in safety."   ***Psalm 4:8 NIV***

I promise my beloveds *sweet sleep.* It is never my will to give restless sleep, unless I am calling you to intercede.

Beloved, I rejoice in your sleeping! I minister spiritual rest and recuperation as you sleep. I anoint your sleep and give you dreams of your heart's desires.

When you love Me, no fear can disturb your sleep if you trust Me with your life. I even work in your behalf as you sleep. I work in others' hearts and arrange circumstances.

Your angels watch over you as you rest in Me—it is a holy thing to receive anointed sleep! I love you! Amen.

August 21

Victory!

"But thanks be to God! He gives us the victory through our Lord Jesus Christ."
I Corinthians 15:57 NIV

Faith does not come by sight but by believing the unseen. Your Lord Jesus Christ is unseen, yet it is through him that you receive *victory!* Incomprehensible? No, but comprehended through the revealed Word of God.

Victory is faith manifested. It is the winning side of the game of life. Victory is above, not beneath—light, not darkness—excitement, not depression.

Victory in the mind and heart is announced by the voice of Jesus Christ. It is the supernatural provision of God for inner peace and quiet tranquility of the soul. True victory is the inner presence of God, my presence in you, soothing and calming you daily. I love you! Amen.

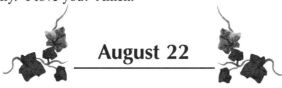

August 22

Mother the Peacemaker

"Peacemakers who sow in peace raise a harvest of righteousness."
James 3:18 NIV

Young mother, tape James 3:18 onto your refrigerator door! This is my promise to you for all of the times you have broken up fights, taught forgiveness, helped little ones repeat "I'm sorry," encouraged hugs, and set children in "time out" chairs (as well as the use of the stick!).

Beloved, what you sow into your children will be what is produced in their crop. The peace that you establish as a foundation in your home will produce a harvest of righteousness. You will see this fruit begin to give bud near the teenage years, and as you faithfully persevere in removing the rocks and debris that blow in from the world's storms, you will have harvests of right relationships with Me in your young adult fields.

Beloved, *mother the peacemaker,* no effort is overlooked. No measure is too great. With a mother of little ones I say, DO NOT LOSE HEART! You are simply planting seeds in this season. If you do not give up or give in to the world's demands upon your children's souls, the day will come (sooner than you presently can imagine) that you will eat the fruit of your labors! I promise you! Amen.

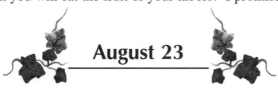

August 23

A Giant in Your Land

"Let us therefore, as many as be perfect, be thus minded: and if in anything ye be otherwise minded, God shall reveal even this unto you."

Philippians 3:15 KJV

In all areas of your life there exists wrinkles of imperfection and sin. As I walk with you as Lord, you submit to Me all areas of your life. Then, I go about ironing out the wrinkles. What once was crinkled and even damaged looking becomes ironed out to where there is even no wrinkle that remains.

Those areas of your life that once seemed laborious, those mountains that once took all of your devotion and strength to climb, slowly dissolve into looking like little mole hills. I have changed you by equipping you with tools to efficiently climb the mountains. We have paved a path together through the wooded hills. We, together in prayer, have removed the obstacles, the rocks and stones that used to block the paths. I have taken you and transformed a weak and stumbling vessel into a mighty person of God.

I make you *a giant in your land*, and as you peer down over the once challenging and nearly seemingly impossible mountain to ascend and conquer, you look down upon the old challenge like a dog's paw upon an ant. The plan is understood. All fear is defeated. The trial is ended. Faith has met her match and has been allowed to grow and overcome. Now, you reign as a king and priest amongst your circumstances!

In every day of your walk with Me in Christ, I purposely lead you to still waters between battles, to minister rest and recuperation, but how will you continue to grow unless I advance you on to more difficult turf? It is good to be steadfast. It is most excellently great to grow! When you, therefore, experience a feeling of frustration, know that I am targeting an area to conquer.

My promise to you is that I will be faithful to add maturity and strength to feeble limbs. I will empower you from on high to be victorious in absolutely every area of your life! This is my word, and this is my promise. I will cause you to overcome in all things, in all areas of your life.

Frustration has roots, and it is a "signal" that an area needs to be stronger. I am the root puller. I am able to root up sin from your soul. Only I can do this supernatural surgery called "change" deep within your own personality. It is called a miracle, conforming you into the image of Jesus.

It is in the revelation of my Word that divine transformation takes place. I promise you, my plan in every area of your life is to transform you into a mighty person of God! Amen.

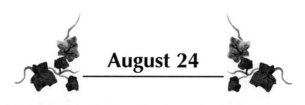

August 24

Turned Upside Down

"These who have turned the world upside down have come here too."
Acts 17:6 NKJV

Have you turned your world upside down with your testimony of my love and power in your life? Beloved, I have placed you in your unique corner of my world to do just this—turn it upside down!

Your nest should be unlike other nests and your tree unlike other trees! In your tree and in your nest, you are in dominion over the enemy.

Sickness and disease bow at your command. Poverty trembles at your demand. Depression takes a hike when you say, "flee!" Despair digs a hole when you rebuke its breath.

Beloved, your little corner of the world is inhabited by unseen forces—my angels! What is "norm" for Joe Blow is not for you. The thief avoids your home, for he is forbidden by the bodyguards at your door.

My world is *turned upside down,* one nest at a time, as salvation is actualized within households. PRAISE GOD FROM WHOM ALL BLESSINGS FLOW! From my throne flows my power to turn your world upside down—in love and in order, for my glory! Amen.

August 25

The Sanctuary

"When I thought how to understand this, It was too painful for me—Until I went into the sanctuary of God; Then I understood their end."
Psalm 73:16-17 NKJV

In my sanctuary, in my house, I dwell. When my house is filled with my people, there am I in your midst. My angels come, my Holy Spirit is at work, and we inhabit your praises.

There is an oil of anointing that I apply on my saints when you gather together in one accord. Heaven touches earth when you congregate in my name. Your songs and hymns draw us to you, and we bask in your worship. Much business in heaven transpires, unknown to carnal eye, as you worship together. Prayers are collected. Prayers are answered. Great power exists when my people gather together and pray in unity.

That is why I can pull clouds of misunderstanding off of you in *the sanctuary.* I honor the gathering together of my saints, and I work to minister to each of my children present.

I love you for gathering together in my name! Amen.

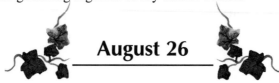

August 26

Distress

"In my distress I called to the Lord, and he answered me."   **Jonah 2:2 NIV**

I will answer you in your *distress.* The problem is that sometimes your ability to hear my voice in return is weakened because the distress has weakened your spirit. Now, this should not be. Distress is like an emergency signal to alert you to a need. Distress means: Pray more! Seek Me! Get help!

The person who calls out in distress will receive my aid, but you may need help from a fellow saint to "clear up" the muddy water that has risen ankle deep.

I would have you not bow to distress. I would have you living on the offensive, strong in my Spirit, fighting and winning!

Yet the human condition bogs down, and that is how I most often teach my children. I want you not to be in distress; but, if you are, I understand, I answer, and I am here to help! Amen!

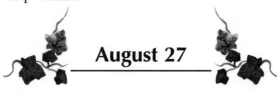

August 27

Eternal Balloons

"My grace is sufficient for thee: for my strength is made perfect in weakness. Most gladly therefore will I rather glory in my infirmities, that the power of Christ may rest upon me."   *II Corinthians 12:9 KJV*

Natural strength brings Me no glory, for it requires no faith. I am glorified through what you do when you are trusting Me to supply the fuel in your tank.

When you depend on Me, I give you my Spirit's breath and strength to accomplish your day's demands. When you have asked Me to be your supply, then a supernatural combustion takes place within your spirit man that raises you up above the carnal level and elevates you into the Spirit realm.

All natural men are given a measure of ability, but I desire to expand you with my divine breath like a balloon. All of the raw materials are in a simple empty balloon, but the difference I make is my helium that expands your natural shape and causes you to rise above the crowd and bring joy to others. In doing this, you bring Me glory.

As one talent after another is given back to Me, and as you learn to yield every aspect of your personality and life, then is when you become a cluster of balloons, all attached on my strings of grace. My hand is holding the clump of strings as you share my beauty and cheer with the world around you.

Each eternal balloon represents the end of your own strength made perfect in weakness. The cluster represents true faithfulness by the power of Christ resting upon you in faith.

Never fear weakness. Many youths produce plush and juicy grapes, but it is the seasoned old grapes that have been allowed to wither that become raisins of meaty nutrition and the sweetest tasting fruit.

It is my business to turn weakness into strength. I am glorified when my strength is made perfect through you! Such works cannot burn like wood, hay, and stubble.

Beyond my Gate, *eternal balloons* will become gems in your crown—worn for eternity.

August 28

Great and Awesome God

"Do not be terrified by them, for the Lord your God, who is among you, is a great and awesome God."
Deuteronomy 7:21 NIV

A *great and awesome God* am I! Oh, if you but only realized the depth of truth and power in my greatness—you would never fear, never!

I am a big Mack truck smashing ants on a highway. I am a heavy boulder loosed to roll down a mountain smashing anything in the way. I am as lightning flashing across the dark summer evening sky, the strength of a storm, the roar of a tornado.

I spoke the world into existence! My power is incomprehensible. I can easily take care of you! There is no enemy too great to warrant your fear because you are not alone. I am with you. My angels work always to respond to your faith in my power and my promise to deliver by my right hand.

You would not expect your small child to fear a dog if you were nearby to protect. I, too, expect you not to fear "the dog" who roams the earth to devour those who are afraid.

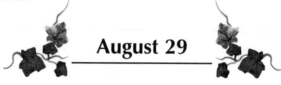

August 29

Not One Hoof

"Our livestock also shall go with us; not a hoof shall be left behind."
Exodus 10:26 NKJV

I am a God of perfection. When I move, I do not perform at half measure. No, my deliverance is complete. My salvation is whole. My purpose is all-consuming. That is why "lukewarm" is spewed from my mouth!

Beloved, I love you, and when I deal with your weaknesses, I am after a perfect work within you. When I move, my sovereign Spirit thoroughly cleanses and wipes away the ordinances of judgment set against you.

I am a God of completion. When allowed to move freely within you and when I am given your patience, I do a complete work. *Not one hoof* is left behind. I give the enemy in your life not one hoof!

Beloved, you must believe in my sovereign and all-consuming fire! I burn to completion. I do perfect works. Your part is to BELIEVE, not fret and worry, which is unbelief. Your complete TRUST in Me guarantees your complete deliverance and my fulfilled promise that not one hoof will be left behind. Amen.

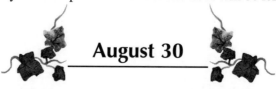

August 30

You Are My Lighthouse

"Then your light shall dawn in the darkness, And your darkness shall be as the noonday."   *Isaiah 58:10 NKJV*

When things don't seem quite right, you need to fast. Sometimes, you just need to pull away from the table, sacrifice a meal, and seek Me.

My light in you is my Spirit. In some, I am a battery flashlight, others, a pleasant table lamp, and still in another, the strong beam of a search light.

Remember that *you are my lighthouse.* I have you placed in your particular corner of the world to shine brightly. In the smallest of ways, you can make a big difference in the lives of those around you. No smile, word, or touch is too small for Me or others to notice or benefit from.

Every ray of my life emitting from you forces darkness to flee—no matter where you go or what you do. Your presence is always emitting light and dispensing meaning to others' lives.

If you have been feeling, lately, like there is a bushel basket over your candle, then respond to Isaiah 58's promise. Fast! Fasting will chase away the darkness. It will destroy the basket and will increase your flame. Your darkness can be as the noonday. Praying instead of eating does wonders for the soul!

August 31

You Win the Title of Champ!

"Many are the afflictions of the righteous, But the Lord delivers him out of them all."   *Psalm 34:19 NKJV*

You may be comforted to know that I never said you would not have affliction, but I have promised that always I will deliver you from it. I never said you would not battle, but I have promised that you will win the war.

You are the overcomer! You are the victor! *You win the title of champ!* Your enemy is defeated always. You can do all things through Christ who strengthens you.

Beloved, your sword is the sharpest weapon in the universe. Though your enemy doesn't war fairly, he sits at a disadvantage because your weapons are mighty to the pulling down of strongholds.

Greater is He that is in you than he that is in the world!

Your enemy's weapons are puff balls compared to the power of your sword. Demon soldiers tremble at the sound of my Word. Your enemy's only weapon is lies. My soldiers believe my Word and place their trust in the power of their Living God to deliver them from any affliction.

My sword cannot fail—it is impossible! Your enemy has no such weapon, no such weapon at all.

If you are fool enough to listen to his lies and fool enough to believe them, then you are fool enough to fall to his attacks.

The only weapon in life you need, will ever need, is my Word. Let the sword of my Spirit be professed through your mouth. Your enemy will freeze, and you, my beloved, will have victory. Amen.

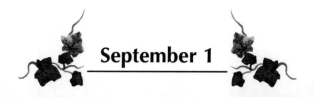

September 1

Boldness in Prayer

"Let us therefore come boldly unto the throne of grace, that we may obtain mercy, and find grace to help in time of need."　　　　*Hebrews 4:16 KJV*

The key to your prayer life with Me is boldness. If you know that you are my child, and if you spend time getting to know Me and being with Me, then when a need arises, your instant reaction is to cry out to your Abba, Father!

Boldness in prayer comes from your assurance of my love and favor towards you. Your boldness rises up inside of you because you have confidence that you are the apple of my eye!

Because you spend many hours at my feet, worshipping and fellowshipping, is it no wonder that you run to Me at the instant there is a need? Your response is that of a child to its loving and nurturing Father, as it should be.

Your boldness before my throne of grace spawns from our intimate relationship with one another, that which religion, alone, can never generate. True boldness from the heart is a courage and confidence in my favor toward you. It is grounded on promises in my Word. Yes, that would be intellectual grasp of my faithfulness. Only a fervent heart can pray the prayer of faith that will open a prison door and set a captive free.

No man can produce a fervent heart. A man's fervency before Me is produced over time by walking and talking with Me, enjoying my presence, and becoming familiar with my voice. It is when you begin to hear Me answer back ten thousand times a day, "I love you," that your fervency grows.

I always have mercy and new grace for you, like a gas station giving out free gas! If you have the boldness to drive up, my nozzle will fill up your tank with power for the next stretch of road.

I am always ready to meet your need because I love you! Amen.

September 2

You Are My Gold Mine

"Before I formed you in the womb I knew you, before you were born I set you apart; I appointed you as a prophet to the nations."   **Jeremiah 1:5 NIV**

Beloved Church, before I formed you in your mother's womb, I knew you! You have always been in my heart! I have always loved you and always known you! Eternity past and future is a difficult concept for the human mind to grasp.

Beloved, I foreknew you and deposited in you my calling unto my Lordship. Jesus Christ has always stood over you awaiting the blossoming of gifts deposited within you.

You are my gold mine. We have known of the wealth hidden within your soul. The excavation of your treasures has been long awaited.

Now is your day! Now is your hour! Allow my Holy Spirit to dig up the jewels of your spirit, and share with my world my gold formed within you.

Your heart glistens with the love of Jesus Christ. Allow my Spirit to "show off" himself through you! Allow us to make fine jewelry from the wealth of your soul. Give back all that we have given you, and we will multiply your eternal wealth by distributing your love throughout the nations.

Let your light shine! Allow your golden heart to express its value and worth in Me to a lost generation. Place upon others my gold bracelets and fine jewels. Share your goods and be not stingy!

My gold in you will never stop being supplied. There will always be more than you can use.

You are my bright shining gold nugget! From the beginning of time, I foreordained your fulfillment of my will in my Kingdom. Send forth your jewelry. Give of my wealth to my people! Sharing my love and giving your gifts is like placing chains of gold around the necks of my people.

You are my jeweler. Enjoy asking no price for my Kingdom's gold.

Open your mouth! Demonstrate my compassion! Record my Words! Ornate my people with my gold excavated from within you! Amen.

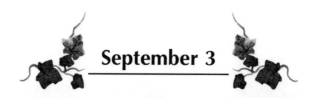

September 3

Power of the Tongue

"Death and life are in the power of the tongue: and they that love it shall eat the fruit thereof."   **Proverbs 18:21 KJV**

Just as I have authority and speak my Word into the universe, you, also, created in my image, have authority through your words.

Words have power! Notice that I did not create a mute world (could have . . . did not). Now, why did I create my people to speak? Because in my image, so you are created!

I speak, and the angels respond. All of creation came into existence through my own spoken word . . . so, now, also in yours. Your faith is proclaimed through words of your mouth. Angels "stand by" to listen, then hearken to your request or to your positive expression of expectation in Me. This is the *power of the tongue.*

Your words are like a painter's brush. Each stroke helps to develop the final portrait. Every word from your mouth creates the "masterpiece life"—you! Therefore, speak only that which you desire fulfilled, for someday we will hang up on eternity's wall (in your mansion) the formed "image" of Jesus—the earthling that was you!

September 4

I Love You, Lord!

"I love you, O Lord, my strength."   **Psalm 18:1 NIV**

This should be your cry to Me. All throughout your day I long to hear you say, "I love you!" My Holy Spirit stirs up this love within you throughout each day. When this happens, simply whisper, *"I love you, Lord!"* and go on about your business.

Your strength to accomplish the works of your hands comes from Me. You are my hands. I am your strength.

If I were to withdraw my strength from you, it would be like a marionette's strings collapsing onto the stage. You would be lifeless and hopeless apart from Me.

I replace your natural strength with my divine strength. Truly, I am your source of fortitude!

September 5

Be Ravished Always

"Let thy fountain be blessed: and rejoice with the wife of thy youth. Let her be as the loving hind and pleasant roe; let her breasts satisfy thee at all times; and be thou ravished always with her love."   *Proverbs 5:18-19 KJV*

It is the marriage bed that is undefiled. What transpires between husband and wife is holy and undefiled. A man's pleasure is his woman's body. She is to be a tower of perpetual honor and pleasure unto him, one upon which he can ascend and reign as king. His tower is adorned with the fragrance of a garden, a sweet-smelling perfume that beckons him continually. One taste of her ointments satisfies momentarily. The sweet ecstasy of her ascent yields only to more desire of her beauty.

Her breasts belong to him and only him. They are his reward and pleasure, my escape for him to pleasure in.

Husband, you shall *be ravished always* with her love, easily wooed from the world's voice into her arms of sensitivity and warmth. She is your retreat of honor. There within her you are lord of the castle; 'tis your domain, your authority.

Beloved, recognize my gift to you in your woman's body. She is to be unto you the scent of 1,000 roses. Her petals are yours to bask in, like a bed of flowers specially chosen and picked for you.

Your bed chamber is holy unto Me. Your union is sanctified, and my oil from heaven drips upon your kisses.

Tender and gentle is my atmosphere of love, like two doves cooing in morning's breeze. Like a raging river, passion's zeal announces its power of devotion and proclaims its ownership of love.

Husband, strum her body's strings as a harp from heaven. Make melody upon her keys, and cause the praise of marital love to ascend to my throne. Your union is holy—is holy—is holy unto Me! Amen.

September 6

Still Small Voice

"And after the earthquake a fire; but the Lord was not in the fire: and after the fire a still small voice."   *I Kings 19:12 KJV*

If I am a big mighty God, why do I speak to you in a *still small voice?* Why do I not shout your name from a mountain top? Why do I not speak your name through the television or radio? Or why do I not contact you through the Internet or call you on the phone?

My voice is as the delicate whispering of the leaves from the breeze of my Words. I am Spirit. You who worship Me worship in spirit and truth. I communicate with you in the Spirit, and my Spirit does not fit into the natural law like capturing a bug in a box. You cannot cramp Me into a corner nor dictate how I shall appear and speak. No. My voice is more like the rustling of leaves, my Spirit like the breeze.

Men would like for Me to speak over a public address system and appear on NBC nightly news, but no. I have given you my Word. If read in the Spirit with the heart, my voice speaks, explains, and touches your soul with its meaning.

My voice is my Word, both on earth and in heaven. Only the born-again spirit can feast upon my Word and be a special guest, banquet after banquet.

I have created your spirit man to know Me and love Me. Your body only houses that spirit, but the flesh is strong and prone to the pull of the earth. It expects demonstrative, audible manifestations of my being.

I ask you, how does the sun know to rise and set? How do the clouds know to save moisture and give back rain? Scientists have discovered natural truth but have forgotten to acknowledge who set these truths into motion.

Beloved, my voice to you is still and quiet. That is how I choose to reveal myself to you—Spirit to spirit.

I sent my Son, and the flesh became the Lamb of God. Now, enjoy my gift of the Holy Spirit sent to earth to comfort and speak my Word.

Many religions will profess a dialogue of extravagant proclamations. I will come to you in a still small voice that no one can take away from you, nor will you ever doubt.

Listen carefully to the center of your inward spirit wherein I dwell. I love you, and I want often to talk with you.

Draw away from the flashing lights of the world. Close your eyes, embrace my Word, and listen to my still small voice in the hidden chambers of your heart.

I want to speak to you. I want to speak! Amen.

September 7

Pure Mourning

"The steadfast love of the Lord never ceases, his mercies never come to an end; they are new every morning; great is thy faithfulness."

Lamentations 3:22-23 RSV

Beloved, I am well pleased with you, for you have rested your weary heart at the foot of my throne. You already know it is impossible for you to carry your present burden of life alone, and you daily kneel before Me and rest your broken heart at my feet. Beloved dear one, there is no other way for you to survive but to allow Me to sustain you through these miserable and lonely months of your widowhood.

Beloved, I love you! Every heartbeat of yours is recorded in my book. Every tear is noticed and saved. My angels hasten to your side when the tears of your soul mist your eyes and cloud your vision.

In all of your sorrow and deepest despair, I am here with you. I feel every pinch of your soul and each stab of the heart. I am nursing your wounded spirit.

I know it seems long, never ending, and impossible to endure, but I am healing and making you whole.

Please, be patient with yourself. You have no apologies to make to anyone! No effort in mourning is wasted when yielded to Me.

Yesterday's pain may be bandaged and repaired, but you abruptly are faced (seemingly out of nowhere) with new pain, fresh heartache, beginning remembrances that are yet surfacing like razor blades against the lining of your soul.

Beloved, I am sorry for your pain—but I promise you Lamentations 3:22-23. My mercies are new every morning!

In this supernatural walk, you are finding and discovering a hiding place in Me, a place of refuge, an immovable rock to your soul that you will literally retain for eternity.

All of this pain does have gain within the private cubicles of your soul and our eternal and everlasting relationship.

You must cling to my new mercies every morning through this present season of mourning. You will learn the "habit" of completely depending on Me for your life—and meeting with Me early in the morning to set your table for the day.

Rise early and drink from my fresh wells of Living Waters—before the world rises. This is my weapon of strategy for you.

Allow my new mercies to apply fresh oil and soothing salve to your bruised, but healing, soul before new wounds of the day come unexpectedly.

I love you. You cannot outgive Me. You have gained fine treasures already in your heart by drawing closer and closer to Me. These fine treasures have more eternal wealth in them than earthly happiness can hold.

You have an edge on heaven that many around you will never experience on

continued

earth. These heavenly jewels come with a great price—Jesus' blood and your heartache; but, because you have looked to your healer, I have transformed and crystallized every tear into a jewel of eternal hope, love, and goodness that reflects the face of Jesus. You are being conformed into the image of Jesus Christ.

Someday, in time, when the razor blade moments pass and you become comfortable with my destiny for the rest of your life, you will realize what a changed and dynamic person you have become in Jesus Christ. You will see the fruits of your *pure mourning* bearing, producing, and feeding others in a most fruitful, victorious, and abundant life on earth.

You will serve with a strength and fortitude that comes only from Me, and I will use you to pray with and touch many with the glimmering light of the life of Jesus in you, gained so very much through those worst of times.

My promise to you is that because you have yielded your mourning to Me, not one tiny speck of your pain has gone for nothing. I have deposited your submitted pain and redeposited in your earthly vessel my presence, my Spirit, and my "jewels of the soul" that will be you for all of eternity! Amen.

September 8

To Die Is Gain

"For to me to live is Christ, and to die is gain."　　　　*Philippians 1:21 KJV*

For you to live on earth is to be always looking into a mirror, seeking to see in you the reflection of Jesus in spirit and in truth of heart.

True, some days the mirror is smudged or dirty. It can even be cracked or shattered. Your life is, nonetheless, your attempt to seek Me, please Me, obey my commandments, and to see Jesus in yourself and others.

Now, life can be good! Walking in my love and blessings of prosperity can be a joy. I can enable you by my Spirit to live life abundantly as you cast all of your cares onto Me and allow Me to heal and keep you whole.

Life in Jesus on earth is meant to be very very good!

To die is gain; so, you see, whether here on earth in the flesh or here in heaven in the spirit—either is with Me and both are good.

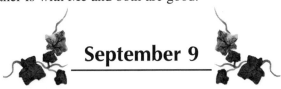

September 9

Be Not Afraid!

"In God, whose word I praise, in God I trust; I will not be afraid. What can mortal man do to me?"   *Psalm 56:4 NIV*

Be not afraid! This is the key to successfully winning battles with the enemy and not being "pulled down" emotionally into oppression and discouragement.

The enemy attacks and stirs the situation that tempts fear into rising up. What do you have to fear when your King of Kings and Lord of Lords has already defeated the enemy?

There is no contest unless you entertain fear and allow the army of the enemy to march onto your land and intimidate your soul.

If you would comprehend how BIG my army of hosted angels is, you would never fear and only LAUGH at the enemy's suggestion to do battle. He is an old fool! Rebuke him and be gone with him. Your King is Jesus Christ, the Son of the Living God!

September 10

Love

"Love never fails."   *I   Corinthians 13:8 NIV*

My game of life has one rule—*LOVE*. The rule book is a precept-by-precept explanation of the one golden rule which is LOVE.

My Word is my love letter to the nations and to my people. In my book is contained the unfolding revelation of my love for my creation, mankind.

Love is eternal. It never dies, and it never fails.

Now, the world's rules and Kingdom's rules to the game of life are different. If you play by worldly standards, you will believe that love can fail. If you play according to my plan book and coaching, you only serve to prove the absoluteness, faithfulness, and undying nature of LOVE!

True love never ever counts the cost—never—and it never ever dies or fails to supply the need. Never, for all of eternity, will or can love end. Never!

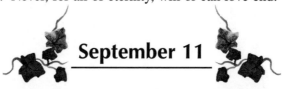

September 11

Cushion Buffer

"Forbearing one another in love."   *Ephesians 4:2 KJV*

When you forbear one another in love, you live not like a prickly porcupine, always ready to poke and pierce your neighbor in defensive air and attitude. No. Rather, you are to be a big spongy cushion that acts as a buffer when another's evil spews from the mouth.

The world will always have wickedness about you, for men are prone to speak out the corruption of their hearts and their offenses against one another. You cannot control the lock on another's lips, but you do have the key to your own. My key is Ephesians 4:2. If you are forbearing one another in love, then you are like a sponge that is able to draw in another's woes and then squeeze them out at the feet of Jesus—without retaining its sinfully tainted moisture.

The world around you needs you. It craves your patience and envies the padlock across your lips.

You need to realize that you are my buffer. Offenses hit you, but you do not strike back. You are a living buffer zone because all around you defenses are not set up. You do not have to return evil for evil!

You are my big foam rubber cushion. Another's irritability does not ignite your fire of wrath. It only kindles intercessory prayer. A true intercessor who stands in the gap must forbear and be the absorbent sponge. Somebody in this earth has to stand in the gap in behalf of his generation. Some intercessor must forbid to take offense, refuse to strike back in the flesh, and empty and squeeze out the burden of mankind in prayer before Me.

Others around you know that you are my *cushion buffer.* They will use you to empty their wrath. You will not intimidate their expressions of evil. It may appear disrespectful, but, in truth, it is releasing ground in which you are given access to intercede.

The hidden things of man's heart, once exposed and expressed, can be labeled and carried by the intercessor to my throne room.

As you forbear another's poison, remember and say, "I have legal right to absorb and empty this before my Father. Now, He can clean and scrub the filth of heart manifested before me. Have mercy, oh, God, have mercy!"

My intercessor is a sponge, a buffer, and a big foam rubber pad—a cushion of love to the wearied soul. Amen.

September 12

Children's Children

"Children's children are the crown of old men; and the glory of children are their fathers."   *Proverbs 17:6 KJV*

When all is said and done, what measure is a man's wealth in face of the grave? Can a man take his bank account with him? What comfort are jewels on the last day of earthly life?

An old man's crown is his *children's children*. Offspring is an inheritance left to earth—particularly righteous seed.

If a man's faith can be passed on to his children's children, then that man has left an invaluable inheritance to earth.

He can behold from heaven his own blood line and watch his inheritance pass on my Spirit to the next generation—from generation to generation.

Abraham has beheld his children multiplied century to century as my Spirit has given birth to father, to son, and to grandson in my faith.

Fathers, children are your glory! They are your own seed planted within earthen soil. They are your contribution to earth's continuance. They are your heritage left to perpetuate your own wisdom and understanding of life.

Glory in your children! You cannot take them with you—but they can follow you.

In heaven, you will fully understand the eternal significance of your contribution to my plan through your righteous seed! Amen.

September 13

My Word

"For you have magnified Your Word above all your name."

Psalm 138:2 NKJV

I am *my Word.* We are One. Father, Son, and Holy Spirit—we are One. We are my Word. We are One.

Jesus Christ is the Living Word sent to earth to manifest the Word in flesh and blood, to walk and talk my Word, to demonstrate in power my Word.

We are One. We breathe together. We sing together—always in perfect harmony and agreement. We are One.

"In the beginning was the Word, and the Word was with God, and the Word was God." John 1:1, KJV.

In heaven, you will see my Word living and breathing like ornaments on a tree that are alive. The ornamentation of my dwelling place is my Word. My Word adorns your mansion, drips from my trees, lines my paths.

My Word is alive. Just as you are alive in the flesh on earth, so, also, my Word is alive in spirit in heaven.

My Word has power and authority, and my Word in your mouth can defeat every foe. My Word is your ammunition available to be used against impending danger. Your enemy understands the authority of my Word. He can only flee in its presence.

My Word is a two-edged sword from your lips. It takes no carnal might but faith to speak. Demons unseen to your eye tremble and run away like scared rats when my Truth is spoken from your lips. Ambushes arranged against you scatter before their execution because of my Word spoken through your lips.

We are One—my Word and I—for you to enjoy, understand, and utilize for your eternal life. Amen.

September 14

Boxing Match

"Let not the foot of pride come against me, and let not the hand of the wicked remove me."   **Psalm 36:11 KJV**

Who is your deliverer? Upon whom do you call when another human being seeks to crush your spirit? When evil is lashed out at you through the lips of a fellow comrade, a daily associate, what course can you take?

I tell you, when evil raises its ugly head against you, first cry out to Me and pray! The foot of pride shall be stopped against you. The hand of the evil doer will be held back.

It is difficult to understand why a child of mine would be cruel to another, but unseen foes lurk beneath deceiving smiles and fake hellos. There are those who are tormented by the evil one, and they know only to lash out at the good.

Anger is cruel when its attempt is to strangle a fellow child of mine. This originates from the pit of hell. Do not fight back and entangle yourself with demonic ropes.

No. Come to Me and pray. Together, we will wrestle the distorted mind and noose the instigator of the attack.

This is not a flesh and blood war. Choose carefully your words to the foe, and allow Me to work to loosen the unseen chains of bondage which harass your enemy.

Do not allow your human emotion to be drawn into this ring where a *boxing match* will follow. Keep your heart clean. Always, daily, forgive. Use this circumstance as an opportunity to pray for the frenzied soul.

This aggression has really nothing to do with you and everything to do with Me. You pray. I will work. Most of all, do not go into the ring! In refraining from this temptation, your foe is forced to box Me, and I always win! Amen.

September 15

Do Not Fret!

"And the Lord, he it is that doth go before thee; he will be with thee, he will not fail thee, neither forsake thee: fear not, neither be dismayed."

Deuteronomy 31:8 KJV

Please, *do not fret!* Where is your faith? Replace fretting with faith. You know better than to worry!

I will provide your strength. My strength in you will increase, and my anointing will flow in your situation.

I have written the last chapter. I know how the story ends. If you STAND IN FAITH, you, too, will be assured of a happy ending, and you will quit fretting about like a chicken in a fuss over her ruffled chicks, scared by the big bad wolf on the outside of the fence.

I tell you, my fence of protection 'round about you cannot nor will not be penetrated as long as you persevere in faith.

Go about your life manifesting the joy of the Lord. You needn't have a care in the world! I am your Abba-Father-Daddy. I watch over you with my protective, guiding, consoling hand. Why fear or lack anything?

I am all sufficient. The more you trust Me, the more I minister in your behalf. Your faith and trust release my energy in your behalf, like pushing in on the accelerator pedal. Your faith pushes, and my motor of love responds! My Holy Ghost tank is always waiting to be used. My energies are absolutely eternally unending!

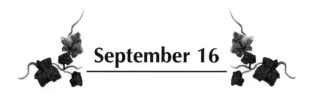

September 16

Bow of Contentment

"Do all things without complaining and disputing, that you may become blameless and harmless, children of God without fault in the midst of a crooked and perverse generation, among whom you shine as lights in the world."

Philippians 2:14-15 NKJV

Don't be a whiner and a complainer! No one wants to listen to you—especially Me! Good children are those who listen and obey without snide comment or complaint.

A squeaky wheel can be oiled. A squeaky soul is quieted less easily. The oil of my Spirit is missing in you who must murmur against my hand of provision and discipline over you.

I say, rather, to rejoice! Be thankful that I love you. Embrace your life and the circumstances you interpret to be irritating. Lasso with your rope of prayer those matters that need change. Leave with Me the disturbing consequences of others' rebellion, for you cannot live another person's life for them.

Seek only to please Me and to nurture our father-son relationship. Find your contentment in Me, in knowing Me and loving Me. The world around you will always let you down, but my Love Eternal can never disappoint you.

Seek Me to oil your joints of complaint with my Holy Spirit presence in your life.

Contentment is a gift from Me, your Holy God and Father. Contentment is my seal of approval. It means you have responded to my discipline and are obeying my will. Contentment is like the bow on a wrapped package, the last thing to go on.

Enjoy being content and uncomplaining! I enjoy you. Your *bow of contentment* brings Me great pleasure! Amen.

September 17

Calves of Your Lips

"Take with you words, and turn to the Lord: say unto him, Take away all iniquity, and receive us graciously: so will we render the calves of our lips."
Hosea 14:2 KJV

Bring Me your words. They are like expensively wrapped gifts, the finest of gifts. Every Word of mine pursed through your lips is a unique gift to Me. Apart from faith, words lie as dormant rocks, but spoken from your spirit man, sent directly zooming through the universe to my throne, they are like jewels coming alive and receiving divine breath! The emerald sings! The dead stones come alive and make music unto Me! My Words are riches hidden to appear plain and dead—only letters—but they give divine breath and transform into power and energy!

Your born-again spirit is the excavator of my Word to you. When you dig up a promise, and the gleam of its brilliance strikes you, the Word becomes alive, empowering your faith to believe and move mountains.

When OWNERSHIP of my Word has taken place, no one person, no measly demon power, and no situation can come in and steal your possession. It has been banked into your spirit man where moth cannot corrupt, nor thieves steal.

Ownership of my Word sets the captive free. Strongholds are broken when you speak from your lips my Word that you own. There is no greater power.

If you are trapped in the snare of a displeasing circumstance, then:

(1) STOP. Search for my promise that covers your need.

(2) Receive the Word into your heart. (This means ponder, write, rewrite, and memorize).

(3) Speak forth my POWER, and watch your atomic bomb have its effect. No foe can stand before faith.

OWN my Words, and SPEAK my Words. I will render to you the *calves of your lips.*

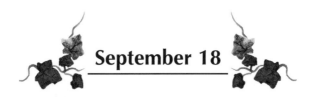

September 18

Holy Mortar of Grace

"The seed of the righteous shall be delivered."   *Proverbs 11:21 KJV*

When you instruct your teenagers, do so using wisdom: discipline, instruction, correction. You are to instruct your children by the Word of God. Withhold discipline until you are able to present scripture to support for instruction. You will, therefore, be building on solid rock, a foundation secure on the rock of Jesus Christ in both their hearts and their minds.

Just as mortar fills the cracks of a foundation, so, also, is my Word the mortar of life. I will fill in the cracks of their foundation with my *holy mortar of grace*.

As your Abba, Father, I, too, love your sons and daughters. I serve as Father-Abba-Daddy, and I work with you when cracks or missed spots appear. My holy mortar of grace comes shining through in teens' lives.

Do not despair, parents. When founded on the cornerstone of the blood of Jesus Christ, I can do anything. Nothing is impossible unto you who believe!

Fear not the shaky monuments that your eyes behold. I am not finished with my work! Many times teens appear the most scarred and incomplete creations. Do not compare them to adult figures. They are still very much in the making. It is at this time in their lives when, for the first time, I release my braces upholding them, to test their strength to stand alone. For the first time, they are allowed the test of wind, and, yes, even the storms must beat against their chests.

It is during this precious time that they begin to settle into realizing who I have structured them to be. What kind of building have I made them? What purpose do they have in my Kingdom? What color have I painted them? What merchandise of my Kingdom comes forth from their vessel?

Depending on the craftsmanship of the particular parent, some teens may settle immediately into their calling. Others may have crooked or broken bricks which must be repaired and corrected.

Remember, my condition for correction, sovereign and divine intervention, is a repentant heart covered with the blood of the Lamb. From this cornerstone, I am able to do reconstruction at low cost and relatively low pain.

You are not God. You struggle daily against sin and the world. You have tried to do your very best. Now, hand over your teens to Me. In faith, allow and request of Me to carve, sand, and rearrange. My holy mortar is an extension of the "golden thread of grace" that you have so faithfully, lovingly, and devotedly sewn around their hearts since conception.

I will be absolutely faithful in rearranging your teens to bring Me glory. Remember, the first solo flights are beginning to take place. The first tests are being done. Your teens are still very much in the making. I am yet very busy refining the construction projects. This is the time in their lives when loose bricks should fall out and when cracks and faulty crevices should be found.

continued

HOLY MORTAR OF GRACE continued

Please, be patient with your teens. Once you have released Me to inspect and refine, your job is to believe—to absolutely stand in faith unwaveringly. If I tear down a whole wall, fear not. My promise to you is that I will rebuild it. You are to praise, applaud, and encourage your teens.

Remember: discipline, correction, instruction—only by the Word of God. If you cannot offer a nugget from my Word, you do not deserve the privilege of correcting. Have them write it down, and refer to it when needed again.

Understand, this is a very trying, tender, sensitive season of their lives. Compare it not to your adult life, but understand it in the light of maturity, the phase of testing the bricks and securing the foundation. This is a glorious season in my sight. I love teenagers! It is with great and tender compassion that I deal in their hearts. Oh, glory! Oh, glory! Oh, glory! The "golden thread of grace" has done its work.

Now, allow the holy mortar to accomplish its work in the final stages of our construction project: CHILDREN! Amen.

September 19

The Joy of Your Salvation

"Restore to me the joy of your salvation and grant me a willing spirit, to sustain me."   *Psalm 51:12 NIV*

This is the deep-rooted cry of a repentant soul looking unto Me as his source for JOY and attitude to endure. This is the very key to humility—absolute and complete trust in Me.

Only I can restore one's JOY in his eternal salvation package. It is like needing the key to unlock the toy chest. The chest is full, but one must be able to get into it to utilize and enjoy the goods.

The key to *the JOY of your salvation* is in my hand, and it must be sought. To walk on ahead of Me without inquiry and daily relationship is spiritual suicide. One must walk with Me to enjoy his purchased salvation of JOY. I am the key! Amen.

September 20

I Inhabit Your Praises!

"I will praise You, O Lord my God, with all my heart, And I will glorify Your name forevermore."   *Psalm 86:12 NKJV*

This cry of your heart voiced in sweet whispers or shouted on top of a mountain . . . this, your heart's deepest cry, brings Me greatest pleasure. This is my love for you returned to Me! I bask in your love cries that glorify Me!

Beloved, I love you most earnestly and affectionately! No love on the face of the earth can compare with my measure of love for you!

Your love praises are sweet nectar to my lips, honey to my ears. They grab my heart with intensity and cause my blessings to fling out into the universe toward your home, your heart.

Remember, *I inhabit your praises!* Your exaltation of Me beckons my angels to your side. They are all about you ministering the power of my Word, the 2-edged sword, over you!

Beloved, find the secret places of my heart, and nestle within my comforting presence. Allow Me to soothe your soul. I love you! I desire to scrape away the crust and grime that the world has left on you and to replenish and sustain you with my power and presence.

You are the salt of the earth; so, allow Me to sprinkle you over those who need my seasoning to spruce and live'n up their daily lives.

Beloved, I love you. Church, you are coming home! You will inhabit my Holy Temple where no sun sets or rises—and where Jesus will shine brightly for all of eternity! Amen.

September 21

Valiant Warrior

"Through God we shall do valiantly: for he it is that shall tread down our enemies."   *Psalm 108:13 KJV*

In Me, you cannot fail because I will not allow failure to happen. The key is "in Me." If you have yielded yourself squarely beneath the Lordship of Jesus Christ, then you are protected from the enemy's snare.

I propose victory! I announce success! I declare you victorious over any attack of pain or disease. I announce you victor over all enemy holds.

It is through Me that you may live valiantly! When you have the Sword of the Spirit in your hand and mouth, there is no weapon that can penetrate you.

Beloved, when you live valiantly in Me, your life brings Me great honor and praise. Live according to my Word—precept upon precept—and I will never fail you in any endeavor of your life. To live a life of peace and joy is my gift from heaven.

True inner peace can only come from Me. It is the precious early morning hours when the air is still and the birds are synchronizing their praises to Me. A quiet anticipation of the day's labor nestles within the sovereign arms of the Creator. Peace is supernatural, a cloak from heaven wrapped about the heart. The enemy is still; the saint is valiant!

Oh, let your heart sing praise unto Me! The *valiant warrior* is robed in righteousness. The valiant warrior basks in PEACE, like in a pool of gardenias. My valiant warrior rises from the battleground prizing the heaven-scented peace of heaven on earth.

War is fought to obtain peace. My valiant warrior's clothing is peace.

I tread down the enemy, and my valiant warrior knows only to sing praises unto Me! Hallelujah! Amen.

September 22

Rich in Love!

"The Lord is gracious and compassionate, slow to anger and rich in love."
Psalm 145:8 NIV

Earthly men find it difficult to grasp my infinite and intimate, deep love for them. They say, "God is love," but they do not realize what their words mean.

Love, as the world knows it, is laced with sensuality, lust, and pride in the ownership of the loved one.

My love is as pure as a clear and cool mountain stream. My love thinks only of your best in an all around attempt to see you conformed to the image of Jesus Christ. It is like an earthly father never losing control and always disciplining and training precisely, correctly at all times.

I am endless mercy and compassion. I always am ready to reach an intervening hand to you, <u>never</u> <u>too</u> <u>busy</u> <u>for</u> <u>you</u>!

I am *rich in love!* I am an all-consuming fire of love! I always seek to uplift you and better you. I forgive you of your sins so that we may love one another more completely.

September 23

Children of God

"How great is the love the Father has lavished on us, that we should be called children of God!"
I John 3:1 NIV

You are my children in the literal sense. In spirit, I have born you as my sons. I rejoice in your lives and jealously watch over your coming and going much like a mother hen and her chicks. I hover over you with my wings of protection, and my pinions wrap their arms around you to keep you safe from the thief that steals, kills, and destroys.

I love you, my precious beloved ones! You are my family—*children of God*—and you are beautiful in my sight.

I love you beyond human capacity to understand. In heaven, I will shower down upon you your rich inheritance and lead you to my eternal green pastures and living waters where no man thirsts. I love you! I love you! I love you!

September 24

As for Me and My House

"But as for me and my house, we will serve the Lord."   ***Joshua 24:15 KJV***

For the man of God, I will brand this Word into his heart and across his chest to wear as armour. I will blaze this commitment into his soul, and he will stand uncompromisingly to face the world in behalf of his family.

Like cement, I will solidify my man's feet in Joshua 24:15. He will stand and not waver against enticing choices that will lead to foolishness for his family.

This man's voice cries, "We will serve the Lord!" stubbornly, relentlessly, without bowing to the world's standards.

This man greets the visitor at his door and discerns good or evil according to the measure stick of my Word within him. Some guests are asked to leave, others, not allowed to enter.

As for me and my house . . . as head of the home, his voice is final. There is no gray area or doubt on the part of a perpetrator.

"Evil will not enter here," is my servant's cry. "We will serve the Lord! We will serve the Lord! We will serve the Lord!" His family rests. There is no doubt, no wavering. The Lord Jesus reigns. All are at peace. The house is in order. Amen.

September 25

My Goodness

"God saw all that he had made, and it was very good."   ***Genesis 1:31 NIV***

I am good and can only be good, for there is no darkness in Me. Every intervention of my life woven into your life is good. (Good means bringing you no harm, but always blessing, richness, and righteousness from Me.)

My created universe was good, but the sin of man has corrupted my creation. I continue to give *my goodness* to earth through men who know Me and love Me. Remember, light chases away darkness. Good chases away evil.

My children, you are now the dispensers of my goodness to a lost and weary generation. I pour my goodness into you daily, and you, in turn, offer it to the broken world around you. This is as it should be. I pour into you, and you pour out onto others the goodness of your God! Amen.

September 26

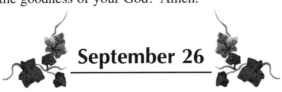

Earth Is An Allegory

"On earth as it is in heaven."   *Matthew 6:10 NIV*

All of *earth is an allegory* to what is in heaven. What is on earth is natural, yet the same earthly gifts are found in heaven, only they are spiritually alive. The only spiritual life on earth is found in the born-again spirit of man; so, in essence, man is spiritual, although your bodies are still natural flesh.

In heaven, all things that are on earth become spiritual. Take grass, for instance. It has no spiritual life on earth, but in heaven, grass is as singular blades of jade, shining and alive—yes, spiritually alive! It breathes the essence of God; and, of course, it grows perfectly, never needing a mow or trim. It is perfection because it is alive in heaven, spiritually.

On earth, grass is alive by the natural laws of earth: oxygen, carbon dioxide, the sun, water, soil, and the root system. In heaven, the earthly laws are dropped. All here thrives by spiritual law.

What you see on earth, all that your eyes behold, is magnified ten million times above and beyond what mind can imagine. Earth is a foretaste of my glory, a foretaste divine.

A foretaste divine . . . a sunrise, the crispness, the freshness of each new day . . . a foretaste of my freshness and regenerating spirit of heaven. You catch a twinkle of heaven's actual glory as the sun rises, in the stillness, the calmness, the purity of a summer's dawn.

Summer in her blooming peak of glory is a foretaste divine, another peek into heaven's glory: the fragrances sweet being emitted from blossoms, the creative, ornamental array of colors flashing their proud flags of color as the winds and soft breezes gently stroke them—a foretaste divine.

In my heaven awaits endless, unimaginable-to-you mega-acreage of flowers, entire crops of one blossom, colors, scents, beauty that cries unto Me always, "Glory, glory, glory!"

September 27

Rest Comes

"Come to me, all you who are weary and burdened, and I will give you rest."
Matthew 11:28 NIV

Jesus died on the cross to give you rest! Rest is faith in my promises and belief in the power of the blood of Jesus Christ against any enemy. No foe is able to steal your peace unless you worry, fret, or fear.

My rest is in knowing and understanding that no power is greater than the name of JESUS! Demons have to flee! Strongholds have to be broken! Demon spirits must flee!

The enemy first roars, and your fear opens the gate for his entrance to manifest in the natural human realm. He always first must announce himself, though disguised, and be allowed to enter. (He does not sneak up and attack because he is unallowed to do so upon his own.)

Rest comes in perfect faith within the redeeming blood of your Lord Jesus Christ. Amen.

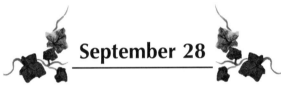

September 28

I Am Always with You!

"I will not leave you nor forsake you."   *Joshua 1:5 NKJV*

I am always with you! I never will leave you or forsake you—never! You can always call upon Me, and I will be near to answer. If you listen for my voice, you will hear Me speak to you. Just stop to listen!

I am mighty to combat the unseen forces that tamper with circumstances and situations unpleasantly. I am mighty to save you from the enemy's snare, hold, and attack. I defeat the enemy, I alone!

I love you and greatly delight in your love for Me! I bask in your love songs of worship to Me. They are beautiful to my Godly ears!

When you are disturbed or worried, I comfort you with my presence and love as you cast your care onto Me. I quiet your worries and sustain your faith. I love you. Amen.

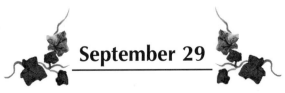

September 29

Secret Police

"And I will give you the keys of the kingdom of heaven, and whatever you bind on earth will be bound in heaven, and whatever you loose on earth will be loosed in heaven."   *Matthew 16:19 NKJV*

Binding and loosing—these are the keys that wield your authority on earth over demon powers and evil.

Through your lips is to come the enemy's command to loosen his grip on the attacked. The savage knows no mercy, shows no pity, feels no remorse—never! Your enemy is ruthless and heartless in his attempts to kill and destroy goodness in men's lives.

Your enemy will greatly attempt to steal whatever and whenever, given the opportunity. When you catch him in action, BIND him and forbid the assault to continue.

You are my *Secret Police*. The State of Heaven gives you the authority to command the thief to STOP and let loose his grip on stolen goods.

Your badge is your redeemed heart. Your club is my Word, like a two-edged sword. The thief is hand-cuffed when you speak my promises, and his deception is revealed. He is powerless before the blood of the Lamb of God.

All of heaven backs you up.

September 30

Angels

"Are they not all ministering spirits, sent forth to minister for them who shall be heirs of salvation?"   *Hebrews 1:14 KJV*

My *angels* hover over you like doddling parents attending to their newborn baby! They are assigned by Me to assist you in all that your hands seek to do. My angels accompany you at all times, and they literally intervene at moments unaware to you, keeping you safe from danger and harm to your body. They protect your belongings and watch over your possessions.

My angels are named, and they are called out by name in assignment over you. They listen to your words of faith and respond accordingly. That is why it is important to speak my Word over your difficult situations. My Word activates the protective host about you. My Word energizes, acts as fuel, and prompts my angelic forces to move and act in your behalf.

If you could see into the spirit realm, you would be in great awe of the extensive activities that take place 'round about you.

Your eyes would bulge from their sockets to realize the interchange that takes place between heaven and earth on your behalf.

I love my angels. They serve and worship Me—my servants who find pleasure in being your unidentified assistants.

Remember, though, I am a God of faith; so, also, my angels' protective measures respond to your level of faith.

If you could see my angelic screen around you, fear would never be a problem. Know that the presence of fear may distance yourself from the Author of Your Faith. Strive to believe and have faith in my promises! Angels enjoy being angelic! They do this best amidst an atmosphere of faith. Amen.

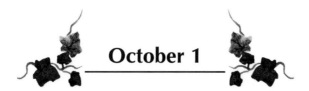

October 1

Marriage Is a Holy Covenant

"But from the beginning of the creation God made them male and female. For this cause shall a man leave his father and mother, and cleave to his wife; and they twain shall be one flesh. What therefore God hath joined together, let no man put asunder." **Mark 10:6-9 KJV**

It is a beautiful gift for Me to behold when a man and a woman live in harmony one with another. Their two hearts, joined as one, reflect the image of Jesus and his Bride unto Me. All of my universe is threaded with my love. My holy loom of sovereign intervention over your life sings the song of unity and joy over a happily married couple.

Your oneness and harmony reach my ears like a well-synchronized orchestra whose strings are tuned and horns correctly play their notes. Your romance and agreement bring Me pleasure.

The earthly life is much work and hard labor that requires harmony between family members. A family whose voice sings praise and honor to Me is a family set aside for my divine purposes.

You seek to please Me and bring Me joy as your Heavenly Father . . . then, love your mate and unceasingly serve one another clothed in humility, exalting one another in honor.

The marriage bed is undefiled, and your holy union is like setting fireworks off in the heavenlies. Man's outward endeavors are all very important to Me, especially your relationship with your spouse.

Seek to give joy and pleasure to your beloved spouse. My oil of anointing drips upon your bed and works always to soothe and minister healing.

I have given you your love to both cherish and honor. Never be cruel in any way or form to your sweetheart. *Marriage is a holy covenant* sealed before my throne, not to be broken or abused.

It is the holiness of your marriage that brings Me joy, for I am a covenant maker. Do not be a covenant breaker. Amen.

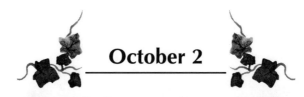

October 2

Gain

"But what things were gain to me, these I have counted loss for Christ. Yet indeed I also count all things loss for the excellence of the knowledge of Christ Jesus my Lord, for whom I have suffered the loss of all things, and count them as rubbish, that I may gain Christ."   *Philippians 3:7-8 NKJV*

Every brick of man's soul not grounded on the foundation of Jesus Christ will be shaken within the course of a life time. It is to your eternal profit that your soul be immovable in Me.

When others appear to be breezing through life lightheartedly and fancy-free, know that this is only an illusion.

All divine construction of your soul is permanent, reaching into the halls of eternity. No element of sorrow can be wasted on earth's side if committed to the Lordship of my Son Jesus Christ.

It is an apparent given that man's soul does not change gracefully or painlessly. No heart tremble is frivolous when I hold the chisel. Being conformed into the image of Jesus Christ is my foremost goal for you.

When you return to Me and behold my face, you will not grimace at the remembrance of earth's pain, but, rather, *gain*. In the twinkling of an eye, you will stand before Me, the Creator of your soul. It is for this destiny that you comply.

The imperishable jewel of your spirit will sparkle and reflect my glory as you stand before Me robed in righteousness.

October 3

Be Ready to Come Home

"Moreover, no man knows when his hour will come: as fish are caught in a cruel net, or birds are taken in a snare, so men are trapped by evil times that fall unexpectedly upon them."   *Ecclesiastes 9:12 NIV*

Life is cruel, and death can sting. The forces upon earth are not the dynamics of heaven. Earth is a prisoner to a curse over natural circumstances that I never originally designed to be in place.

That is why life is cruel. Death can come as a thief and steal a beloved member in the twinkling of an eye. This is the unmerciful truth of earth's right.

There is no victory for death because death is swallowed up by the promise of eternal life.

Heaven rejoices over that which earth mourns. The saint's entrance into his mansion is a glorious occasion, this side of heaven. My Holy Spirit on earth, my Comforter, comforts the widow and consoles the brokenhearted, healing the wounds of the soul.

Evil times fall unexpectedly. That is why it is important to carry your purchased visa to my throne at all times, bought with the blood of Jesus my Son.

People know when their time is near. I tell them. They often do not listen, but I do tell them. I tell others around them, also, but many times they do not rightly interpret my stirring within them and my voice 'round about them. I speak it into the universe: "You are coming home soon!"

Death can come unannounced. Always *be ready to come home.*

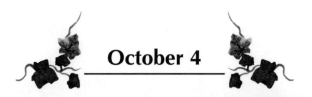

October 4

Repentance

"The Lord is not slack concerning his promise, as some men count slackness; but is longsuffering to us-ward, not willing that any should perish, but that all should come to repentance."   *2 Peter 3:9 KJV*

When you see the fall leaves blowing in the wind, your eyes observe the swaying of the tree limbs and the dancing, frolicking of my colored leaves. You perceive my wind, but, can you catch my wind? Can you store it in a jar? Can you hold my wind in your hand or take it into your home in your pocket? No. You see the effects of my wind only. You feel and experience my breeze across your cheeks, but you cannot contain it.

Beloved Church, I love you! You must TRUST Me as you pray! I do hear your cries and your intercession for yourselves and for others. I am able to take care of you swiftly because you hear my voice, you obey, and I deliver and bring peace. Yet, in my dealings with your loved ones who have not yet bowed their hearts to Me, you must trust, just as you trust in watching my breezes comb through a tree's hair, its glory of leaves.

My Spirit is working! When you pray for the lost, my Spirit does respond, but there is sometimes a preparation of the heart that you humanly do not understand.

Look closely into the person that you are praying for. You will see the leaves moving. You will see the manifestation of my Spirit dealing in their life, but some trees must enter into many seasons before they are ready to respond unto Me. I promise you: when the heart is ready, the *repentance* will come! You must TRUST Me in this and occupy yourself with loving Me and enjoying my presence. The preparation of a soul is no more mysterious than my wind whistling through fall leaves. I am stirring and drawing, and I am patient (long-suffering), not willing that any should perish, but that all come to repentance.

Beloved, **never give up** on the souls I have planted in your life 'round about you who don't know Me fully. I have planted them alongside you. Please, continue to water them with my love, patiently, as I am patient with them. Seasons come. Seasons go. Then, when the time is right, when the heart is readied, when the fruit of repentance is ripe: glory will break forth!

Beloved, I need you to express my long-suffering love to a crying world. Never give up on the seedlings planted around your garden that appear weak or disabled. Like the wind, my Spirit is moving and responding to your intercession for a lost world. I am unwilling for any to perish. Help Me by believing and rejoicing when you see the leaves stirring in a person's life. The wind of repentance is blowing. It will increase in intensity. The fruits of repentance shall come! Amen.

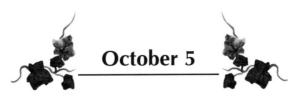

October 5

Trust Me

"Trust in the Lord and do good; dwell in the land and enjoy safe pasture."
Psalm 37:3 NIV

This is my simple command of life: *TRUST Me*—do good—and enjoy my provision for you in every way. This is the simple solution of a simple man.

TRUST denies all doubt, fear, and worry. TRUST announces faith in all situations and circumstances.

TRUST releases my Fatherhood provision onto earth over your needs.

TRUST keeps your soul in the bosom of your Savior, out of the world's grip and snare where you are safe, sound, and content in Me!

Human enjoyment comes in safety—good health and positive well-being over all of your needs.

I keep you safe!

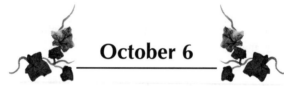

October 6

Life Insurance

"The Lord is my strength and my song; he has become my salvation. He is my God, and I will praise him, my father's God, and I will exalt him."
Exodus 15:2 NIV

This is the response of a humble man who recognizes the Lordship of Jesus Christ in his heart. The humble know from where and whom come their strength, taking no thought to their own pride in self-accomplishments.

The man of my heart always hears the song of my Spirit rising up from the voice of his spirit. This is the song of celebrating the contents of the package salvation. Salvation is my comprehensive *life insurance* plan for the human soul, already bought and purchased for you by the blood of Jesus Christ!

In the realization of who I am and what my salvation delivers, the true man of God bows in humble praise and adoration of Me, his God. I am highly exalted by the one who humbly cries, "You are my everything, oh, God!"

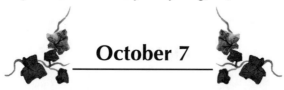

October 7

Servitude Brings Me Glory

"But he that is greatest among you shall be your servant." Matthew 23:11 KJV

If you want to be great in my Kingdom, SERVE OTHERS! The miserable, pitiful soul is the selfish one bound by chains of self-centeredness that disallows movement toward others' needs.

Beloved, I love you, and I want you to look like and act like JESUS my Son! I desire that your heart be flooded with my goodness, which is goodness enough to meet any need that presents itself before you.

Live not only unto yourself. Wood, hay, and stubble will burn up before your eyes at my gates of entry into heaven, but servitude unto others will be like shining silver armor that remains, stands, and goes with you throughout eternity.

Serving others is the attitude: "What can I do for you?" To be a servant is to taste the sweet breath of Jesus within your own throat.

Servitude is glorifying! Done in Jesus' name, *servitude brings Me glory* and honor. It is the opposite of the world's way. The enemy's personality is none other than fully selfish.

True servitude counts not the cost. Its JOY comes from hearing my voice say, "Well done!"

I love you, my beloved servant. I love you! Amen.

October 8

Family Baskets

"For son dishonors father, Daughter rises against her mother, Daughter-in-law against her mother-in-law; A man's enemies are the men of his own household. Therefore I will look to the Lord; I will wait for the God of my salvation; My God will hear me."   *Micah 7:6-7 NKJV*

The spirit of rebellion seeks to turn upside down baskets of families. The basket is turned, an upheaval of events and eruptions transpires, and my basic unit of love on earth disintegrates.

My families, stay together! Pray together! I will tell you that the enemy thrives on upsetting and emptying *family baskets.*

Now, what to do when yours has been targeted? First of all, I charge you, fathers, stand up to the enemy and disallow his dominion in your home! Take stand after stand against evil influence upon your children. Men of God, protect your family. Make it your business to contend with rebellion as it sprouts up in your young ones. Do not rest this duty on your wife alone. You have a voice of authority in your home that will cause the demons to tremble when you take a stand against evil seen in your children. Disallow enemy tampering! If you see, smell, or hear rebellion, address it! Rebuke it! Forbid its ugly face to present itself amongst your family ranks.

As man and wife, your affront towards rebellion will determine precisely the degree to which the perpetrator is allowed to infect and steal purity of heart. It takes both of you. Work together, and keep high standards for your beloveds. Your children are your heritage. It is your responsibility to address sin when its ugly head is raised.

The denial of rebellion's presence in your home will greatly increase the power of my love in your children's hearts. The positive will flow much more easily when the negative is dealt with and the firm hand of the parent says "stop!" to rebellion's voice.

Overbearing? Absolutely! Rebellion is like water seeking small cracks in a foundation that eventually gives way to large cracks, broken walls, and a tumbled foundation. Allow no leakage! Permit no cracks! Protect your children's walls.

The enemy, rebellion, has no right to come near your "basket of love," but he is ruthless and will make the attempt. Parents, stand guard, and the result will be a defeated foe and an abounding basket of fruitfulness—your family!

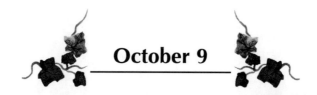

October 9

Love One Another!

"Return to the Lord your God, for he is gracious and compassionate, slow to anger and abounding in love."   *Joel 2:13 NIV*

This is how I want you to be—created in my image. I would have you be gracious, compassionate, slow to anger, and abounding in love. These are the characteristics of Jesus your Lord exemplified through your unique personality.

I desire to fill you with tender mercies toward all men so that even when they attempt to offend you, your loving compassion is stronger, and your response is one of gracious understanding and forgiveness.

Be like Me—slow to anger. Your anger works not the righteousness of God.

I want only that you love one another tenderly, fervently, and with a pure heart.

Little children, *LOVE one another!*

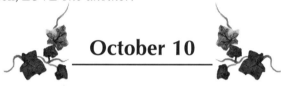

October 10

Be Still

"Be still, and know that I am God; I will be exalted among the nations, I will be exalted in the earth."   *Psalm 46:10 NIV*

There are times when all you should do is stop and *be still* before Me, especially in the gathering of the congregation when my Spirit is moving amongst you. There are times when I desire you to be absolutely still before Me so that you can hear my voice.

The world is always speaking, yelling, and bringing diversions away from my voice. One must listen carefully to discern my voice. Be not afraid of silence! There is a hidden treasure of beauty wrapped in my cloak of stillness amidst the congregation.

I encourage you to stand in silence before Me. I will speak to your hearts—and then will you rejoice! Amen.

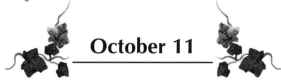

October 11

Increasing Brightness

"The path of the just is as the shining light, that shineth more and more unto the perfect day."   *Proverbs 4:18 KJV*

When you walk with Me, I pave a path for you that leads to eternity. Your steps are carefully monitored. Angels are assigned to your path.

As you progress up the path, my light upon you shines more brightly day by day.

As I deposit myself into you and you learn to walk in faith, then my light in you shines brighter and brighter daily.

This is an *increasing brightness* that continues throughout your lifetime.

The "perfect day" is my perfect will unfolding before you. All that I have created you to be is planted along your path.

Like a bright shining light, you grow to become "my will"—even unto your day of entrance into my Heavenly Kingdom. I love you! Amen.

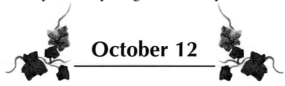

October 12

Songs of Praise

"How good it is to sing praises to our God, how pleasant and fitting to praise him!"   *Psalm 147:1 NIV*

My nature in you is praise. You see, I am song. I am music. I am melody! Praise is my name! Just as a young lover longs to serenade his bride-to-be, so, also, we in heaven long to receive your songs of adoration. They are sweet courtship to our ears! All of heaven resounds with praise and song!

Approach Me with *songs of praise,* and my heart opens up to you. Fill my halls with your song, and you receive my listening ear. Your songs of praise come directly before Me. My courts are entered via praise!

I cannot resist any praising child. He has my ear, my blessing, and my consent toward his desires of the heart. Our will becomes one as we melt together in love! Amen.

October 13

I Come to Heal

"I said, Lord be merciful unto me: heal my soul; for I have sinned against thee!"   *Psalm 41:4 KJV*

This is the cry of the repentant heart entering into my presence. It is only by my Spirit that man is able to see the condition of his soul, the true need for daily revival and healing of man's nature.

This cry of Psalm 41:4 is the cry for mercy to a Living Father God, given by revelation of the Holy Spirit. Surely, *I come to heal* not only the brokenhearted and deserted, but I come to heal each man's state of soul that he might be free to receive my gifts and blessings of good health and prosperity apart from restrictions.

You can do all things through Christ who strengthens you!

Greater is He that is in you than he that is in the world!

You are more than conquerors!

In praying Psalm 41:4, you are humbling yourself before your God. My response is to heal and then exalt you. Daily, one should confess sin. Daily, I should heal the soul.

The secret of your Heavenly Father is this: it is in the humility of Psalm 41:4 that you receive my favor and promise of verse 11:

"By this I know that thou favourest me, because mine enemy doth not triumph over me." Psalm 41:11, KJV.

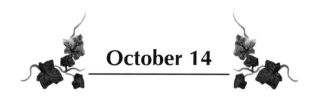

October 14

Rope of Love

"I have loved you with an everlasting love; Therefore with loving kindness have I drawn you."   *Jeremiah 31:3 NKJV*

From the beginning of time, I have known you and loved you. Always you have been in my bosom of love! Always I have cradled you as a proud papa nestles his newborn close to his chest. I kiss your forehead and gently squeeze you. You are my creation, my seed, and I love you!

My love for you is everlasting. It always has been and always will be. You cannot frustrate my devotion to you. It is like a rope weaved into one complete circle without ends. The fibers of the rope are my diverse aspects of love: my compassion, my concern, my sovereign plan, my will, my care, my protection, my provision, my prosperity for you, my package of skills and talents, and, yes, my very purpose for your existence on earth!

I place you in the middle of this *rope of love,* my eternal, everlasting longing for you. You are kept safe—eternally protected—in my everlasting love.

No matter how many times you fall away or goof up, I will always draw you back into my rope of love. If you fall ten thousand times, my everlasting love will entwine itself around your circumstances and draw you back into the safety of my arms.

Beloved, it is I who have chosen you! It is I who brings you back around to my awareness time and time again. It is my patient loving kindness that refuses to give up on you. I love you far too much to allow my rope of love to break one thread.

No! My love is perfect, strong, and nonnegotiable. No enemy will tear one fragment of my everlasting love entwined about your heart. You are my child, born and created by Me to do good works. I will never leave you nor forsake you! Only will I perpetually draw you with my everlasting love—because I love you, no matter what! Amen.

October 15

Be Bruised No More!

"The Spirit of the Lord is upon me . . . to set at liberty them that are bruised."
Luke 4:18 KJV

One of my greatest joys is bringing the healing touch of my Son Jesus to the brokenhearted. Jesus, too, had a broken heart—for mankind and Jerusalem—and for you.

I love to see the broken heart mend in the presence of my love. My needle of love, like a surgeon's, stitches up the wound, and my salve of the Spirit from heaven is applied.

If you have a broken heart, please bring it to Me. I want to heal you. I do not desire that you carry around that wounded soul to bleed and drain you of strength and, thus, productivity.

No! I have future plans for you, and your destiny in my hand is like a rose whose petals unfold and whose fragrance emits a precious ministry to others in my Kingdom.

Why waste days hurting and being of no use to anyone except the Kleenex company?

(1) Forgive your offender.

(2) Ask Me to forgive you for your struggles with unforgiveness.

(3) Give up the source of your pain. Set the wound at my feet to be healed.

(4) Believe in my promise of Luke 4:18. Jesus came to set you free!

(5) *Be bruised no more!* Be healed in the mighty name of Jesus Christ. Amen.

October 16

A Way That Seems Right

"There is a way that seems right to a man, But its end is the way of death."
Proverbs 14:12 NKJV

That which often seems "right to man" is not my will. Man so often pedals feverishly, but the wheels are off the pavement like an exercise bike—a lot of effort with no gain. That is because without Me, men's plans are foiled. They are tainted with "self-will" and "self-improvement." If the hidden agendas of men's hearts were revealed, few men would be left standing as good and honest. Few men have pure hearts unto Me.

The unfortunate outcome of a man seeking his own kingdom and building his own city for his own glory is: the way that seems right leads to death.

Life is a maze of paths intricately woven unto the day of death. For the man who has not paved with my stones, he will look back and see torn and upheaved pavement where he has tried so hard to build his own way.

At the door of death, man is given the opportunity to look back. Before Me, we take account of the earthly path he has taken. The world's riches and methods do not build the path that opens to the reward of eternal life in the end. For the Godly man, it is the beginning.

A way that seems right to man is based on personal opinion and personal philosophy. It is not safe because the foundations fall through at death's call. The only sure cornerstone is Jesus Christ. Any other building blocks in man's thinking will crumble at the end of the earthly life.

It is important to draw your building materials from my Word, not to create or invest or own or borrow from the world's supply. Every tool and material for the construction of your "path of life" is available in my Word. Wisdom enough for all ages past, present, and to come is stored within my Word. Every promise is eternal and infallible, unshakable for eternity.

I honor the careful and patient paving of your path as you allow Me to watch over my Word to perform my life in your life. Together we pave. Together we build, stone upon stone, mixing right materials of eternal value that cannot crack or deteriorate.

Any deviation from my Word's "specks" will end in death. All building apart from my plans is futile.

I love you! As you rely upon Me to be your engineer, I design and unfold the plan and then equip you to conduct the construction, stone by stone.

That which seems "right to Me" leads to life, where all investments are eternal.

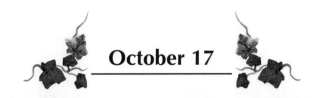

October 17

Accuser of the Brethren

"Then I heard a loud voice saying in heaven, "Now salvation, and strength, and the kingdom of our God, and the power of his Christ have come, for the accuser of our brethren, who accused them before our God day and night, has been cast down."   ***Revelation 12:10 NKJV***

The *accuser of the brethren* is the voice of the enemy against you. It comes in many shapes and sizes and is masqueraded to appear noble and true. Satan is an angel of light. He can only lie. He is only deception. He can only distort truth.

When you are being hammered against with resistance to doing my will . . . when others blaspheme the name of your God that you openly serve . . . when you walk in obedience and are scorned for every step . . . when you choose to take a stand and the world laughs, know that the "accuser of the brethren" is spouting off his lies . . . lies, lies, and more lies!

The spirit of condemnation will wreck your ship of faith. You must come to discern between my voice of conviction and the screamer's darts of accusational condemnation.

True guilt will produce repentance and your cry for the cleansing blood of Jesus. Accusation only produces confusion and torment.

Beloved, don't get off track just because you may hear the accuser's voice through others around you. Of course, he wants you stopped! You are a threat to his puny little kingdom on earth.

Others will try to stifle your attempts to broadcast the gospel. There will be those who question, scorn, and ridicule your spiritual sharpness. Of course, you will be assailed with criticism. Why would an enemy wage an attack on a weak and sick vessel that forges no threat?

Beloved, it is a compliment to be "accused," for that verifies the threat you are posing. Know who you are in Me, and the enemy will flee. Amen.

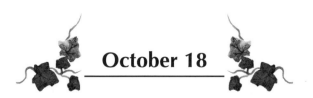

October 18

Feed My Sheep

"He said to him the third time, 'Simon, son of Jonah, do you love me?' Peter was grieved because he said to him the third time, 'Do you love me?' And he said to him, 'Lord, you know all things; you know that I love you.' Jesus said to him, 'Feed my sheep.'"   *John 21:17 NKJV*

Feed my sheep! If you love Me, the expression of that love will come in your outreach to souls. If you love Me, you will desire to evangelize, and you will express your love for Me to a lost generation. If you love Me, you will not sit idly, but you will seek out those who hunger for Me, and you will find my Word to feed them.

It is important to Me that you feed my sheep! Every man needs an encouraging word, a friendly "hello!" and a morsel of my wisdom. You are to be the bearer of good words to your fellow man. Look to edify your neighbor or to comfort the brokenhearted. Whether you are dispensing joy or concern, always you are seeking to feed my sheep with my Word of Life as you testify of my goodness in your personal life.

Even if you are weeping with those who weep, you are feeding my sheep as you pray together and comfort with my Holy Spirit's presence in you.

Beloved, your love for Me becomes concrete and purposeful when I send you into the world as my missionary. Anywhere off of your property is your evangelistic field of missions. Every word that comes from your mouth represents Me. Even in your own home, your constant ministry to your family is unending.

You feed my sheep daily! Hourly, you dispense buckets of my grain of goodness on your job.

You didn't know that a big smile or pat on the back, given in Jesus' name, is like an ear of corn to a hungry lamb?

Beloved, you are called to feed my sheep. Every hour of the day I prepare you to look beyond yourself into the harvest at hand. The harvest is great, and the laborers are few. When you say, "Lord, I love you," I respond by crying, "Go! Feed my sheep! Teach them to love Me, too!"

Perfection

"Every good and perfect gift is from above, coming down from the Father of the heavenly lights."   **James 1:17 NIV**

A sunrise is the reflection of my glory. My *perfection* can be observed in the colorfully arrayed beams of light welcoming and announcing the new day.

A sunrise has no sin. A sunrise is a small glimpse into heaven's home. The breathtaking eloquence of the sunrise is a partial peak into your future home with Me!

Perfection is always my gift because it is unattainable by man's efforts. When I intervene and give a spiritual gift, the giving is pure. The gift is pure, but the use of it becomes incomplete and imperfect.

Your knowledge and prophecies are imperfect. The gifts are pure. The vessels are men, so you prophesy in part and know in part. When you personify Jesus Christ, those moments are perfection in my sight through the blood of the Lamb of God—through the blood of my Son, JESUS. Through his blood, you are perfected. Amen.

October 20

Cast Your Cares Upon Me

"Cast your anxiety on him because he cares for you."   **I Peter 5:7 NIV**

I care for you! I love you! I sent my very Son to die for you! I watch over you as a young mother who nurtures her newborn baby. I am always watching and beholding all that you do!

I am pleased when you bring your worries and concerns to Me. You bring Me pleasure as I receive your anxieties. I love for you to *cast your cares upon Me.* In my hands, they turn into opportunities for miracles, openings for my Holy Spirit to intervene with power and might—and to conquer enemy holdings. I transform your worries into faith.

I watch you always, but it is because of your prayers that I intervene. In casting your cares upon Me, you are loosing, by your very own mouth and will, the power of God on earth in your behalf. I love to meet your needs! Amen.

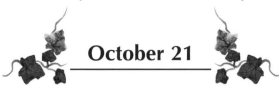

October 21

Doing What Comes Naturally

prophetic song

"And they sing the song of Moses the servant of God, and the song of the Lamb, saying, Great and marvellous are thy works, Lord God Almighty; just and true are thy ways, thou King of saints."　　　　　　　　*Revelation 15:3 KJV*

Doing what comes naturally to the spirit man,
　　This is my call to you, and now you understand.
Walking with Me and holding my hand,
　　Praising Me, now you understand.

Doing what comes naturally to the spirit man,
　　Singing praises to my name, now you understand.
I have created your spirit man to bring
　　The sacrifice of praise through your lips as you sing.

Doing what comes naturally to your spirit man,
　　Now you understand,
That doing what comes naturally to your spirit man
　　Is praising my name.
Now you understand!

Doing what comes naturally to your spirit man
　　Is singing praises to my name, now you understand.
Now you know my plan,
　　While doing what comes naturally to your spirit man.

I love you . . . I love you . . .
　　I love you . . . I love you.
Doing what comes naturally to your spirit man,
　　To your spirit man.

I love you . . . I love you . . .
　　I love you!

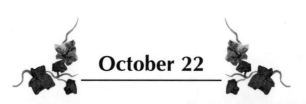

October 22

Joy Tracks

"Behold, God is my salvation; I will trust, and not be afraid: for the Lord Jehovah is my strength and my song; he also is become my salvation. Therefore with joy shall ye draw water out of the wells of salvation."   *Isaiah 12:2-3 KJV*

Your born-again spirit is a well of my salvation. Every cup that you drink from this well feeds you my joy, working to quench your thirst for happiness.

You need to learn to drink freely and frequently from your very own well of salvation that always goes with you! What is this gloominess I observe? Where did the voice of depression come from? Did I send either? No! Nor do they dwell in your well of salvation.

You have need of utilizing that which I have already deposited within you—my joy. Declare openly, aloud, for all your enemy to hear:

"God is my salvation.

Lord Jehovah is my strength and song!

I shall draw water out of my well of salvation with JOY!

with JOY!

with JOY!"

Beloved, when you do not have joy, you are short-circuiting yourself from heaven's already purchased provisions for you. Even in intercession, joy comes in the morning.

How can the world be drawn to a joyless Church? It must see Jesus' joy in you—sparkling through your eyes and formed upon your lips.

Beloved, *joy tracks* follow you—holy prints—that prove my Spirit's presence. Look behind you. Do you see "joy prints?" If not, run to your well of salvation and drink. Drink! You must have joy, or else the world will never see Me living in you!

Joy tracks must follow everywhere you go! That way, others can trail your walk with Me.

I love you, beloved. Amen.

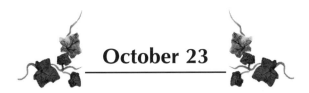

October 23

Promises

"God is not a man, that He should lie, Nor a son of man, that He should repent. Has He said, and will He not do? Or has He spoken, and will He not make it good?"   ***Numbers 23:19 NKJV***

I NEVER LIE! It would be impossible for Me to do so! I can only speak truth and seek to reveal truth and teach truth to my children.

What I have promised, I will perform! My Word is my Promise Book to you. As you receive in your heart a promise from Me, you then allow faith to lift it up as upon wings of the Spirit. Then, faith rises up to Me, and when I behold the faith before my throne, the promise is completed. Your only job then is to listen, watch, and wait for Me to perform that which you have believed.

These are "golden moments" when a promise is conceived and faith rises to my throne. It is like the miracle of a newborn baby!

Only unbelief will abort the child, and my gifts, once promised, die.

Beloved, regard not faith lightly. To believe in Me and my *promises* is a gift from heaven. When you have experienced my touch of faith for a matter, you then allow my Spirit to implant within the womb of your heart my promise. Then, faith's promise will come to full gestation.

A mother does not abort her baby because of impatience. A mother waits and walks through the pregnancy with joy and excitement, preparing for the birth and the outward cradling of the promise in the arms of flesh.

Beloved, BELIEVE! I will bring forth the birth of those promises, in Jesus' name. Amen.

October 24

Called

"Faithful is he that calleth you, who also will do it." I Thessalonians 5:24 KJV

If I have *called* you to perform a certain task, then I also will equip you to do it. I will not leave you without water to drink in the desert. I will not pump you up only to pop your side with the pin of disappointment and allow you to fall head first.

When I call, there is an accompanying divine excitement. That is because you have been on line in communication with Me! You receive your marching orders, and you are off to trot . . . for awhile.

Then the true colors of the task emerge. There are roadblocks to hurdle and problems to solve. There is the fatigue factor and the rubbing elbows with fellow cohorts about which the plans did not forewarn you. Your flesh begins to scream. Fear or frustration needles its way into your heart, and then your wheels become stuck in deepening muddy waters. You are at a standstill, and you ask, "Now, what's gone wrong?"

The dawn of understanding begins to surface after much prayer . . . somewhere down the line, my strength was taken over by your own self-strength.

If I call you, then I equip you, and no task is too difficult for Me! Just remember to rely on my strength, not your own. I will be absolutely faithful in enabling you to perform the task I have called you to do! Amen.

October 25

Flowers

"This people have I formed for myself; they shall shew forth my praise."
Isaiah 43:21 KJV

All *flowers* are a reflection of my glory. They sing of my praises as their heads are raised toward the Son of God. They seek light and pursue light. Apart from light, they wither and die, just as men apart from the Light of Jesus wither and die.

The aroma of my flowers speak sweet scents of praise unto Me, just as your own lips of praise glorify Me as you offer up sweet-smelling fragrances of praise and worship.

Just as petals fall to the ground and die to bring forth multiplication of new petals, you, as a grain of wheat, fall to the ground and die to your own self-will that you might serve Me in my will.

Your life is as a flower. You continually emit sweet fragrances of praise, and you are my seed on earth to bring forth the furtherance of the Kingdom of God on earth as it is in heaven, amen!

My people are as a wild but comely flower garden. You are a diversified people in race, creed, and gifts but not in doctrine of the love of Jesus Christ!

All across the land your worship services offer up to Me pristinely designed flower arrangements prepared to say, "Father, Abba, Jesus, Holy Spirit, I love you!"

You are a sweet-smelling sacrifice to Me as you lay down your life for your friends. The fragrance of earthly flowers are the foretaste of the fragrance of heaven.

Flowers grow for only one purpose: to give GLORY to God. You, too, need to live out one purpose on earth, that is to give GLORY to Me in all you say and all that you do.

Live to bring Me GLORY! This is the purpose of flowers on earth. Their color, their beauty, and their praises are all a foretaste divine reminding mankind of his human nature and frailty. The purpose of my creation is to shine in beauty and give GLORY in all that you do!

October 26

Art of Womanhood

"Who can find a virtuous woman? for her price is far above rubies."
Proverbs 31:10 KJV

In Proverbs 31:10, I describe the *art of womanhood*. The holy woman of God is not idle. She swiftly works with her hands diligently because of that which is born in her heart: holy womanhood.

A holy woman of God possesses a meek and quiet spirit that sings to her heart's content in the pleasures of her home. She reigns in her home. Her children and family are her calling. She rejoices in time to come because her heart is pure and understands my call of servitude found within the walls of her own home.

A pure woman of God will see with eyes of deep spiritual understanding that my greatest gifts to her are linked to family. She will uphold her loved ones in prayer-support throughout her life.

The art of womanhood comes in discovering who she is in Jesus Christ and what my purpose and plan for her life is. It hinges on priority. She is first and foremost my sweet and dear child. She offers herself to Me in daily communion and brings her Father's heart joy and pleasure in her worship and love songs to Me, morning by morning.

When I join her with a man, her next priority becomes her servitude unto him. She understands my calling to her as a humble servant to aid and uphold this man in both prayer and physical nurturance. They must serve one another, enabling one another to be better servants in my Kingdom.

Her third priority then becomes the fruit of his loins. She bears him children. They lovingly, humbly, receive my gifts—children—and wrap their caring arms 'round about them for the rest of their days on earth, giving their lives over unto prayer in behalf of these children.

The holy woman of God enjoys divine contentment when her heart is pure and able to receive my simple plan of family into her home. She is the woman that glows and thrives on being all that she can be in Jesus Christ by humbling herself to serve her husband and their offspring with all of her heart. She finds contentment in her husband, in her family, and contentment within the walls of her home.

My plan is the architect's original drawing and fulfills my dream by building the family as designed. Now, I never said this purity of blessed womanhood could not apply to the single, the divorced, the separated, or the woman working a career. Many women will vary widely in circumstances. I will anoint the art of womanhood as I am sought. My perfect dream and plan for purity of heart is possible to all Godly women who call upon my name. Amen.

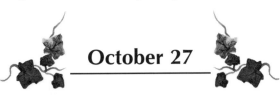

October 27

A Wise Son

"The father of a righteous man has great joy; he who has a wise son delights in him. May your father and mother be glad; may she who gave you birth rejoice!"
                                                                    Proverbs 23:24-25 NIV

There is no greater reward on the face of the earth than bestowing righteous seed. The opposite is, of course, also true. There is no deeper grief than to behold foolishness and dishonor in a grown son who has been trained to know better.

A man looks at his son and sees a reflection of himself. His heart is encouraged and thrilled when the son excels the father in strength, character, wisdom, and eternal insight.

A man's soul swells with the goodness of satisfaction when he beholds *a wise son* pursuing his own manhood in wisdom and sincerity.

The gifts of the soul are imperishable and impossible to purchase monetarily. A wise son invests jewels of wealth into the hearts of his parents. These can be treasures that live eternally in the born-again man.

A man can die penniless, but richer than 12 pounds of gold in heart, if his son has grown up as a solid and healthy giving tree of love that extends its branches to help others.

A wise son makes a dad's wealth, the richness of which can never be torn away, stolen, moth eaten, or corrupted.

Who can weigh the value of a wise son? Only the heart of a parent can answer. Only the heart can know—only the heart.

October 28

Scripture

"For everything that was written in the past was written to teach us, so that through endurance and the encouragement of the scriptures we might have hope."   *Romans 15:4 NIV*

You are blessed! You have the written, recorded Word of my love to study and cherish day in and day out. You do not have to be dependent upon ancestors or scribes to teach and preach your Heavenly Father's love for you. No. All you have to do is open my Book, and you can pour yourself into the annals of my Kingdom history.

Your very ancestors' lives are recorded in my Book! You can eat, breathe, and live their lives by studying my Word.

Their lives of faith should inspire you to have your own walk of dynamic faith with Me!

Beloved, *scripture* is the music of your soul. You will discover your Father's heart when you draw close to my Holy Word. Amen.

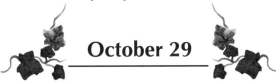

October 29

I Am Joy

"I will be joyful in God my Savior."   *Habakkuk 3:18 NIV*

This is the declaration of my mature man, the decision to live life in my Joy (or in other words, in my manifested presence). Life with Me is a decision, and it is your decision. You determine your walk with Me. The measure of Me you desire is the measure I dispense.

It is true revelation to understand that *I am JOY*. Amidst an onslaught of enemy lies, one must stand firm and shout unto the enemy's hosts, "As for me, I will be joyful in God my Savior."

This man of revelation understands the meaning of "Savior." He knows that his Savior will indeed save him from the enemy's plot against him; therefore, he will rejoice.

The enemy will fear his JOY and flee because following after JOY is the Savior's sword to save, crying, "Flee, flee, flee!"

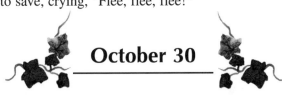

October 30

Hedge Builder

"And I sought for a man among them, that should make up the hedge, and stand in the gap before me for the land, that I should not destroy it: but I found none."
Ezekiel 22:30 KJV

I sought for a man who would stand in the gap, and I found you! I sought for a man who would make up the hedge, who would build walls around my people, and I found you! I sought for a man who would press his ear close to my heartbeat and understand my need for intercession in behalf of my children, and I found you!

Beloved, you have heard my call to pray for your nation. You have hearkened to my voice, and you have listened to my cares and concerns for the lost.

You have given over your time unto Me, hour heaped upon hour, to stand in the gap for your fellow man.

You have taken my sword and pressed into the fears and strongholds of enemy territory.

Beloved, you are my *hedge builder,* and I love you! Build and construct my walls around my people! Construct the hedge of intercession that will protect my Church and allow her to flourish within my protection.

Beloved, I love you! Without you, who would cry for the lost? Who would plead for the diseased? Who would stand in the gap and build the bridge between heaven and earth?

Jesus, my Son, is your intercessor. He is your example. He is your bridge, but I need human intercessors on earth to fortify the prayer force in my Kingdom.

Oh, to be like Jesus! He rose a great deal before dawn and went to a lonely place and prayed unto Me crying, "Abba, Father! Abba, Father!"

Stand in the gap between heaven and earth, and utilize my divine resources to build hedges around your church, your loved ones, your schools, and your homes. Build my hedges, and disallow the thief from stealing, killing, and destroying in Jesus' name. Amen.

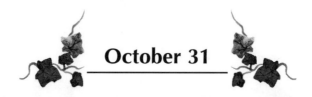

October 31

Prayer for Perfecting

"The Lord will perfect that which concerns me; Your mercy, O Lord, endures forever; Do not forsake the works of Your hands." **Psalm 138:8 NKJV**

Psalm 138:8 is an excellent prayer when you feel concern about Me accomplishing a certain task through you. You may speak this *prayer for perfecting:*

Beloved Heavenly Father, I thank You for perfecting that which concerns me.

For all the frayed edges and undone matters, I entrust unto You their completion.

Your mercy, O Lord, endures forever!

Thank You for forgiving me of procrastination and worry.

Empower me by your Spirit to accomplish that which You have placed before me to do.

Lord, thank You for not forsaking the works of your hands through my hands.

Thank You for never giving up on me.

I praise You for enabling me to do above and beyond what I could ask or think!

In Jesus' name. Amen.

November 1

Bull's Eye Life

"Thy will be done, as in heaven, so in earth."   *Luke 11:2 KJV*

How do you know if you are in my perfect will? You know that you indeed are when you repeatedly hit the bull's eye. Imagine a target: darts (or attempts at life's pursuits) can be thrown at the target. You may hit far or near the eye, depending upon your accuracy and skill in correctly aiming . . . so it is with your walk in Me.

When you walk fluently in my Spirit from morning to night in good health, productivity, and prosperity, then you know you are walking in the blessings of my perfect will because angels have paved your day's path, and all things work together for your good and "fall into place" to benefit you and yours.

Out of my will, you begin missing the target. Mistakes mount up. Lack of peace enters. Joy diminishes. Condemnation begins to scream. You know you have goofed!

My perfect will for you will be doors gently opening as you simply and obediently take steady, faithful steps forward in my direction.

All you have to do is watch your mark to know if you have wandered from my perfect will.

The *bull's eye life* is what I have for every child of mine, and it only requires obedience and a listening ear to "flow in my Spirit" and take gentle steps toward my voice.

If you have not been missing the mark, and if your joy is strong and steadfast, then rejoice! You are walking with Me, and you are sheltered inside the arms of my perfect will for you at this time.

Love, your Heavenly Father.

November 2

Giving Comfort

"That we may be able to comfort them which are in any trouble, by the same comfort wherewith we ourselves are comforted of God."

II Corinthians 1:4 KJV

Your responsibility in my Kingdom is to give that which you have been given. The more you have, the more you give, in both talent and money, in both blessing and understanding.

If I fill your bucket half full with gold coins, I expect you to dispense them to others—utilize and invest their value—until the bucket is empty, so that I might refill your bucket with even more coins.

It is the same with *giving comfort.* As I deliver you and instruct you with understanding over the rough spots in your personal life, so, also, I am equipping you at the same time to be my instructor to another who is in the same rut.

Be not selfish with the revelations of my good news! On your tongue shall be readied encouragement to those who have yet to conquer areas that you have already mastered.

Let your leading be done with great compassion and mercy, remembering always my free gift of grace that has mercifully dug you out of the pit over and over again.

I require of you only that which I have given. Know that if I have led you down a path and brought you over the bridge of faith into victory, then you, too, will be required to lead and encourage others down that same path.

Never be selfish with my revealed wisdom invested in you. The price of pain is a great price. Be about your Father's business aiding and assisting those who also must learn Jesus' Lordship in all areas of their lives.

Be a willing vessel used by Me, and I will open and create opportunities for you to give that which I have given unto you. This is how my Church is meant to function. Give and give and give! Amen.

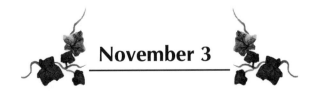

November 3

It Is Not Enough to Believe

"Then Peter said to them, 'Repent, and let every one of you be baptized in the name of Jesus Christ for the remission of sins; and you shall receive the gift of the Holy Spirit.'"   *Acts 2:38 NKJV*

My three steps into our Kingdom are so easily laid out before you in Acts 2:38. There should be no question as to the meaning of this verse. Once again, as in John 3:16, in a nutshell, I have given you my plan for salvation.

Jesus Christ is the cornerstone rock of his Church. He simply announces through this verse his three steps:

(1) Repent (turn from your old flesh and admit that you need Me).

(2) Be baptized (allow Me to circumcise your heart and wash away your sin).

(3) Receive my gift, the Holy Spirit.

The message of entrance into my Kingdom was preached by Peter and should be taught by all believing men one to another.

It is not enough to believe. Even demons believe that Jesus Christ is the Son of God! One must confess and repent. One must exemplify in obedience the Lordship of Jesus Christ through baptism. One must be filled with my Holy Spirit to be empowered to do my work.

To not be baptized would be like creating a car without a paint job. To not be filled with my Spirit would be like owning a brand new car without gas in the tank to make it run.

How long will a car last without finish? How far will a car go without fuel? Preachers and teachers, hold up my standard, my Word, and fully equip my children to be abundant and influential citizens in my Kingdom. Remember, it is not enough to believe!

November 4

Language of Heaven

"I will sing of your love and justice; to you, O Lord, I will sing praise."
Psalm 101:1 NIV

You should sing and make melody in your heart unto the Lord all of your days. There should always be a song strumming the strings of your heart. That song is my Spirit within you always wooing you to praise and concentrate on your expression of love to Me.

Remember, the *language of heaven* is song and worship and rejoicing. As you sever yourself from the world, you will be increasingly more able to hear the distinct and divine sounds of heaven echoing in your soul.

Listen for Me! I am the very song of your heart. Love songs flow between us, because I love you . . . because I love you . . . BECAUSE I LOVE YOU!

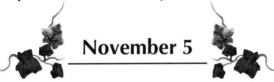

November 5

My Word Is My Voice

"Your word is a lamp to my feet and a light for my path." **Psalm 119:105 NIV**

The revelation of my Word into your heart and mind is like nuggets of gold stored in the pouch of your soul. With each new understanding of my Word, you grow more wealthy and rich in the spirit man.

Wherever you go, my Word should lead and guide you. My Word is a lamp for your feet. No steps should be taken in your earthly life without the equipping of the Word to sustain you to your destination. Your steps are guided according to my Word.

In heaven, you will rejoice to audibly hear my voice. Yet, presently, you have my voice in written form—my Word.

My Word is sufficient to meet every need in your life. Your generation may bask in my Word, bathe in my Word, and rejoice in my Word.

My Word is my voice, is Me—I love you. Love my Word!

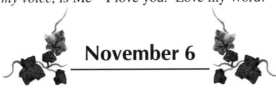

November 6

Secret to Revival

"Wilt thou not revive us again: that thy people may rejoice in thee?"
Psalm 85:6 KJV

I delight in empowering the average man to perform the impossible! Great honor is given to Me when a simple man releases my anointing and others are touched by my Spirit.

There are big names in my Kingdom and prominent ministries. They all rise to the dimension of grace given; but, oh, my joy, when a man with whom I have invested a small measure, performs in large measure. Then I am blessed in heaven!

I am a God of multiplicity. I love to multiply! The simple humble man offers Me his best, and I double his anointing to continue in his witness of Me.

This is the *secret to revival*. I am always searching the earth for vessels of humility—the common man who has the heart of a lion! When sincere humility mixes with repentant intercession in behalf of the body of Christ, sparks of revival begin to ignite. They literally find combustion deep within the inner working canals of my servant's heart.

When a humble man with a small measure begins to ignite my Spirit's fervor for revival, then is when I multiply with intensity the outpouring of my Spirit.

Pride quenches the Spirit, like a pitcher of water on a campfire, but the opposite is true of revival. The repentant servant-intercessor can tip my bowels from heaven and pour out tanks of fuel upon your kindled flame of love for Me.

Beloved, revival will begin when the spontaneous combustion of flesh and spirit strike the heart of your God. In true and sincere humility, revival will ignite because I love you! Amen.

November 7

Law of Kindness

"She opens her mouth with wisdom, And on her tongue is the law of kindness."
Proverbs 31:26 NKJV

On the tip of your tongue should reign the *law of kindness.* It is like a filter that screens out harsh words. It is a demand upon the soul to retain a clean heart and, therefore, a clean tongue.

A virtuous woman seeks to drip honey from her mouth. She looks for ways to sweeten the atmosphere with words of encouragement and good cheer to those around her.

Words have great power! They can make or break another's day. They are strong as a Cat bulldozer that can tear down self-image in an instant and leave it shattered in pieces for another to put back together.

A sincere woman of God chooses her words carefully. Her mouth is like a seamstress sewing stitches in people's hearts. Some words mend. Other words create new pieces of stitching that add to another's self-worth and character.

A ridiculing tongue is like a sharp razor blade that can leave hearts bleeding. A wicked tongue is filled with cursing and condemnation.

My woman of God learns to be a carpenter with her tongue, building up her home and constructing secure little lives in her children. Each good word is a nail added for a lifetime. She consistently builds with praise and admiration. Her super glue is Love that sticks forever because the nature of Love is eternal and never ending.

The Law of Kindness is a precious gift, and he who is married to the woman abiding by this law is a fortunate man, indeed.

Is it any wonder why the children of such a woman grow up to praise their mother? They are simply returning what they have been given for a lifetime— the language of praise!

November 8

My Name

"O Lord, our Lord, how majestic is your name in all the earth!"

Psalm 8:1 NIV

Oh, that my creation would recognize *my name*. Oh, that my children would know and be instructed to call upon my name above all names.

In my name, I give victory over the enemy. My name is backed up by all of heaven and all the hosts of angels!

My Spirit cries, "Come!" unto the churches.

I cry, "Come, Come! Come!"

At the sound of my name, angels rejoice, but demons tremble. The evil spirits are afraid of my name.

To dwell on my name is to be drawn into the finer things of life, to be drawn above the earthly realm into areas that even angels long to dwell in.

To behold my majesty is to have entered into the bosom of your Daddy's heart.

I am love, and I love you. Bathe in my love and be whole. Amen.

November 9

You Love Because!

"Love the Lord your God with all your heart and with all your soul and with all your strength."

Deuteronomy 6:5 NIV

This is my most important command, for from your love for Me will flow the rest of obedience necessary to secure my life of abundant blessing in you.

The only motivation you should have in your heart is to please Me because you love Me. This love alone will prompt you to seek my face, search my Word, and walk my path.

No other motivation suffices. Your unquenchable thirst for my Word stems from loving devotion to Me.

I love you! I do not manipulate your love or quest for Me.

YOU LOVE BECAUSE! This love erupts from your very spirit man and feeds into your soul. Your love for Me covers all circumstances and situations.

Your depth of love for Me is a mystery to your mind but not to mine. It is directly connected to your unique free will. You choose to love Me and how much. It is that simple.

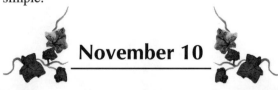

November 10

Purehearted Vase

"Now the purpose of the commandment is love from a pure heart."
I Timothy 1:5 NKJV

A pure heart is like a glass vase that you can see through. It has its unique shape designed by my hand, and it has its purpose to serve by holding up flowers for others to enjoy.

A vase is a servant. It has its own original beauty in the design of the craftsman, yet its purpose is to uplift the flower, accent the bouquet's beauty, and to be "upstaged" by the loveliness of the arrangement's scent. Others might acknowledge the craftsmanship of the vase alone, yet this is largely ignored as the servant yields its own beauty to humbly accent the glory of the flowers.

Man's heart is like a vase that I have created in my image, yet molded and designed to be a particular color, shape, and size. Each vase is my original cut of beauty, distinct from any other, lovely in its own right.

My call is to humbly lay down its own glory to be supportive of others. This is the quest of the pure heart. He who possesses a pure heart will not be driven with hidden agendas and ulterior motives. The person of a pure heart seeks to uplift another, seeks to edify others, looks to build up always and never to tear down another with open ridicule nor cynical attitude toward them.

A pure heart is the vase that daily is washed by the blood of the Lamb, lest scum build up on the inside of the vase and the clear glass becomes clouded with the wastes of water residue.

In servitude, there is a price to pay, and sometimes old water is left stagnant to smell and stain your inward vases. The sin of the world has a stench that is unavoidable, but my purehearted servant knows to apply and utilize the cleansing and forgiving blood of my Son.

The purehearted seeks Me to daily apply my glass cleaner to his inward man. Even when negligence produces scummy and putrid circumstances that you must serve through to the end, the inside of your heart remains clean and unscarred by others' sin.

A pure heart is a servant. In that servitude, I honor and promote my child, the vase. It is the *purehearted vase* that can stand alone in the center of the table with no flowers in it and still glisten and shine as the light of Jesus glows brightly through it.

Resentment and bitterness leave a scum, rings of use that grow unbecoming with time. The purehearted vase, cleansed by the blood, remains ever ready to serve Me and please Me.

Let my Light so shine through you that the world may see Jesus in your face —in your vase.

November 11

Love of the Groom

"And so were the churches established in the faith, and increased in number daily."
                                                                    Acts 16:5 KJV

I love my Church! My heartbeat is the very breath of my Church. With passion and zeal we oversee her work, her growth, and her love.

Jesus is Lord over the Church! His great compassion covers his Bride with arms of protection that reach across the globe. His love is the universal language that entwines all segments of his Church into one.

It is with wells of mercy that Jesus comes and pours into his Bride forgiveness of sin. The very blood of her Savior has redeemed her from poverty and sickness. Jesus clothes her with his own righteousness, and she stands before him white as snow, as sparkling emeralds and diamonds that reflect the glory of the Savior and his sacrificial blood of the New Covenant.

Before Jesus' eyes, his Bride glimmers as a gown of one million finely cut stones adorning her shape and announcing her beauty to him.

Jesus tends to the growth of faith and increase of his Bride with the heart of a groom deeming precious her every move. His yearning for her is like that of a seaman who has long awaited his lover's welcome and embrace after a lengthy journey apart.

Words fall short in describing Jesus' love for his Bride, the *love of the groom*. Human logic cannot contain his intensity of pain for her. She is his life! She is his love! She is his Bride!

In Fasting

"Howbeit this kind goeth not out but by prayer and fasting."

Matthew 17:21 KJV

In fasting, you have the heartbeat of Jesus pounding in your soul for others— not so much for yourself. Fasting is the only way by which some men will be saved. Many are wrapped with chains of the enemy, strongholds linked 'round about the captives. Only by prayer and fasting will they be released.

Pure fasting has intercession for the lost at heart. Pure fasting takes on a selfless cloak of righteousness. It is not self-seeking, but rather self-sacrificing. It is willing to sacrifice the fleshly pleasure and demanding appetite, the only pure motive from which the promises of Isaiah 58 of blessing will come forth.

In fasting, my hand, my supernatural grip, is beckoned to slowly place pressure within a stronghold's link, press it open, release it from the rest of the chain, and disintegrate it. Evil spirits are linked together. That is why fasting is so effectual. Spiritual law demands and gives liberty over satanic hold. Authority is reeled. I am able, logistically, to remove strongholds and minister deliverance apart from the captive's knowledge.

This is the only way deliverance can take place for an unsaved loved one prior to his own acknowledgment of salvation—through prayer and fasting.

When enough chains are loosened and cast away, then is when the captive is free to begin to experience my warm calling and drawing on his life.

I take one stronghold at a time. Sometimes I show you the name of it. Often times I do not. The light of the Word exposes darkness. You speak the Word over the captive, and I execute deliverance in his behalf. I am motivated by and respond expediently to the Word of God.

Father has been drawing your loved one, but the chains of bondage have prohibited him from moving. The chains must be addressed. I execute power and judgment. I am able to respond to my holy, heart-pleading intercessor.

I will not turn my face away from my fasting intercessor. I am bound by my Word in Isaiah to respond, deliver, and I shall. It is my JOY to loosen the bands of wickedness, to respond to your intercession, to deliver, and to set free the captive. Amen.

November 13

Listen and Obey

"To obey is better than sacrifice."   *I Samuel 15:22 KJV*

To obey my voice brings Me great honor and glory! For you to hear my voice is one accomplishment, then to obey is another. You are to *listen and obey.*

Beloved, I love you as a mother doe attends to her newborn fawn, in gentleness, but, also, defensiveness. My ears are perked to fend off enemies, to protect you from harm. To remain protected in the shadow of my wings, you must slow down and not go the pace of the world around you. I have a speed that matches heaven wherein there is no anxiousness or hurriedness.

Beloved, I love you! Listen to my heart beat. Draw in to Me, and press your ear close unto my breast of love. Listen to my voice! I am calling your name gently and slowly. I desire that we walk together. I will not chase you down as you run ahead of my will for you.

You will know you are walking in my perfect timing when doors open before you without ever first reaching towards the knob. My angels are equipped to go before you! They have your day's path lined with sweet-smelling rose petals, like a bridal's ascent to the altar to meet her groom. Each day can be a dream come true in your heart as you behold Me intervening in your behalf. Few are able to walk this blessed path because my people are lazy before Me. If you do not hear my voice, then do not proceed. Simply wait! Waiting is a beautiful gift to Me! It demonstrates faith in my ability to intervene promptly and efficiently in the right timing of events.

A good chef does not merely dump all ingredients into the bowl at once and mix on high. No, certain steps are observed as he carefully prepares the recipe according to his learned wisdom in cookery. In the same manner, I, too, desire to stir together your day in prestigious chef fashion. There is always a "best" way, and that is my planned and ordained path for your day.

In faith, walk slowly. I will bring your day's mission to you. In waiting, you will hear my will for you.

When you clearly hear my voice on a matter, then obey and go! Proceed in love, but remember not to go the speed of the world. If you will keep listening as you go, I will hum in your ear a precious love song, and you will know my voice as you know my way and my speed. Amen.

 **November 14**

To Have Joy Is to Have Faith

"Be joyful always; pray continually; give thanks in all circumstances, for this is God's will for you in Christ Jesus."　　　　　*1 Thessalonians 5:16-18 NIV*

This is my will for you, to always pray unto Me about all of your concerns and needs, for I, in turn, answer, and you, in turn, have need of nothing, nothing to fear.

The thankful heart reflects the nature of Jesus in you. Anything opposite of thanksgiving is not Jesus' nature in you.

Worry and fear will rob you of my Godly nature flowing from you.

If you give Me your needs, then I will answer and give you only reason to rejoice!

The enemy will steal joy and kill every ounce of good in you if you continue to entertain worry, doubt, and fear. Satan is afraid of faith because it immobilizes him and thwarts his evil plans against you. *To have JOY is to have FAITH* in my ability to take care of uncomfortable situations. Amen.

November 15

My Unfailing Love

"May your unfailing love be my comfort, according to your promise to your servant."　　　　　*Psalm 119:76 NIV*

This is the heart-rending cry of my servant who truly, deeply, and intimately knows Me, loves Me, and daily communes with Me. My true servant knows that my love for him/her is absolutely unfailing, undying, and inexhaustible. The true servant of my heart knows even amidst adversity that, without a doubt, I love him/her and would never forsake my anointed one.

This servant knows my voice and has spent time before Me listening to my promises of love and faithfulness. This servant has found the heart of his/her God, and nothing else will satisfy the thirst of his/her soul but my love. He/She rests in *my unfailing love* and dwells in my perfect peace. Amen.

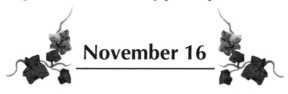
November 16

Roots of Hope

"Hope deferred makes the heart sick, But when the desire comes, it is a tree of life."　　　　　　　　　　　　　　　　　　　　　　　　*Proverbs 13:12 NKJV*

The nature of man requires hope. Like water to the body, hope is to the spirit of man. When hope is destroyed, the spirit of man dries up like a shrunken prune. The sparks of the fire die out. Little life of the soul is left.

A man's soul must have hope in his tomorrow, an anticipated desire for his probable existence and success.

When hope is shattered like a broken window, the heart collapses, and the protection of the pane of glass ceases. Weather elements, wind, and unwanted debris soon fill up the house with confusion and depression. The neat and orderly home of blessing and servitude becomes a cluttered, confused mess, and giving stops.

It is of utmost importance not to lose hope, and quick repair is essential. Hope, like windows, is easily repaired, and the heart, like a home, can be readily cleaned and reset into order. The very nature of hope is to spring back quickly and not hold grudges. The very fibre of man's soul is lined with divine hope. It is the nature of man to have good hope in his tomorrow and future.

Now, hope sustains the weary man and empowers him not to give up. Without hope, you would unplug the alarm clock and not get out of bed.

The beauty of hope is that it gives birth to the desires of the heart. When this happens, when hope is actualized and the baby is cradled in the arms of flesh—seen, touched, and smelled—then is when man becomes a tree of life.

The *roots of hope* sustain the desire, and new branches, leaves, and twigs sprawl their wide arms out to give shelter, shade, and beauty to its world. A tree has much to give; but the eye only sees its glory, not the serving roots of hope that labor hard in and out of season until the tree matures.

Every tree of life—each fulfilled dream—can give credence to hope's sustaining breath, whose purpose is to never give up.

November 17

My Peace

"Peace I leave with you; my peace I give you. Do not let your hearts be troubled and do not be afraid."   **John 14:27 NIV**

My peace is salve to your soul. My peace is the still sunrise peeping over a Colorado foothill. My peace is a fresh drink from a cool mountain stream. My peace is a soothing song of comfort to a weary and grieved heart.

My peace is still and motionless. It is void of strife and hardship. My peace is the quiet of a still summer night, the breath of a sleeping newborn.

Jesus' blood purchased peace. That is why you mustn't allow your heart to be troubled, for it is needless and wasted human energy because Jesus has already paid the price for your peace of mind and quietness of heart.

Beloved, I love you. No gift on earth can duplicate my gift of peace. No salve or apothecary oil can replace my peace. Nothing on earth compares to my heaven's peace applied to your soul, for it heals and makes whole your otherwise lonely self. Peace to you! Amen.

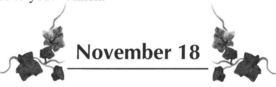

November 18

Contentment

"I am not saying this because I am in need, for I have learned to be content whatever the circumstances."   **Philippians 4:11 NIV**

Contentment is fruit from a mature tree that has stood strong and sturdy through many seasons of diverse weather.

The content tree has learned not to scream out in fright at the sound of a loud clap of thunder, for I have proven my faithfulness through prior storms.

Contentment clothes the tree that has weathered severe drought, for this tree's roots run exceedingly deep into the soil of my Word, and there is never an inward dryness or lack of drink.

Even the most bitter circumstances have not frostbitten my content trees in the dead of winter.

The content tree has learned in whatever state to be content, for the nurturance comes not from without but from within the vital supply of spirit-power rooted deep in the center soil of my heart. This is intimacy! Amen.

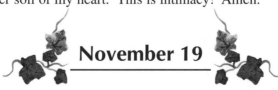

November 19

Dry Morsel

"Better is a dry morsel, and quietness therewith, than an house full of sacrifices with strife."   *Proverbs 17:1 KJV*

STRIVE NOT! Do not wrestle with one another. I have called you to live in peace one with another. Truly, quietness in a home or in a relationship wins merit over constant bickering and debating of critical or useless topics.

Beloved, be not ashamed when with quietness you clothe your home, your job, or your family. There are many times that saying nothing is your gift of love to the hour. Flopping jaws fuel the fire of strife and division. Learn contentment in quietness, for it is a safety net from the enemy's alert to pounce at an opportune moment.

Strife is poison to the soul. It kills joy of my Spirit in you. It separates close friends. It can spoil the loveliest feasts.

Hold your tongue, and you will hold peace, for a lashing tongue is sharper than a knife blade. It literally punctures the tender soul, and souls take time to heal, if they forgive. The unforgiving remain permanently harmed.

Fear no condemnation when you are quiet around strife. It is good to secure the tongue, latching it tightly, refraining it from freedom.

There are those filled with the enemy who come to harbor strife, come to "pick a fight." There are those who are "strifers" who seek out confrontation.

Open, verbal strife brings an onslaught of demonic activity to the scene.

In quietness, pray for the beloved one perplexed with frenzy and a heart of war. Enter into no battle with this one. Leave him be and pray!

A *dry morsel* is better than strife with steak. Given time, the angered and confused one will come to peace—especially as you pray for him or her.

Dry morsels are not a glamorous, enticing meal, but they sustain the relationship until better times.

Never apologize for quietness. A wise person understands its defense.

November 20

Rise Early to Pray

"And in the morning, rising up a great while before day, he went out, and departed into a solitary place, and there prayed."   *Mark 1:35 KJV*

The life of my Son Jesus Christ was that of holiness and chasteness. He was wholly divine and fully pure—yet he learned obedience through that which he suffered. You see, he also was fully man; therefore, his chain of command and resource of strength always had to come from Me in heaven.

Jesus had to pray because he was man on earth. Because he was flesh and blood, he sought my face just as you do.

Jesus had tremendous power, but his source was always Me. While in the flesh, he had to *rise early to pray* and call upon heaven, my glory and power, to manifest the miracles that came through him.

Jesus was a conduit of my love and power. The secret of the power surge is the prayer urge. Jesus refueled with Me. His human flesh required meat and drink but also long segments of time before Me.

In the same manner, you would be wise to schedule early morning staff meetings with Me. How else can you make it through one day of the world's stench? You need my daily cleansing and the refreshing meal of my Word, the Bread of Life.

How can we conduct Kingdom Business if we haven't discussed the day's demands and schedule?

The secret to effective prayer life is TIME. If my only begotten Son found it necessary to rise early and meet with Me, shouldn't you?

Power does not come without a price. You will seek Me and find Me when you seek Me with all of your heart. Every day can be a miracle—it is up to you, for I am always here listening, ready to empower and give my touch and presence. You must ask.

November 21

Your Pilgrimage

"Your statutes have been my songs in the house of my pilgrimage."
Psalm 119:54 NKJV

In the house of *your pilgrimage,* I rejoice to hear your praises and songs unto Me! Beloved, in my house—your Father's house—are many mansions! In your present life, you are housed in your pilgrimage home on earth, but your permanent mansion is in glory land.

Your pilgrimage is precious to Me! It is here on earth that you are granted the priceless gift of salvation! Even though you grow weary here and your feet callous and pain from the hard roads of earthly life, it will all come together in the end. Your eyes will behold your Eternal City whose light is Jesus, in whom can be found no darkness!

Your pilgrimage is sweet unto Me because this is your only opportunity to affect the lost soul for Jesus Christ. It is an eternal privilege to have taught the gospel of Jesus Christ on earth and to have testified of his grace in an earthen vessel!

Mankind is my creation. My plan of redemption is very precious to Me, so much so that I sent my own Son to die as your sacrificial lamb. Your home is heaven, and your pilgrimage is a time of "passing through" to your eternal mansion.

While you are here, serve Me and work for my Kingdom's sake! Influence others to know Me and love Me! Let your light so shine before men! It is in the days of your pilgrimage that this privilege is granted, for no unregenerate men dwell past heaven's gates. They mourn at the sight of our Light beyond the gate! Repentance is earth's gift. Please, hasten to live daily and spread daily my good Spirit to lost souls.

The clock always ticks. The sand always slides through the hour glass. You are here for a moment, in light of eternity. Never begrudge these days; but, rather, rejoice in my songs of your pilgrimage! I love you. Amen.

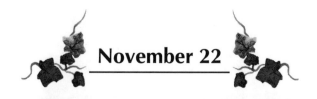

November 22

Belt of Goodness

"The goodness of God leads you to repentance."   *Romans 2:4 NKJV*

It is my goodness working in your life that brings you to repentance. It is my goodness that draws you to your knees and reveals your human heart.

Sometimes the circumstances that entangle themselves around you—the very ones that serve to bring you to the end of yourself—seem cruel and unfair. You may feel like a child that is repeatedly whipped, as if I am always after you!

Well, beloved, I take the consequences of sin and use the harsh circumstances to bear down heavy upon you—so that from your own weakness you will cry unto Me for my strength. That is my goodness.

It is within my goodness that I delicately watch my pressure gauge on your soul, allowing just enough to produce my desired results!

Beloved, I love you, and my goodness follows after you and examines your situations and motives. When they do not measure up correctly, I ring the bell of sorrow (a grieved spirit), and I wrap my *belt of goodness* around you, tightening until you cry out with the voice of repentance.

I enable you to turn around and go the opposite direction.

If my belt of goodness is buckled around you, then you will be responsive to my pangs of tightening, and you will be quick to say, "I'm sorry." Repentance is a precious, priceless gift.

As you value Me more, my goodness increases upon you—and repentance comes easily because you always wear my belt of goodness. Amen.

November 23

Strength to Strength

"They go from strength to strength, every one of them in Zion appeareth before God."   *Psalm 84:7 KJV*

This is what I give you in exchange for the old man and his worldly ways. I may have your will, but you have my STRENGTH. My desire for you is to live your life day in and day out going from one strength to another strength.

Weakness brings Me no glory! I desire you strong in spirit, healed and made whole, dancing and making melody in your heart unto Me.

My stepping stones of growth in Jesus are a paved path to heaven. Each stone reinforces you a little more and a little more. It is not my will for you to slip on a stone nor to fall backwards down the inclined path and scar your spirit.

My growth is steady and sure, like an onion skin that wraps and rewraps itself around the internal core of seed. Layer after layer of my strength I invest in you. This is why reaching age 50 shall be a great monumental moment of glory in your life! The world says that your body is older, achier, and less ambitious.

Ha! I say that my layers of strength and path of stone have you more empowered than ever to stand in fortitude against the enemy. He is a mere chase towards your dust at this point in your life if you have earnestly sought Me for a life time.

The second half of your life should be filled with my roses from heaven adorning your path. The sweet scent of heaven should be increasing around you, as you have forsaken youthful lusts and childish pursuits.

You are a saint of God empowered with wisdom and knowledge. It is good to grow old in Me—because *strength to strength* is power and holiness in my Spirit. Amen!

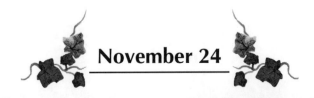

November 24

A Cheerful Giver

"God loves a cheerful giver."   *2 Corinthians 9:7 NKJV*

Cheerful giving is my attribute placed within you. I love to see myself in you! When you give unselfishly, you are talking and walking and looking like your Heavenly Father. Oh, how I love to see my traits in my children!

There is nothing I will not do for my giving saint. I love you, and I am thrilled with your pleasure in giving!

Of course, it is impossible to outgive Me, so your gifts only require my angels to respond with our giving back into your bosom and account!

A cheerful giver does not tithe because of obligation, duty, or obedience. No, a cheerful giver is like a bubbling brook, a mountain stream of fresh and invigorating water that lives to give and flows to meet the thirst of others.

A cheerful giver enjoys sharing that which I have given him. He understands that I pour into him, and he pours out to others. Ownership, to a cheerful giver, means "co-ownership" with Me!

A cheerful giver brings Me great pleasure! You are experiencing my heart in yours when you joyfully dispense of my goods to others. Isn't it fun, being a giver of good things? Kingdom fun is giving! It has a thrill all its own!

November 25

My Compassion Endures Forever

"The Lord is good to all; he has compassion on all he has made."
Psalm 145:9 NIV

I rain on the just and the unjust. My gift of life and prosperity is offered to many who despise Me. I am full of compassion towards my children. I send the warmth of my sun upon all, and the beauty of my holiness reigns down upon good and bad, right and evil.

I send my blessings of natural life, daily, the air you breathe and the water you drink. My life is in all of your physical elements. It is forgotten or unknown that I am the chemist who first formed, designed, and master-minded the universe!

My compassion upon the sons of men is sent forth daily in my consistent provision of the natural life. Were it not for compassion, earth's crust would have burned up centuries ago.

My compassion endures forever, but earth will not always remain. There will come the day, the appointed time, and then my love gifts through earth's hands will end.

November 26

High Praises

"The Lord lives! Praise be to my Rock! Exalted be God, the Rock, my Savior!"
2 Samuel 22:47 NIV

How often does your heart cry out with such humble praise? Daily, I would have you rejoice from the inner most depths of your soul, crying out my praises and your adoration and worship of Me! It is within the *high praises* of my Lordship that my Holy Spirit is released in behalf of your life to perform above and beyond what you could imagine.

It is not for selfish pursuit that I long to be worshipped. It is more so for my return release unto you to have notable mercy and grace increased upon you. Worship releases your Father's heart of inexhaustible attributes and escorts you into realms unpioneered before.

This, in my inexhaustible presence, is where you will want and choose to dwell now and unto eternity. Amen.

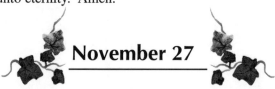

November 27

To Will and to Do

"For it is God who works in you both to will and to do His good pleasure."
Philippians 2:13 NKJV

It is my good pleasure to have you serving Me willingly with a glad and energetic heart. I desire that you desire to do my will!

Sometimes you long for the opposite of my perfect will for you. Sometimes your heart cannot be trusted. That is why I work always in you to will and do my good pleasure. To do other than my will only brings frustration and heartache in the end.

Remain open and supple to my will, remembering that you are the child, and you may not agree with your Father's choices for you initially. You are always my child. I am always your Father. Even at age 90, you may disagree with my will for you.

It is, therefore, important not to assume that your own heart's desires are necessarily mine for you. Listen and be sensitive to my Spirit's voice. If your heart is purposed to obey and please Me, then you will not be tripped up by wrong desire. Many plans may appear noble and good, but there is only one road that is my chosen path. It is the best one for your feet to travel.

I am always working in you both *to will and to do* my good pleasure. I strive always to line up your desires with my will and make them one. I am always working to perfect your desires so that they match mine. Sometimes this does not come so easily because of the influence of your own will upon the desires of your heart.

I love you! Allow Me to mesh my will and your desires to do—into one! Amen.

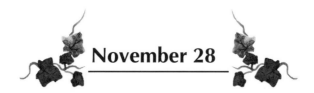

November 28

You Yourself Have Cursed

"Do not pay attention to every word people say, or you may hear your servant cursing you—for you know in your heart that many times you yourself have cursed others."   *Ecclesiastes 7:21-22 NIV*

Be careful in judging another too sternly for the very same error in which you commit, for *you yourself have cursed.*

Anger has taken you further from my light than you have wanted to go. Anger will destroy your destiny if allowed to rage unaccountable.

Attempt to take lightly another's offense toward you, for you, also, have committed similar offenses toward others. Be honest. Offense comes with unforgiveness. True love from God forgives and forgets the grudge.

Some people's words need to glide off your back like water on a wet duck.

Only sponge in love, not offense.

All men error. All men fail. Show mercy to your brother because I show mercy unto you every day. I wash away your sins; so, too, you need to forgive. Playing God is not wise. Judgment is mine. Forgiveness is yours.

Walk in mercy, and you will walk in my love and, therefore, be very pleasing to Me. Amen.

November 29

What Do I Require?

"He has showed you, O man, what is good. And what does the Lord require of you? To act justly and to love mercy and to walk humbly with your God."
Micah 6:8 NIV

You ask, *"What do I require?"* My answer is that your walk on earth is to be simple and upright, walking fairly (justly), mercifully (tender–heartedly towards other men), and clothed with the humility of Jesus Christ.

ACT JUSTLY—Be fair and not partial in your dealings with the just and the unjust. Every man is my creation whom I love. Show not favoritism!

LOVE MERCY—Forgive always and immediately any wrong done unto you, and do not stop the flow from heaven to earth through you to others. Never stop being my "angel of mercy" to all around you.

WALK HUMBLY—Walking humbly with your God is depending on Me for all things and not presumptuously assuming self-centeredness at any given moment. Humility is dependency on Me, and it always produces good success.

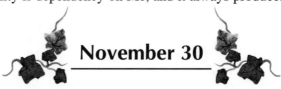

November 30

I Build Your Home

"Unless the Lord build the house, They labor in vain who build it."
Psalm 127:1 NKJV

Brick by brick, *I build your home*, beginning with a man's love for a woman and her returned loyalty to him.

Unless a marriage be built on the rock of faith in Jesus, it will not withstand the currents that will come to beat against its walls.

Human love is good. Divine love is better. Human love is earthly. Divine love is eternal.

Allow the Mason—Me—to build your home in my love and tender care. I will place your bricks in perfect order and see that no faulty brick is set that will later crack under the daily pressures of laborsome life.

It is futile to attempt to sustain that which I have not ordained. Life is designed to test foundations.

Your foundation in Me will never give way to the pressures of temptation and the attacks of the enemy. His roar will not shatter your windows.

I will sustain that which I build and fortify your walls.

The vain man builds alone. He is wise who allows Me to build the house.

December 1

Doing What We Do in Heaven

"Serve the Lord with gladness; come before him with joyful songs."
Psalm 100:2 NIV

I am song. I am gladness. You draw closer into my presence, and my glory expands your soul as you sing high praises unto Me. *Doing what we do in heaven* is what I am wanting you to do on earth. This is written in my Word for your instruction of truth. Not many men would sing glad songs unto Me apart from revelation understanding of who I am.

Do you want to draw closer to Me? Do you want to bring Me into your heart to line your soul with my JOY and to breathe new and fresh anointed oil into your spirit?

Then, rejoice before Me with glad songs and joyful spirit.

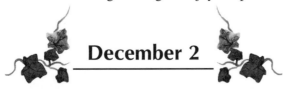

December 2

A Wounded Spirit

"The spirit of a man will sustain his infirmity; but a wounded spirit who can bear?"   *Proverbs 18:14 KJV*

It is easier for you to receive physical healing than it is to receive spiritual healing. The pharmacy shelves are lined with ample supplies to soothe the healing of the wounded or diseased flesh, but what apothecary can give adequate service to the spirit's wound?

The laws of the flesh are scientific, as doctors utilize their knowledge to facilitate my healing, but the healing of the spirit falls under spiritual laws. No science will ever be able to dissect the human spirit. Psychology has been man's attempt, which I laugh at. Hands cannot touch the spirit.

In my Word are the dictates of the spirit life. My wisdom is hidden and concealed within my Word—available for mankind to utilize.

My creation of man's spirit is quite different than the flesh. The body falls under physical laws of the earth, and it remains on earth. The spirit originates in heaven and is a pilgrim on earth. Its laws are in heaven; therefore, it is much more sensitive and vulnerable than the body.

That is why Christian families are admonished to raise children up in the tender love and arms of the Church. Parents are to train the spirit and protect the spirit of their children. That is why I admonish in Ephesians to be not harsh with them.

If children are not shielded and protected from the world, they will lose their sensitivity to Me and their innate desire for Me. A man loses hunger for Me as his spirit is beaten down by insensitive parental hands, and sometimes it takes Me a lifetime to restore and draw back my child unto Me. Parents determine the destiny of their children's spirits, and many perish in hell because mom and dad could not shield and protect the delicacy of their child's spirit.

No man can bear *a wounded spirit* without being destroyed. The destruction of the soul is inevitable apart from the healing touch of Jesus.

December 3

You Will Not Be Shaken

"I have set the Lord always before me. Because he is at my right hand, I will not be shaken."   *Psalm 16:8 NIV*

This is the nonarrogant heart attitude of my servant—total dependence upon Me.

This is the man of God that will not be tempted to move to the right or turn to the left.

This is the man of God whose face is set as flint towards my saving right hand. He is confident of this very thing: that I who began a good work in him will perform it in the day of Jesus Christ. Within the days of Jesus' Lordship, I will be strong upon you because you are holding strong upon Me; therefore, *you will not be shaken.* It is impossible for you to be shaken—can't happen, won't happen, and shall ever more not happen as long as your heart is fixed and in line with Psalm 16:8. Amen.

December 4

Always Listening

"For the eyes of the Lord are on the righteous and his ears are attentive to their prayer."   *I Peter 3:12 NIV*

My ears are *always listening* carefully to your conversations with Me. This is right relationship: conversing with your heavenly Father—both speaking and listening.

You are righteous in your Lord and Savior Jesus, my Son, your King of Kings and Lord of Lords. You are righteous in his blood. You are righteous in our relationship one with another.

It is your Abba-Daddy's delight to hear your heart spoken through your human lips.

Redemption and salvation are my plan! You bring Me glory and honor as you speak your prayers and trust Me with your cares.

I love you desperately and endlessly. You are the apple of my eye, so, of course, I will listen and answer because I LOVE YOU!

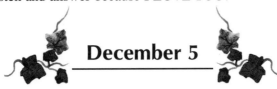

December 5

I Am the Potter

"Yet, O Lord, you are our Father. We are the clay, you are the potter; we are all the work of your hand."   *Isaiah 64:8 NIV*

I am your Father, and *I am the potter.* You are the clay in my hand, and even before conception, my hand is squeezing, forming, and preparing your divine destiny in Me.

You are the work of my hands! Some vessels I mold and design for great feats. These vessels are strong and are placed in my oven for long hours in preparation for service to Me.

Other vessels I mold to be less ornate and weaker. I have need in my Kingdom for the differing parts of the body of Christ wherein a toe's service unto Me is no less regarded than an arm or shoulder. You are all members of one body.

You should never judge a book by its cover nor a vessel by its shape. What appears to the human eye often is not what exists spiritually.

Some of my tiniest frames perform precision tasks for Me in little corners of the world where my more bulky pots could not fit.

Every man is of equal worth to Me. That is why I tarry, so that all may come to repentance . . . to Me. I want not one to burn. I have hand-designed each pot, and my heart breaks when the pot does not stop to ask Me "how" to fulfill its divine purpose on earth.

You, the body of Christ, exalt one and abase another. Nonsense! Even the tiniest of jars hold tiny nuggets, ones that would otherwise become lost or misplaced in a larger vessel.

I know every corner of the world. I send out my pottery to shine as lights in the world.

Remember, I am the potter. You are the clay. While molding you, I have a special purpose and plan for your life breathed into the very DNA makeup and package of gifts invested in you. Ask, and I will reveal to you my purpose for your particular shape, color, and size. I am the potter, and you are the beautiful works of my hand!

December 6

Clothe Yourself with My Love!

"Let love and faithfulness never leave you; bind them around your neck, write them on the tablet of your heart."   *Proverbs 3:3 NIV*

Proverbs 3:3 is an admonishment, an exhortation of caution. Literally wear your love for Me! *Clothe yourself with my love!*

Take the effort of time to prepare yourself before a day's battle. Do not presume that love and faithfulness will follow you around like a toddling duck. No! You must put forth effort to perpetuate my gifts. To receive requires a receptive and polite response and an opening of the package.

One must persevere in my love. One must be dedicated in heart to perfect the walk of faithfulness.

You pen my words onto your heart where they can never leave you or be stolen from you. Persevere, and yours shall be the Kingdom of Heaven! Amen.

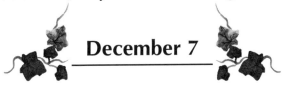

December 7

No Hidden Secrets

"For there is nothing covered, that shall not be revealed; neither hid, that shall not be known."   *Luke 12:2 KJV*

There are *no hidden secrets* in my Kingdom. In the arms of eternity, all mysteries of my nature, purpose, and being will be revealed.

It is the opposite nature of man to conceal, hide, lie, and veil the truth. Deception is the enemy's strongest trait. He can only lie and distort truth.

That is why one man can read my Word and see only words, and another man can read and receive the Words of eternal life. One man wallows cold stones in his mouth while another banquets at my lavish table! One feasts, another starves.

Why is this? The fallen nature of man is not alive unto Me, nor does hunger stir in his belly for Me.

It is my will to reveal all good things to my children. Many veils exist over man on earth. These veils shield the eyes of my glory shining from heaven!

My desire is to rid people of shielding veils, that I might pluck their heart strings with hunger and love for Me and our intimacy.

In my Kingdom, there are no hidden secrets—only truths waiting to be discovered.

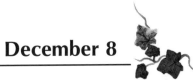

December 8

On the Sabbath

"Remember the sabbath day, to keep it holy."   *Exodus 20:8 KJV*

Today is your Sabbath day. Keep it holy—set apart as unto Me. Do no grueling labor on this day. This shall be a day you look forward to. Your labors end on this day. Take time to enjoy your family or friends. Be light-hearted. Relax, enjoy my blessings, and be thankful for all that I have given you. This shall be a day of thanksgiving.

As you labor through your week, you shall have my Sabbath day to soothe you, to anticipate, to reward you—a day to take a deep breath. Do not clutter your day with obligations.

Rest! My people need rest. You are designed by my hand to need this rest, both physically and psychologically. This day should give you greatest JOY out of the week. If Friday or Saturday night climax your week, something is wrong (your heart). Worshipping Me in the great congregation with fellow saints should be to you, and is, a high privilege, particularly in the light of history!

You have so much for which to be thankful. The beauty of it all . . . rejoice! Prize and cherish each moment you have amidst the congregation. I am there! My angels and I are there! Set your eyes not on human imperfection, but, rather, set the eyes of your heart on Me. I am there to nurture in a way unlike the other six days of labor.

On the Sabbath, I send forth a special anointed portion of my gifts of grace to each participant because I am overjoyed with your gathering. You know not what you do! Go to receive of Me increased grace to strengthen you through your new week.

I love you with my everlasting love. I designed you to need to worship on the Sabbath. You will malfunction apart from this free dispensation of my renewing grace—something like your weekly vitamin. You could say that those who attend multiple services are your fanatic body builders. I love you all!

Go now. Sin no more. Embrace my Sabbath with thanksgiving and appreciation for this, my special gift of allowance to you. I give you my Sabbath because I love you, and I know how to effectually sustain and maintain my creation—you!

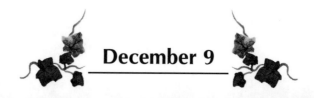

December 9

My Word Is Perfection

"As for God, his way is perfect; the word of the Lord is flawless."

2 Samuel 22:31 NIV

Human minds cannot understand true perfection. Every aspect of your earthly life rotates around imperfection. You have grown accustomed to less than perfect, for you have never known true perfection as found in heaven.

My Word is perfection. It is true, holy, and right. The closest you may be to perfection on earth is my Word!

All of heaven echoes the voice of perfection. That is why you cannot peer into my heavenly realm. You could not stand. You would melt in the presence of the Lord. Perfection melts away imperfection just as light exposes darkness.

Seek perfection by being an absorbent sponge to my Word. My Word will perfect you. Then, when you are squeezed by life circumstances, there will pour forth the beauty and perfection of my Spirit, not the carnal flesh of man.

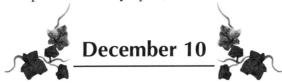

December 10

Spiritual Gifts

"Follow the way of love and eagerly desire spiritual gifts."

I Corinthians 14:1 NIV

I would have you be excited about spiritual gifts as little children are at Christmas time over presents. *Spiritual gifts* thrill the body of Christ because they, like Christmas toys, are new and fresh and fun! I have designed them and given them to my Church to edify, build up, comfort, and exhort. There is always a touch of my supernatural in spiritual gifts because natural man cannot duplicate an authentic gift from heaven.

My gifts bring a fresh anointing to the body of Christ. There can be no staleness in spiritual gifts as they are used and dispersed in the Church.

I desire for spiritual gifts to freely flow with spontaneity amongst many brethren when my people gather together. They manifest my presence like mirrors reflecting heaven.

December 11

Royal Rescue Crew

"For I am persuaded, that neither death, nor life, nor angels, nor principalities, nor powers, nor things present, nor things to come, nor height, nor depth, nor any creature, shall be able to separate us from the love of God, which is in Christ Jesus our Lord."   *Romans 8:38-39 KJV*

Nothing can separate you from Me! I will never allow the pressures of your earthly life to squeeze out of you my love. At the worst of times, I am with you!

Even when you have turned down the wrong path and made terrible choices . . . and even when the consequences of those wrong choices come catapulting hard against you . . . even when you have run away far from my hand of goodness and you have set yourself stupidly up for defeat . . . I am still there for you.

Now, you may never turn your back on Me, but circumstances of the world may come in like a raging flood that seeks to drown out your very breath of life . . . disease may cram its wicked claws into your flesh and seek to consume you . . . divorce, infidelity, or heartache may drop its unfair weight on you and crush your tender spirit . . . the enemy, death, may steal a loved one out from under your feet, too soon, too early, mercilessly . . . depression may wrap its dark cloak about you hovering to take your very life away.

I tell you, no attack of the enemy can separate you from my love which is in Christ Jesus your Lord. Even in the belly of the whale, I am there! I love you. I love you! I LOVE YOU! You cannot frustrate my love for you. My love is eternal, everlasting, and unconquerable. I will always be seeking to rescue you, heal you, and redeem you from the consequences of sin.

I am total mercy—complete in compassion—fully tender and all forgiving. The blood of Jesus Christ was spilled for your rescue! Even when you are lost, I find you because I love you! I am here to rescue you because I love you!

I am your *Royal Rescue Crew*, and I know how to snap you from the snares of disaster and calamity. I love you, and your beeper "beeps" when in need. I know where you are and what you need—because I love you! Amen.

December 12

Fasting

"Now there was one, Anna, a prophetess . . . who did not depart from the temple, but served God with fastings and prayers night and day."

Luke 2:36-37 NKJV

Fasting is a way to purify the heart. Fasting is a way to draw closer to Me.

Fasting is a way to secure greater power from on high in behalf of your earthly needs or loved ones or endeavors.

Fasting is a time of setting yourself apart to concentrate more fully on Me while you intercede.

Fasting is you taking the "extra effort."

Fasting takes hold of your need and "catapults" it, beelines it to my throne, like sending it air mail instead of pony express. The prayers of fasting are accompanied with an urgency, a serenity, a heart to heart throbbing of the soul that painstakingly pulls against my heart. I cannot resist the heartfelt prayer of my beloved. The prayer of earnestness reaches my ear and prompts a response.

Fasting helps to tear away some of the fleshly obstacles that lie between asking and openly receiving. The earnestness of the plea demands my attention.

When you pray, I hear. I know your every breath and every movement. You cannot hide under a blanket or pretense. I know you inside out. I understand your prayers completely, and I work within you so that faith (genuine, unadulterated faith) might grow, to the glory of God, in Jesus' name. Amen.

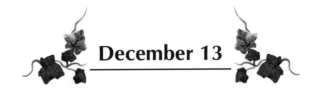

December 13

Basic Instinct

"I the Lord search the heart, I try the reins, even to give every man according to his ways, and according to the fruit of his doings."　　　　*Jeremiah 17:10 KJV*

No man knows his own heart unless I press upon his chest burdens too great for him to bear. It is the breaking point that determines the test outcome. Does one break "out" and explode the filth of the heart upon others like a miniature atomic bomb? Or does one break before Me in humble, contrite repentance for the sin nature revealed under pressure?

It is only in repentance that I can refine. It is in the breaking of the vessel's pride that I am able to remold the pot more completely. Earthen pots are designed to break; otherwise, I would have made you out of steel or robotic agents. No, I designed your hearts of flesh to be moldable, implorable, breakable, and cleanable.

Apart from the cleansing blood of Jesus Christ, what hope is there? I cleanse the soul. I scrape the wickedness. I scour the vessel. Apart from Me, no man can improve his *basic instinct* of iniquity.

Only I truly know your heart, and it is in repentance of sin that I am able to buff and shine you!

December 14

Peace

"Peace be with you!"　　　　*John 20:21 NIV*

Jesus Christ came to earth to give you *peace.* No other gift of mine soothes like my peace. My peace is like salve to an aching wound, like a blanket's warmth to a trembling and cold body, like white clouds in the sky that appear as billowy cotton balls on a summer day.

My peace settles into the center of your soul and brings a calm and quietness to your spirit unlike the world knows. My peace is like a still lake's surface that perfectly reflects the sky as a glassy mirror.

My peace cannot be manufactured or duplicated. It is your constant companion, even as it keeps you in the eye of the storm.

My peace does not worry or hurry. It basks in my presence soaking up the rays of the Son of God.

December 15

Fully Persuaded!

"He staggered not at the promise of God through unbelief, but was strong in faith, giving glory to God: and being fully persuaded that, what he had promised, he was able also to perform."   *Romans 4:20-21 KJV*

This faith of Abraham is also your faith. I desire for you to walk in the same manner of faith as your father, Abe. Abraham staggered not. I would have you not being tossed about like a buoy afloat turbulent waters. I want you to be firm and stable like the concrete boulders that hold up the bridge, that budge not when the wind of storms beat against you.

I do not lie! My promises are true and sure, and I am not a covenant breaker. I always keep my promises. In my time, they come to pass! You error in anticipating results in your time frame, not mine. You must also trust Me to bring to pass my promises at my appointed time.

In faith, you are able to be thankful even before the package is unwrapped. You hold in your lap my gift of promise. You embrace the answered prayer and giggle with excitement like a child holding a packaged gift. The wrapping is your faith.

Like a child, you well remember your request for a specific item of which Grandpa has now handed you a package resembling its size. You do not doubt for one moment "Papa's" undying love and loyalty to you. Grandpa asked what you wanted for Christmas, and with a gleam in his eye, he smiled and whispered, "Okay!" Your child heart leapt with joy! It would soon be yours!

I am able to perform that which you ask, so do not stagger in unbelief and doubt. Like Abraham, be *fully persuaded!* Ask in faith. Receive by faith. Embrace your package with childlike anticipation and joy!

In my perfect time, you may unwrap your gift. Simply be patient and wait upon the Lord! Amen.

December 16

Paid in Full!

"As far as the east is from the west, So far has He removed our transgressions from us."   *Psalm 103:12 NKJV*

When the accuser screams in your ear and publicizes flashbacks of past sin, you are to do one of two things. Either say, "The Lord rebuke you!" Then, praise Me for my cleansing blood of the Lamb, or in matter of fact fashion state, "It is written, as far as the east is from the west, so are my sins removed from me."

Beloved, I do not store away videos of sin forgiven. The remembrance of your forgiven transgression ceases to exist. The blood of Jesus Christ is a thorough cleansing that leaves no residue. It is a powerful cleansing detergent that destroys even the remembrance of your transgression.

Beloved, life will stack itself against you without a Savior to knock down the blocks of guilt and condemnation. No man can stand clean before Me apart from the cleansing blood of Jesus Christ.

The price has already been paid, the debt already cleared. I, the loving Father, have purchased your gift—eternal salvation—through the blood of my Son. My gift need only be RECEIVED!

If your earthly father took your inheritance and purchased in cash a mansion set on a hill, would you not rejoice and inhabit the gift? Of course! You would be thankful for your father's love. You would not call the bank to enquire of the balance left due for you to reimburse. No. You would trust your dad's word and believe that the home was a token of his love.

In the same manner, I have purchased your eternal mansion, and you are debt free! You need only receive daily the cleansing blood of Jesus Christ over your life, and then rejoice and enjoy my gift of salvation every day.

If a false accuser knocks at the door, disguises himself as a bank representative, and seeks the payment of notes due on your gift-mansion, look him straight in the eye and announce Psalm 103:12: "As far as the east is from the west, so have my debts been *paid in full!*" Amen.

December 17

Eternal Abundance

"The thief cometh not, but for to steal, and to kill, and to destroy: I am come that they might have life, and that they might have it more abundantly."

John 10:10 KJV

The thief and I are the difference between black and white, light and dark, cold and hot.

The enemy steals your joy, but I give you JOY! The thief kills your love, but I spawn love in your heart. The thief tears down walls and destroys homes, but I build and reshape the very foundation of your families.

Know your enemy's goals so that you might recognize his footprints. I give you divine health, but the thief steals your well being and delights in doctor bills. He loves runny noses, broken arms, HIV, and the flu.

I rejoice in the longitude of a 50th wedding anniversary . . . the thief inspires nasty divorces. It is my good pleasure to receive your tithe and pay the bills . . . the thief keeps his prisoners in the red. Debt is his glory! Prosperity is mine. The thief's triumph is a broken relationship. Mine is peace and harmony between brethren.

Jesus came to earth to purchase for you *eternal abundance* that lasts forever. There is no need in Jesus!

 **December 18**

Secret of True Worship

"To him be the glory and the power for ever and ever."   *I Peter 4:11 NIV*

The *secret of true worship* is when you realize that I am your total power and complete GLORY! forever and ever and ever. Then all else has no voice. The world becomes silent around you as you seek to hear only my voice beckoning you to the Throne of Grace.

Beloved, I am your glory! Beloved, I am your power! I am your all in all, your breath, your drink, your cup.

When you give Me true honor and acknowledge my sovereign power, then is when nothing stands between you and Me, and no stench of flesh divides our hearts. Then is when we are truly, experientially, one in Spirit.

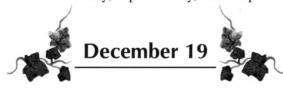 **December 19**

Welcome Mat of Love

"And though I have the gift of prophecy, and understand all mysteries and all knowledge, and though I have all faith, so that I could remove mountains, but have not love, I am nothing."   *I Corinthians 13:2 NKJV*

"I am nothing!" should be the repentant cry of he who stands before the congregation proclaiming gospel truths but simultaneously demonstrating no love to the people. It is hypocrisy to say one thing and do another. To be a Pharisee is to know the law, all the rules—but not to demonstrate the greatest command which is love.

In heaven, if eyebrows could be raised, you would raise yours when you beheld just "who's who" in my inner heavenly Kingdom! The gentleman who faithfully sweeps your floors daily (commonly known as janitor) may be the one with the whitest robes and most honor. The last shall be first, and the first shall be last.

All equipment of the mind and spirit must be soaked with LOVE. Armor without love is useless. Love is the final coat. It is the expression of who I am to others.

Love is not the "feeling." It is the "action." To feel sorry for someone is futile apart from the expression of that sorrow in a constructive and acceptable token of compassion or friendship.

LOVE is interest in your fellow man. It is an inquiry with a listening ear. It is a handshake, a hug, and a "how do you do!"

Preachers who preach my Word but cannot relate to people are useless—nothing. The expression of love—simple friendly concern—is basic to my gospel. That is why I say that having knowledge and faith and prophecy can be nothing. No gift impresses Me apart from love.

You wonder sometimes why my Spirit is quenched in a worship service? I tell you, love must be flowing from my throne, into your hearts, and out onto one another; or else, it is as if beavers have built their dams and stopped my flow. A stagnancy prevails.

Seek to express and display LOVE in every aspect of your life, then your prophecies will ignite into bonfire influence. Your faith will move boulders. Your knowledge will incite fervor and inspiration, and your gifts will function with excited anointing.

Your heart should always be a big *welcome mat of love* to others. Always put the outreach and expression of love first before anything else. If you allow love to be your priority, all other calling and ministries for which I have chosen you will flourish effortlessly because my Spirit will pour itself out upon you and your good works.

December 20

Pure in Heart

"Blessed are the pure in heart: for they shall see God."　　　*Matthew 5:8 KJV*

The *pure in heart* always chooses to forgive, does not take offense, sees the "good" not "bad" in people and in situations.

The pure in heart views life differently from the "average Joe." The pure in heart sees through eyes of beauty. Daily life has lace sewn 'round about its edges. One man sees grass and dreads mowing. The pure in heart interprets grass as a carpet of green to rejoice in, as a reflection of the glory of God.

The pure in heart does not take offense at a wrong done, does often not even notice a wrong was done.

The pure in heart sees Me in everything. There is no slice of life void of Me in his eyes. He virtually sees Me in every situation and view of creation. Rightly so, for I am in everything that exists on the face of the earth.

December 21

Gifts Have Great Power

"If your enemy is hungry, give him bread to eat; And if he is thirsty, give him water to drink; For so you will heap coals of fire on his head, And the Lord will reward you."　　　*Proverbs 25:21-22 NKJV*

The quickest way to appease your enemy is by giving him gifts and meeting his needs. *Gifts have great power* when given with a spirit of forgiveness and humility.

The last thing on earth your self-centered feelings want to do is give good gifts to your enemy. Rather, your flesh desires the opposite of good. If you will swallow your pride and forgive with a clean heart, then I will touch the hardened heart of your enemy through your gift.

This is a spiritual equation that works. Your enemy will respond! Hot coals on one's head cannot be ignored! The discomfort of the coals will cause his conviction, and he will seek out relief. He will want to reconcile.

The giving of gifts is not a bribe. From a pure heart, it is your attempt to end strife and bridge over differences. This gift of reconciliation is honored by Me, and my anointing is on it to burn away division.

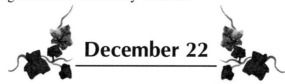

December 22

The Drama "You"

"This is the assurance we have in approaching God: that is if we ask anything according to his will, he hears us."   *I John 5:14 NIV*

Asking, then receiving, brings Me great Glory! For it is my pleasure to meet your needs. I, of course, desire my will to be played out by you. I am the director—you, the actor. I write the script—you speak it. I instruct you with coaching—you speak the lines.

Now, what if you make up your own lines not written down on my script? Well, this brings confusion to the master plan. Therefore, I hear only my will. All else falls as dead and wasted seed to the ground for the wind to escort away.

As you speak my will (my script), other actors take their cues and correspondingly interact. The divine drama becomes delightful, and cast members learn to walk with Me more clearly and obediently. I patiently long for and await to hear the lines of my will and see *the drama "you"* unfold upon life's stage.

December 23

Peace Is the Seal

"Therefore, since we have been justified through faith, we have peace with God through our Lord Jesus Christ."   *Romans 5:1 NIV*

Peace is the seal of my Holy Spirit upon your life. Like an envelope ready to be mailed, I ready you to be sent unto the nations as my servant, into the world as my bond slave, and into the church as my friend.

In all that you do, I seal you up with my peace, my sweet adhesive, that protects you from the thief tampering with my prepared goods within. Those goods are meant to meet the needs of others, not so much yourself.

Peace is my seal of preparedness and readiness. (Not that you are tamper proof!) Now, when the seal is broken, you are alerted, and you seek to find the cause of your discerned awareness of need. It acts as a censor to know when all is well, or is not.

Peace feels like sunshine on a winter's day. It comforts, soothes, and sustains steadfastly, reliably, and forever with Me in charge.

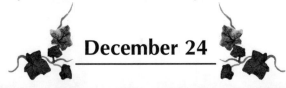

December 24

Luke One

"For with God nothing shall be impossible.   And Mary said, Behold the handmaid of the Lord; be it unto me according to thy word.   And the angel departed from her."   *Luke 1:37-38 KJV*

Luke One is a "peek hole" into my eternal wisdom, like looking through a key hole into my mind and into heaven's purpose manifested on earth.   Luke One is the heartbeat of your Father as the "Drama of Life" through my holy remnant unfolds being played out through human bodies, spoken through human voices. The preciousness of my creation is culminated in the wisdom of Luke One.

In human mind, you measure time and distance and depth of waiting. Your understanding is confined to human degrees of longevity, width, and height.   In heaven's mind, we are as one, and each man is a participant of the divine drama culminated in the eternal reign of Jesus Christ yet to be orchestrated.

Beloved, you are participating in a holy drama, a story begun at the beginning of earth's creation.   You have your role in this time to fill.   You are a link in the chain of centuries that makes up earth's story and manifests your Father's heart and love for you.

In your finite mind, you ponder how long waiting can be; but, in my mind, earth's clock is ticking in perfect rhythm with my ultimate plan for the universe. How many generations waited for the Son of God to come to earth? How long awaiting had my prophets been in foretelling the coming Messiah? How had hearts longed for their Redeemer to save them?

Truly, all of earth's creation has groaned for the curtain that is being drawn on this last impending act of my provision for mankind.   You have been appointed for such a time as this to participate in my human drama of redemption and love.   You are no mistake.   I have appointed you.   I have sent you.   I have called you.

I tarry only because I have authored the perfect timing of events.   You are a member of the divine eternal story I have orchestrated upon earth's stage.   The final scene is about to unfold, and you are standing upon the threshold of my most exciting and powerful chapters written for mankind.

Nothing is impossible with God when it is time.   Live your life and play out your part—as the star actor/actress upon my stage.   Your role is important to Me! Inhabit the earth, and seek Me with all of your heart, that you might reflect my glory.

All you have to offer Me is your own life, the life I have given you.   See that you speak your lines and maneuver upon my stage as predestined for you in my book of human drama.

December 25

Through All Generations

"For the Lord is good and his love endures forever, his faithfulness continues through all generations."   ***Psalm 100:5 NIV***

Through all generations my LOVE has been constant for you, my sheep, my children. Since the beginning of mankind, I have jealously watched over the maturation of the generations, leading, prompting, guiding, and directing.

Now, here we are! This generation cries out for love and mercy! I send you out to go and give of my holy water to the thirsty and parched souls of my creation.

You are called to give to this, your generation. This is your hour, your time, your opportunity. I created you for such a time as this!

Go, beloved! Go, beloved, run to the weary, embrace them, take them by hand, and lead them to Me! Lead them to Me! I will draw, but you take their hands. I love you. Amen.

December 26

Say "Thank You!"

"Let them give thanks to the Lord for his unfailing love and his wonderful deeds for men."   ***Psalm 107:8 NIV***

When you give a gift, do you not consider its cost, and do you not carefully consider purchase options and diversities in products?

I, too, have carefully pursued my gift of eternal salvation to you. My investment in mankind covers centuries of investment in individuals much like yourself who heard my voice, answered my call, and obeyed my leading.

As your Father, I desire to be "thanked," for my gifts of creation are much more far reaching and intricately patterned than your consciousness allows you to be aware.

The miracle of a single cell . . . I created, designed, and blew life into. All that I am is a marvel, and in heaven, you will fully understand my glory. Please, *say "thank you!"*

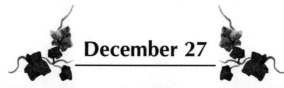

December 27

The Prophet

"Verily I say unto you, no prophet is accepted in his own country."

Luke 4:24 KJV

The familiar does not command respect. It is the nature of men to belittle their own of spiritual expertise.

The prophet owns the mouth of a sword. His words are my words. They can sometimes be rigid and seemingly harsh to ears who are not accustomed to being fine tuned to my voice.

The prophet easily offends the local. "You are one of us," they surmise, not believing in faith that I really could speak through and choose one of their own to do extraordinary miracles.

Spiritual pride is a very deceitful evil force. It masquerades itself as not existing, yet it blinds good people from seeing my gifts to them.

Few locals will embrace their own prophet. They have walked the same roads, shared the same table, worked the same fields. "What right has he to speak the Word of the Lord when I, too, have ears to hear?" the skeptic asks.

It is important for the prophet to not take offense. A prophet's call has a prophet's reward. It matters not who receives him or who does not. My Word goes forth and accomplishes that which I choose for it to accomplish.

Let the prophet be comforted: there is always a small remnant close to you who recognize my gift and honor you as such.

A prophet's call receives a prophet's rewards, many of which come in my Kingdom of Heaven. Amen.

December 28

Pinions

"He will cover you with His pinions, and under His wings shall you trust and find refuge."   ***Psalm 91:4 AMP***

My *pinions* are wrapped around you. Do not fear what man can do unto you. My arms are wrapped around you, for I understand your weakness and your vulnerability. Do not fear. It is I! I will never lead you apart from my protection.

I will keep you and yours safe because you are doing your Father's business. My pinions are wrapped around you tightly. You are my crystal of sunshine beaming on earth, reflecting the glory of Jesus Christ on earth!

I have chosen you. I have equipped you. You are my yielded tool. I will implement my plan and purpose for your life and talents. I am in control, so only trust and wait to walk gracefully through the doors I have prepared for you.

I love you. You are my servant, and my pinions will protect you from the enemy. Amen.

December 29

Under Your Feet!

"And the God of peace shall bruise satan under your feet shortly."   ***Romans 16:20 KJV***

You have authority over the enemy. I have given you the name of JESUS to be your authority. In his name, you have the right to command and reprimand the thief.

Your feet smash the enemy like stomping on a battalion of ants. The Word of God spoken through your lips electrifies your shoes. His plans are electrocuted and fall dead at your heels.

Beloved, there exists far more power in my name than you realize or utilize. It is my desire to see my Church stomping down disease, discord, strife, and division.

He is *under your feet!*

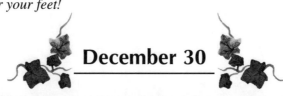

December 30

Lead Your Children to Me

"The secret things belong unto the Lord our God: but those things which are revealed belong unto us and to our children for ever, that we may do all the words of this law."   *Deuteronomy 29:29 KJV*

All that you know of Me belongs also to your children. You have in your heart a treasure chest of nuggets, emeralds, pearls, and costly jewels. These are revealed Word deposited by my hand.

Now, you must, through prayer and testimony, convey the value of your treasure chest to your own offspring.

In light of the world's loud screams and sharp claws, this task is a serious challenge laid before you.

Do not naively assume that your family will take the bait and bite the worm just because you did. No. Children's tiny hands need a big grown-up hand to grasp, to lead, to guide, to walk with into the House of the Lord and into my wells of living waters.

Hand-in-hand, you must come to Me sharing your faith, speaking of my goodness. They will come to know Me, as you also know Me, only as you, together, drink from my living waters.

Take them cup after cup of my drink. Be my servant by serving them the refreshing drink from my River of Life.

Be not lazy or slothful in your training of your sons and daughters, for they must also teach my truths to their children.

You must be keen and sharp in prayer to ward off the sneaky stealing hands of the enemy whose greatest triumph is to steal a child of God.

Watch and place always before you my call to *lead your children to Me.* Amen.

December 31

Topical Index

Continued next page

Topical Index

The Father's Voice
by Rose Marie Jones

ORDER FORM

NAME _____

STREET _____

CITY _____ STATE _____ ZIP _____

_____ @ $15.95 .... $ _____
NUMBER OF
BOOKS

SHIPPING: $2.00 PER BOOK .... $ _____

SALES TAX: PLEASE ADD $1.00 PER BOOK FOR
SHIPMENT TO ILLINOIS ADDRESS $ _____

TOTAL .... $ _____

PLEASE RETURN ORDER FORM AND CHECK PAYABLE TO:
VOICE PUBLISHING
54 ALBION
JACKSONVILLE, ILLINOIS 62650